Pro Java Microservices with Quarkus and Kubernetes

A Hands-on Guide

Nebrass Lamouchi

Apress®

Pro Java Microservices with Quarkus and Kubernetes: A Hands-on Guide

Nebrass Lamouchi
Paris, France

ISBN-13 (pbk): 978-1-4842-7169-8   ISBN-13 (electronic): 978-1-4842-7170-4
https://doi.org/10.1007/978-1-4842-7170-4

Managing Director, Apress Media LLC: Welmoed Spahr
Acquisitions Editor: Steve Anglin
Development Editor: Matthew Moodie
Coordinating Editor: Mark Powers

Cover designed by eStudioCalamar

Cover image by Robert Shunev on Unsplash (www.unsplash.com)

Distributed to the book trade worldwide by Apress Media, LLC, 1 New York Plaza, New York, NY 10004, U.S.A. Phone 1-800-SPRINGER, fax (201) 348-4505, e-mail orders-ny@springer-sbm.com, or visit www.springeronline.com. Apress Media, LLC is a California LLC and the sole member (owner) is Springer Science + Business Media Finance Inc (SSBM Finance Inc). SSBM Finance Inc is a **Delaware** corporation.

For information on translations, please e-mail booktranslations@springernature.com; for reprint, paperback, or audio rights, please e-mail bookpermissions@springernature.com.

Apress titles may be purchased in bulk for academic, corporate, or promotional use. eBook versions and licenses are also available for most titles. For more information, reference our Print and eBook Bulk Sales web page at http://www.apress.com/bulk-sales.

Any source code or other supplementary material referenced by the author in this book is available to readers on GitHub via the book's product page, located at www.apress.com/9781484271698. For more detailed information, please visit http://www.apress.com/source-code.

Printed on acid-free paper

To Mom, it's impossible to thank you adequately for everything you've done.

To the soul of Dad, I miss you every day...

To Firass, you are the best, may God bless you...

To my sweetheart, since you've come into my life, there are so many new emotions and feelings begging to come out...

Table of Contents

About the Author

Nebrass Lamouchi is a senior software engineer at ▦ Microsoft who is addicted to Java and cloud technologies. He is also a former NetBeans Dream Team member. Nebrass was one of the four happy winners 🏆 of the Oracle Groundbreaker Awards ⚇ in May, 2019.

He has also been a project leader on the Barbarus Project for the OWASP Foundation since March, 2013.

He is the author of the following books:

- 📖 *Playing with Java Microservices on Kubernetes and OpenShift,* published with Leanpub, November 2018.

- 📖 *Pairing Apache Shiro with Java EE 7*, published with InfoQ, May 2016.

Nebrass graduated with an M.Sc Degree in Information Systems Security and a Bachelor's Degree in Computing Sciences and Management from the Higher Institute of Management of Tunis, Tunisia.

Over the past eight years, he has worked on Java SE/EE projects in many sectors, including business management, petroleum, finance and banking, medical and healthcare, and defense and space. He has developed applications using many frameworks and Java-related technologies, such as native Java EE APIs and third-party frameworks and tools (Spring, Quarkus, Hibernate, Primefaces, JBoss Forge). He has managed and used infrastructure and programming tools such as DBMS, Java EE servers (Glassfish and JBoss), quality and continuous integration/deployment tools (Sonar, Jenkins, and Azure DevOps), and Docker, Kubernetes, and OpenShift.

About the Technical Reviewer

Georgios Andrianakis is a principal software engineer working for Red Hat. He works on Java frameworks like Spring and Quarkus, while also exploring their synergies with cloud-native systems like Kubernetes and OpenShift.

Acknowledgments

I would like to express my gratitude to the many people who saw me through this book.

To all those who provided support, read, wrote, offered comments, and assisted in its editing and design.

Many thanks to the great Georgios Andrianakis for his technical review and guidelines that helped me write this book.

To my wife and my family, thank you for all your great support and encouragement.

To Laurent Ellerbach, thank you for all your support and guidance!

Last and not least, I beg forgiveness from all those who have been with me over the course of many years and whose names I have failed to mention.

Preface

Pro Java Microservices with Quarkus and Kubernetes will teach you how to build and design microservices using Java and the Quarkus platform.

This book covers topics related to developing Java microservices and deploying them to Kubernetes.

Traditionally, Java developers are used to developing large, complex, monolithic applications. The process of developing and deploying monoliths has always been slow and painful. This book will help Java developers quickly get started with the features and concerns of the microservices architecture. It will introduce Docker and Kubernetes for the deployment in the cloud.

This book is aimed at Java developers who want to build microservices using the new stack and who want to deploy them to Kubernetes.

You will be guided on how to install the appropriate tools, and for those who are new to enterprise development using Quarkus, you will be introduced to its core principles and main features through a deep step-by-step tutorial of its many components. For those who have prior experience using Quarkus for enterprise development, this book offers some recipes that illustrate how to split monoliths and implement microservices and deploy them as containers to Kubernetes.

Here are some of the key challenges that I address in this book:

- Introducing containerization with Docker

- Introducing Quarkus for beginners

- Implementing a sample monolithic application

- Splitting a monolith using the domain driven design (DDD) approach

- Implementing the cloud patterns

- Rethinking the deployment process

- Introducing the Kubernetes world

- Introducing best practices and the recommended patterns while creating cloud-native applications

By the end of this book, you will have practical hands-on experience building microservices using Quarkus and you will be able to deploy them as containers to Kubernetes.

What This Book Covers

- Chapter 1, "Getting Started with Containerization," presents containerization with Docker and Podman.

- Chapter 2, "Introduction to the Monolithic Architecture," provides an introduction to monolithic architecture with a focus on its advantages and drawbacks.

- Chapter 3, "Coding a Monolithic Application," includes a step-by-step tutorial for modeling and creating a monolith using Maven, Java 11, and Quarkus.

- Chapter 4, "Upgrading a Monolithic Application," lists some upgrades for our monolithic application, such as adding tests and most-wanted features.

- Chapter 5, "Building and Deploying a Monolithic Application," covers how to build and package the example application before showing how to deploy it in the runtime environment.

- Chapter 6, "Adding Anti-Disaster Layers," introduces how to implement the security and monitoring layers to help the application avoid disasters.

- Chapter 7, "Microservices Architecture Pattern," presents the drawbacks that can be faced in a typical monolithic architecture and illustrates the need something new, like the Microservices Architecture Pattern.

- Chapter 8, "Splitting the Monolith: Bombarding the Domain," presents domain driven design concepts to help you understand the business domain of a monolithic application, and to be able to split it into subdomains.

- Chapter 9, "Applying DDD to the Code," shows how to apply all the DDD concepts to the monolithic application source code and to successfully split the monolith into bounded contexts.

- Chapter 10, "Meeting the Microservices Concerns and Patterns," offers a deep presentation of the concerns and cloud patterns related to the Microservices Architecture Pattern.

- Chapter 11, "Getting Started with Kubernetes," covers how to build real standalone business microservices.

- Chapter 12, "Implementing Cloud Patterns," presents an in-depth examination of the most efficient container orchestrator: Kubernetes.

- Chapter 13, "Building Kubernetized Microservices," shows how to migrate a monolith's code to build microservices while applying Kubernetes concepts and features.

- Chapter 14, "Flying all Over the Sky with Quarkus and Kubernetes," explains how implement additional cloud patterns using Quarkus and Kubernetes.

- And more 😊

The source code of this book is available via the Download Source Code link located at www.apress.com/9781484271698.

Reader Feedback

I always welcome feedback from my great readers. ☺ Please let me know what you thought about this book—what you liked or disliked.

If you have any questions or inquiries, feel free to get in touch by emailing me at lnibrass@gmail.com.

Introduction

Quarkus is the latest Java Framework project in the long list of frameworks created by Red Hat. First released in 2018, it's the successor to the WildFly Swarm and Thorntail frameworks. These two frameworks came to market in the golden age of the Spring Boot Framework. This is why they were defeated and didn't win the battle. After test-running WildFly Swarm on my own projects, I decided not to adopt it.

Why did Red Hat make another framework? What does this framework bring to the table?

Red Hat is one of the biggest contributors to the Java platform, from design and specifications to providing implementations and tooling. While contributing to the GraalVM project, Red Hat spotted an opportunity to create a framework specifically geared toward this great project and to the cloud.

Wait! What is GraalVM, and what is its added value?

From the Oracle official documentation:

> GraalVM is a high-performance runtime that provides significant improvements in application performance and efficiency, which is ideal for μservices. It is designed for applications written in Java, JavaScript, LLVM-based languages such as C and C++, and other dynamic languages. It removes the isolation between programming languages and enables interoperability in a shared runtime. It can run either standalone or in the context of OpenJDK, Node.js, or Oracle Database.

> GraalVM can run in the context of OpenJDK to make Java applications run faster with a new just-in-time compilation technology. GraalVM takes over the compilation of Java bytecode to machine code.

> The compiler of GraalVM provides performance advantages for highly abstracted programs due to its ability to remove costly object allocations in many scenarios.

> —Official GraalVM Documentation from Oracle at
> https://www.graalvm.org/docs/why-graal/

This abstract definition probably doesn't give you a clear view of this runtime. But what's sure is that you can see how many times the word "performance" appears in it.

In my words, GraalVM offers the ability to compile your Java code into a native executable binary, which will be executed natively in the operating system without the Java runtime. The native executable binary offers two main features:

- Much faster startup

- Lower memory footprint

Here, Red Hat found a big opportunity to make a Java Framework dedicated to this high-performance runtime. This is what encouraged them to give Quarkus a slogan: *Supersonic Subatomic Java.*

It's not sufficient to make a framework just based on a specific runtime. Red Hat had the same point of view, so they added more features (that we will cover later) to their checklist so that their framework can compete against Spring Boot!

This is what attracted me to Quarkus! I wanted to see how Red Hat compared to Spring Boot.

In this book, I try to introduce Quarkus and GraalVM to you in a soft way. If you are a beginner, you will not have a lot of problems dealing with it. Maybe you will not see many differences between it and Spring Boot, and I try to make the picture clear for you! 😄

We will start by building a small "Hello World" application using Quarkus and then begin making our monolith, which we will migrate to the microservices architecture.

You can jump to Chapter 2 if you are already familiar with the Quarkus platform.

CHAPTER 1

Getting Started with Containerization

Introducing Containerization

In the Java world, applications are packaged in many formats before being deployed to the runtime. These environments can be physical machines (bare metal) or virtual machines.

The major risk for software applications are runtime updates that can break the application. For example, an operating system update might include other updates, with libraries that are incompatible with the running application.

Generally, software can coexist with applications on the same host, like databases or proxies. They all share the same operating systems and libraries. So, even if an update does not cause a direct application crash, any of the other services could be adversely affected.

Although these upgrades are risky, we cannot ignore them because of their interest in the matters of security and stability. They include bug fixes and enhances. But we can test our application and its context to see if the updates will cause issues. This task can be daunting, especially when the application is huge.

Keep calm! There is an excellent solution. We can use *containers*, which are a kind of isolated partition inside a single operating system. They provide many of the same benefits as virtual machines, such as security, storage, and network isolation, yet they require far fewer hardware resources. Containers are great because they are quicker to launch and to terminate.

Containerization allows isolating and tracking resource utilization. This isolation protects our applications from the many risks linked to host OS updates.

1

© Nebrass Lamouchi 2021
N. Lamouchi, *Pro Java Microservices with Quarkus and Kubernetes*,
https://doi.org/10.1007/978-1-4842-7170-4_1

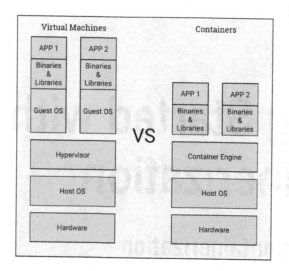

Containers have many benefits:

- **Consistent environment**: Containers are the best way to package applications and all their dependencies. This provides us with a unique opportunity to exactly define the Production environment during the Development and Test phases.

- **Write once, run everywhere**: Containers can be executed anywhere: on any machine, on any OS, and on any cloud provider.

- **Isolation and abstraction**: Containers use OS-level isolation in order to abstract the resources.

There are many container solutions available. 🐳 Docker is a popular, open-source container format.

Introducing Docker

🐳 *Docker* is a platform for developers that aims to package, deploy, and run applications as containers. The adoption of containers as the new application packaging format is called *containerization*.

The Dockerfile

A *Dockerfile* is the source code of a Docker container. It is a descriptor file that holds the instructions that will make a Docker image.

Images and Containers

A *Docker image* is the origin of a Docker container. When we build a Dockerfile, we get the image and, when we run a Docker image, we get a Docker container.

Installing Docker

To start playing with Docker, you need to install it. You can grab the version that is compatible with your platform from `https://docs.docker.com/install/`.

When you visit that page, you will find two versions: Docker CE and Docker EE:

- Docker CE is suitable for development and basic needs.

- Docker EE is an enterprise-grade edition that has many extra features needed to use highly scaled production-grade Docker clusters.

Installing Docker is very easy and you don't need a tutorial to do it. ☺

---

❶   For ⊞ Windows users, ensure that 🐳 Docker Desktop for Windows uses 🐧 the Linux containers.

To check if Docker is installed properly, you can start by checking the installed version by running the Docker `version` command:

```
Client: Docker Engine - Community                    ②
 Cloud integration: 1.0.7
 Version:           20.10.2
 API version:       1.41
 Go version:        go1.13.15
 Git commit:        2291f61
 Built:             Mon Dec 28 16:12:42 2020
 OS/Arch:           darwin/amd64
```

3

```
Context:          default
Experimental:     true

Server: Docker Engine - Community                    ①
 Engine:
  Version:         20.10.2
  API version:     1.41 (minimum version 1.12)
  Go version:      go1.13.15
  Git commit:      8891c58
  Built:           Mon Dec 28 16:15:28 2020
  OS/Arch:         linux/amd64
  Experimental:    false
 containerd:
  Version:         1.4.3
  GitCommit:       269548fa27e0089a8b8278fc4fc781d7f65a939b
 runc:
  Version:         1.0.0-rc92
  GitCommit:       ff819c7e9184c13b7c2607fe6c30ae19403a7aff
 docker-init:
  Version:         0.19.0
  GitCommit:       de40ad0
```

Running Your First Container

As with every programming language, we will start by creating a Hello World example. In the Docker world, we have the hello-world image, which can be used as a starting point: 😛

```
$ docker run hello-world

Unable to find image "hello-world:latest" locally
latest: Pulling from library/hello-world
0e03bdcc26d7: Pull complete
Digest: sha256:31b9c7d48790f0d8c50ab433d9c3b7e17666d6993084c002c2ff1ca09b96391d
Status: Downloaded newer image for hello-world:latest
```

```
Hello from Docker!
This message shows that your installation appears to be working correctly.
...
```

When running this Docker image, we get the typical `Hello from Docker!` message. The source code of this image is available in the Docker Library GitHub repository.

This image is pulled from the Docker Hub, as it's not found locally.

WHAT IS DOCKER HUB?

Docker Hub is a public Docker product that offers many services to Docker users:

- Stores Docker images in public and private repositories.
- Makes continuous integration pipelines to build images when the source code is updated.
- Handles users and groups authorization and access management.
- Includes GitHub and BitBucket integration for making automated builds.

To list the existing local Docker images, use this command:

```
$ docker images
```

REPOSITORY	TAG	IMAGE ID	CREATED	SIZE
hello-world	latest	bf756fb1ae65	13 months ago	13.3kB

ℹ️ Image ID is a random generated *HEX* value that identifies each image.

To list all the Docker containers, use this command:

```
$ docker ps -a
```

| CONTAINER ID | IMAGE | COMMAND | CREATED | STATUS |
	PORTS	NAMES		
42feaf1ce560	hello-world	"/hello"	37 minutes ago	Exited (0) 37
minutes ago	vigilant			

Some details are explained here:

- The `Container ID` is a random generated HEX value that identifies the container.

- The `Container Name` you see here is a randomly generated string name that the Docker Daemon created for you, as you didn't specify one.

Understanding the Docker Architecture

All this is great! But how does Docker work? 😄

Docker uses a client-server architecture:

- On the *server-side*, Docker is exposing a REST API that will receive commands from a client caller. Then the REST API will forward the requests to a core component called the *Docker Daemon* (dockerd), which will make the operations and send back responses to the REST API. The API then sends them back to the caller.

- On the *client-side*, we have the Docker CLI that we are using to type Docker commands.

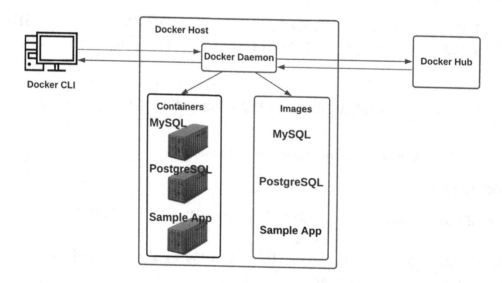

Docker Objects

We already talked briefly about Docker images and containers. In this section, we will discuss these and many other Docker objects in more detail.

Images

As mentioned, a Docker image is the origin of a Docker container. When we build a Dockerfile, we get the image and when we run a Docker image, we get a Docker container.

Each Docker image is based on a specific image. For example, we can use openjdk as the base image for a Java-based Docker image. Otherwise, it can be based on the Ubuntu image and then install the Java runtime in the image instructions.

An image is built using a *Dockerfile*, which is a simple text file containing instructions composing an image. Each instruction in a Dockerfile will create a separate layer inside the Docker image. So, when we change instructions in the Dockerfile and rebuild the image, only the new instruction's layer is built. This way, we get lightweight images that can be updated very quickly, which is not the case with other virtualization technologies.

Containers

When we run an image, we get a container. The container structure and behavior are defined by the image's content.

Docker containers are managed via the Docker CLI. We can have many designs for the containers. For example, we can plug storage into a container or even connect it to a network.

When a container is deleted, its state will be lost if it's not persisted to storage.

Docker Machine

The Docker Machine is a tool that makes it easy to provision and manage multiple Docker hosts remotely. This tool manages the hosts with the docker-machine commands: we can start, inspect, stop, and restart a managed host, and upgrade the Docker installation. We can even use it to configure a Docker client to talk to the given host. Then, we can use the local CLI directly on that remote host.

For example, say we have a Docker Machine on Azure called `azure-env`. If we do `docker-machine env azure-env`, we are pointing our local `docker` commands to be executed on that `azure-env` Docker Engine.

Diving Into Docker Containers

The best way to learn more about Docker is to write an app the Docker way.

Docker Containers in Development Environments

In many projects, the Development environment is different from the Production environment. This can lead to problems when deploying the application for Production. Sometimes, a small difference between environments can create huge problems. Here is where Docker can help: you can have the same image for both environments. Developers and testers can be using the same image as the Production environment.

Other than packaging the application codebase, the Docker image will also package all the required dependencies. This can guarantee a perfect match between environments.

Define a Container with Dockerfile

As discussed, the Dockerfile defines the container and determines how it will be executed. Consider the example in Listing 1-1.

Listing 1-1. Example of a Dockerfile

```
# Use an OpenJDK Runtime as a parent image
FROM openjdk:11-jre-alpine

# Add Maintainer Info
LABEL maintainer="lnibrass@gmail.com"

# Define environment variables
ENV JAVA_OPTS="-Xmx2048m"
```

```
# Set the working directory to /app
WORKDIR /app

# Copy the artifact into the container at /app
ADD some-application-built-somewhere.jar app.jar

# Make port 8080 available to the world outside this container
EXPOSE 8080

# Run app.jar when the container launches
CMD ["java", "-Djava.security.egd=file:/dev/./urandom", "-jar", "/app/app.jar"]
```

This Dockerfile will:

- Create a container based on OpenJDK 11

- Define an environment variable of the maximum memory allocation pool for the JVM to 2GB

- Define the working directory to /app

- Copy the some-application-built-somewhere.jar file from the local path as app.jar

- Open the port 8080

- Define the startup command that will be executed when the container starts

Create a Sample Application

We will create sample-app: a HelloWorld Quarkus application using code.quarkus.io. We need just to define the GroupId and the ArtifactId. For the extensions, let's pick the RESTEasy JAX-RS:

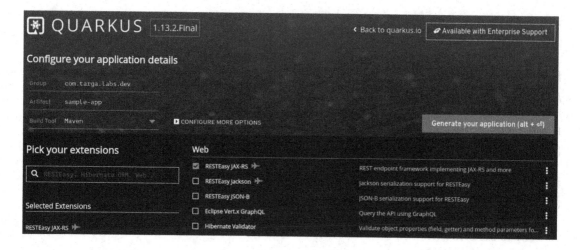

The generated application comes with a sample Rest API:

```
@Path("/hello-resteasy")
public class GreetingResource {

    @GET
    @Produces(MediaType.TEXT_PLAIN)
    public String hello() {
        return "Hello RESTEasy";
    }
}
```

When we compile this application using mvn clean install, our JAR will be available in the target folder.

Running this command in the target folder will show only the files in the current folder:

```
$ ls -p target/ | grep -v /
```

```
quarkus-artifact.properties
sample-app-1.0.0-SNAPSHOT.jar
```

Instead of writing our own Dockerfile when generating a new project, Quarkus comes with a set of Dockerfiles available in the src/main/docker folder:

```
$ ls -p src/main/docker | grep -v /
```

Dockerfile.jvm   ①
Dockerfile.legacy-jar   ②
Dockerfile.native   ③
Dockerfile.native-distroless   ④

These Dockerfiles are used to build a container that runs the Quarkus application:

① In JVM mode with the fast-jar packaging format, which was designed to provide faster startup times.

② In JVM mode with the legacy-jar packaging.

③ In Native mode (no JVM). ⟲ We will talk a lot about Native mode in the next chapters. ☺

④ In a Distroless container. ☞ It contains the application and its runtime dependencies, without any extra components like package managers, shells, or any other programs usually available in any standard Linux distribution.

Let's build the JVM mode-based Docker container and tag it as nebrass/sample-jvm:1.0.0-SNAPSHOT:

```
> mvn package && docker build -f src/main/docker/Dockerfile.jvm -t nebrass/
sample-jvm:1.0.0-SNAPSHOT .
```

```
Sending build context to Docker daemon  51.09MB
Step 1/11 : FROM registry.access.redhat.com/ubi8/ubi-minimal:8.3          ①
8.3: Pulling from ubi8/ubi-minimal                                        ①
77a02d8cede1: Pull complete                                               ①
7777f1ac6191: Pull complete                                               ①
Digest: sha256:e72e188c6b20281e241fb3cf6f8fc974dec4cc6ed0c9d8f2d5460c30
c35893b3                                                                  ①
Status: Downloaded newer image for registry.access.redhat.com/ubi8/
ubi-minimal:8.3                                                           ①
 ---> 91d23a64fdf2                                                         ②
Step 2/11 : ARG JAVA_PACKAGE=java-11-openjdk-headless
 ---> Running in 6f73b83ed808
```

```
Removing intermediate container 6f73b83ed808
 ---> 35ba9340154b                                                          ②
Step 3/11 : ARG RUN_JAVA_VERSION=1.3.8
 ---> Running in 695d7dcf4639
Removing intermediate container 695d7dcf4639
 ---> 04e28e22951e                                                          ②
Step 4/11 : ENV LANG="en_US.UTF-8" LANGUAGE="en_US:en"
 ---> Running in 71dc02dbee31
Removing intermediate container 71dc02dbee31
 ---> 7c7c69eead06                                                          ②
Step 5/11 : RUN microdnf install curl ca-certificates ${JAVA_PACKAGE} \
    && microdnf update \
    && microdnf clean all \
    && mkdir /deployments \
    && chown 1001 /deployments \
    && chmod "g+rwX" /deployments \
    && chown 1001:root /deployments \
    && curl https://repo1.maven.org/maven2/io/fabric8/run-java-sh/${RUN_
    JAVA_VERSION}/run-java-sh-${RUN_JAVA_VERSION}-sh.sh -o /deployments/
    run-java.sh \
    && chown 1001 /deployments/run-java.sh \
    && chmod 540 /deployments/run-java.sh \
    && echo "securerandom.source=file:/dev/urandom" >> /etc/alternatives/
    jre/lib/security/java.security
 ---> Running in 2274fdc94d6f
Removing intermediate container 2274fdc94d6f
 ---> 9fd48c2d9482                                                          ②
Step 6/11 : ENV JAVA_OPTIONS="-Dquarkus.http.host=0.0.0.0 -Djava.util.
logging.manager=org.jboss.logmanager.LogManager"
 ---> Running in c0e3ddc80993
Removing intermediate container c0e3ddc80993
 ---> 26f287fde6f6                                                          ②
Step 7/11 : COPY target/lib/* /deployments/lib/
 ---> 1c3aa9a683a6                                                          ②
Step 8/11 : COPY target/*-runner.jar /deployments/app.jar
```

```
---> d1bdd5e96e5e                                                    ②
Step 9/11 : EXPOSE 8080
 ---> Running in 728f82b270d2
Removing intermediate container 728f82b270d2
 ---> 704cd49fd439                                                   ②
Step 10/11 : USER 1001
 ---> Running in 5f7aef93c3d7
Removing intermediate container 5f7aef93c3d7
 ---> 5a773add2a6d                                                   ②
Step 11/11 : ENTRYPOINT [ "/deployments/run-java.sh" ]
 ---> Running in cb6d917592bc
Removing intermediate container cb6d917592bc
 ---> 9bc81f158728                                                   ②
Successfully built 9bc81f158728                                      ③
Successfully tagged nebrass/sample-jvm:latest                       ④
```

① As Docker didn't find the ubi8/ubi-minimal image locally, it downloads it from the registry.access.redhat.com/ubi8/ubi-minimal:8.3.

② Every instruction in the Dockerfile is built in a dedicated step and it generates a separated LAYER in the IMAGE. The HEX code is shown at the end of each step is the ID of the LAYER.

③ The built IMAGE ID.

④ Our built image is tagged with nebrass/sample-jvm:latest; we specified the name (nebrass/sample-jvm:latest) and Docker added the latest version tag automatically.

WHAT IS THE UBI BASE IMAGE?

The provided Dockerfiles use UBI (*Universal Base Image*) as the parent image. This base image has been tailored to work perfectly in containers. The Dockerfiles use the minimal version of the base image to reduce the size of the produced image.

Where is the image that you just built? It's in your machine's local Docker image registry:

```
$ docker images
```

REPOSITORY	TAG	IMAGE ID	CREATED	SIZE
nebrass/sample-jvm	1.0.0-SNAPSHOT	9bc81f158728	5 minutes ago	501MB
ubi8/ubi-minimal	8.3	ccfb0c83b2fe	4 weeks ago	107MB

Locally, there are two images—ubi8/ubi-minimal is the base image and nebrass/sample-jvm is the built image.

Run the App

Now run the built container, mapping your machine's port 28080 to the container's published port 8080 using -p:

```
$ docker run --rm -p 28080:8080 nebrass/sample-jvm:1.0.0-SNAPSHOT
1 exec java -Dquarkus.http.host=0.0.0.0 -Djava.util.logging.manager=org.
  jboss.logmanager.LogManager -XX:+ExitOnOutOfMemoryError -cp . -jar /
  deployments/app.jar
2 __  ____  __  _____   ___  __ ____  _____
3 --/ __ \/ / / / _ | / _ \/ //_/ / / / __/
4 -/ /_/ / /_/ / __ |/ , _/ ,< / /_/ /\ \
5 --_____/_/ |_/_/|_/_/|_|\____/___/
6 2020-08-05 13:53:44,198 INFO  [io.quarkus] (main) sample-app
  1.0.0-SNAPSHOT on JVM (powered by Quarkus 1.6.1.Final) started in 0.588s.
  Listening on: http://0.0.0.0:8080
7 2020-08-05 13:53:44,218 INFO  [io.quarkus] (main) Profile prod activated.
8 2020-08-05 13:53:44,219 INFO  [io.quarkus] (main) Installed features:
  [cdi, resteasy]
```

- Line 1 shows the command that will start the Java application in the container.

- Lines 2-8 are listing the logs of the Quarkus application.
  There you will see a message mentioning Listening on:
  http://0.0.0.0:8080. This log is printed by the instance packaged

in the container, which is not aware by our tweak: we mapped the container port 8080 to our custom 28080, which obviously makes the URL http://localhost:28080.

If you open the URL http://localhost:28080 in a web browser, you will land on the default Quarkus index.html file, as shown in the image:

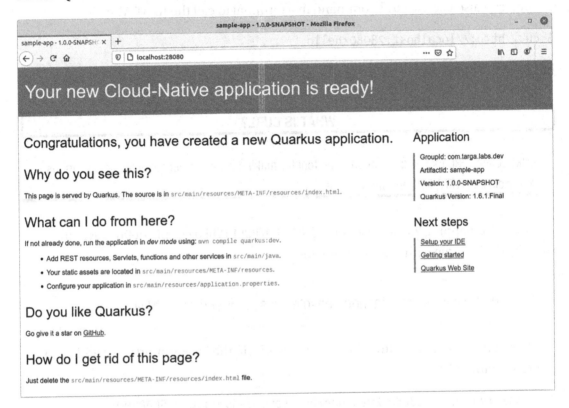

If you go to http://localhost:28080/hello in a web browser, you will see the response of the ExampleResource REST API.

ℹ   If you are using Docker Toolbox on Windows 7 and you couldn't access the container using the localhost, you need to use the Docker Machine IP. Use the command `docker-machine ip` to find it.

You can also use the `curl` command in a terminal to call the REST API:

```
$ curl http://localhost:28080/hello

hello%
```

```
WHAT IS CURL?
```

cURL (Client URL tool) is a command-line tool for making client-server requests using various protocols like HTTP, FTP, and many more.

The port mapping 28080:8080 is the EXPOSED/PUBLISHED couple defined when running `docker run` with the -p parameter.

ℹ   To quit a container-attached console session, just press Ctrl+C.

To run the Docker container in *detached mode* (in the background), just add -d to the run command:

```
$ docker run -d -p 28080:8080 nebrass/sample-jvm:1.0.0-SNAPSHOT

fbf2fba8e9b14a43e3b25aea1cb94b751bbbb6b73af05b84aab3f686ba5019c8
```

Here we get the long container ID for the app and then are kicked back to the terminal. ☺ The container is running in the background.

We can also see that there is an abbreviated container identifier with `docker ps`. We can use the long or short format when running any command:

```
$ docker ps

CONTAINER ID   IMAGE                 COMMAND                 STATUS
PORTS
fbf2fba8e9b1   nebrass/sample-jvm..  "/deployments/run-ja..."  Up
28080->8080/tcp
```

We can see that we have a running container, which has our custom ports mapping. We will use its CONTAINER ID to manage it. For example to stop this container, we will run:

```
docker stop fbf2fba8e9b1
```

After running the command, in order to confirm the operation, Docker will print the container ID again.

Publish Your Image

A local image is not useful at all.😊 Images need to be stored in a centralized location, in order to be pulled from different environments.

Docker images are stored in a centralized place called the *Docker Registry*. The Docker Hub's main responsibility is the registry. Each image collection is hosted in the registry as a repository.

By default, the Docker CLI is on the Docker Hub.

Log In with Your Docker ID

We will be using the free tier of the Docker Hub in this section. You can create a free account at https://hub.docker.com/ if you don't have one.

To authenticate your Docker client to the Docker Hub, just enter this command:

```
docker login -u <username> -p <password>
```

ℹ️   Recall that Docker Hub is by default the Docker Registry. If you want to change this, just specify a Registry URL using the docker login command.

Tag the Image

An image stored on a registry has a name format that looks like `username/repository:tag`. The `tag` contains versioning information, which is optional but highly recommended. If you don't explicitly specify a tag, Docker will define the tag as `latest`, which cannot provide any information about the packaged application version.

The Docker command used to define a tag for an image is as follows:

```
docker tag image username/repository:tag
```

For example, if you want to promote a `SNAPSHOT` version to `Final`, you do this:

```
docker tag nebrass/sample-jvm:1.0.0-SNAPSHOT nebrass/sample-jvm:1.0.0-Final
```

Run the `docker images` command to see your newly tagged image:

```
$ docker images
```

REPOSITORY	TAG	IMAGE ID	CREATED	SIZE
nebrass/sample-jvm	1.0.0-Final	598712377440	43 minutes ago	501MB
nebrass/sample-jvm	1.0.0-SNAPSHOT	598712377440	43 minutes ago	501MB
ubi8/ubi-minimal	8.1	91d23a64fdf2	4 weeks ago	107MB

Publish the Image

Publishing an image is making it available in some container's registry. In our case, we will push the tagged image to the registry:

```
docker push username/repository:tag
```

The tagged image is now available on the Docker Hub. If you go to `https://hub.docker.com/r/username/repository`, you will find the new image there.

💡 You need to be authenticated using the `docker login` command before pushing images.

Let's push the nebrass/sample-jvm:1.0.0-Final tagged image:

```
docker push nebrass/sample-jvm:1.0.0-Final
```

```
The push refers to repository [docker.io/nebrass/sample-jvm]
0f8895a56cf0: Pushed
9c443a7a1622: Pushed
fb6a9f86c4e7: Pushed
eddba477a8ae: Pushed
f80c95f61fff: Pushed
1.0.0-Final: digest: sha256:30342f5f4a432a2818040438a24525c8ef9d046f29e3283
ed2e84fdbdbe3af55 size: 1371
```

Pull and Run the Image from Docker Hub

The application packaged inside the nebrass/sample-jvm Docker image can now be executed on any Docker host. When you run docker run nebrass/sample-jvm, if the image is not available locally, it will be pulled from the Docker Hub. Let's remove all the local containers related to nebrass/sample-jvm:

```
docker ps -a | awk '{ print $1,$2 }' | grep nebrass/sample-jvm | awk
'{print $1 }' | xargs -I {} docker rm {}
```

Let's remove all the local images related to nebrass/sample-jvm:

```
docker images | awk '{ print $1":"$2 }' | grep nebrass/sample-jvm | xargs
-I {} docker rmi {}
```

If the image is not available locally, it will be pulled from the Docker Hub:

```
$ docker run -p 28080:8080 nebrass/sample-jvm:1.0.0-Final
```

```
Unable to find image 'nebrass/sample-jvm:1.0.0-Final' locally
1.0.0-Final: Pulling from nebrass/sample-jvm
b26afdf22be4: Already exists
218f593046ab: Already exists
284bc7c3a139: Pull complete
775c3b820c36: Pull complete
4d033ca6332d: Pull complete
```

```
Digest: sha256:30342f5f4a432a2818040438a24525c8ef9d046f29e3283ed2e84fdbdbe3af55
Status: Downloaded newer image for nebrass/sample-jvm:1.0.0-Final
...
```

The application packaged inside the nebrass/sample-jvm:1.0.0-Final image is now available with all its dependencies inside your machine. There's no need to install the Java runtime or to do any configuration. Everything is ready!

Play with Google Jib

Google created the Jib Maven plugin to build Docker images for Java applications. With Jib, you don't need to create a Dockerfile for your application. You don't even need to have Docker installed on your local machine. Jib will automatically analyze, build, make, and push the Docker Image.

The Docker workflow is shown here:

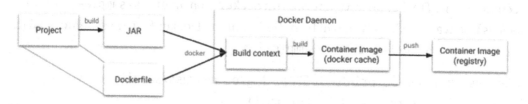

The Jib workflow is shown here:

Jib is not only available for Maven, it's also available for Gradle. It has a wide possibilities of configurations and tweaks that help you override any default configuration or fill a specific need, such as pushing the built image into a private Docker Registry.

💡 To use the Google Jib plugin with a private registry, you need to provide Jib with a credentials helper, such as described in the official Jib documentation at https://goo.gl/gDs66G.

In the Quarkus ecosystem, we have a Jib extension ready to use, called `quarkus-container-image-jib`. This extension is powered by Jib for performing container image builds. The major benefit of using Jib with Quarkus is that all the dependencies (everything found under `target/lib`) are cached in a different layer than the actual application, therefore making rebuilds really fast and small (when it comes to pushing). Another important benefit of using this extension is that it provides the ability to create a container image without having any dedicated client side tooling (like Docker) or running daemon processes (like the Docker daemon), when all that is needed is the ability to push to a container image registry.

To use this feature, add the following extension to your project:

```
./mvnw quarkus:add-extension -Dextensions="container-image-jib"
```

ℹ   When all you need to do is build a container image and not push to a registry (essentially by having set `quarkus.container-image.build=true` and left `quarkus.container-image.push` unset; it defaults to `false`), this extension creates a container image and registers it with the Docker daemon. This means that, although Docker isn't used to build the image, it is nevertheless necessary.

Also note that when using this mode, the built container image will show up when executing `docker images`.

Build with Google Jib

Build your container image without pushing it to a container image registry with this command:

```
mvn clean package -Dquarkus.container-image.build=true
```

If you want to build an image and push it to the authenticated container image registry, use this command:

```
mvn clean package -Dquarkus.container-image.build=true -Dquarkus.container-image.push=true
```

There are may configuration options available to customize the image or to do specific actions:

Configuration Property	Purpose
quarkus.container-image.group	The group the container image will be part of. If not set, it defaults to the logged-in user.
quarkus.container-image.name	The name of the container image. If not set, it defaults to the application name.
quarkus.container-image.tag	The tag of the container image. If not set, it defaults to the application version.
quarkus.container-image.registry	The container registry to use. If not set, it defaults to the authenticated registry.
quarkus.container-image.username	The username to use to authenticate with the registry where the built image will be pushed.
quarkus.container-image.password	The password to use to authenticate with the registry where the built image is pushed.

You can dig more into the great Jib extension using the "Quarkus Container Images Guide."

Meeting the Docker Services

In the enterprise world, applications are composed of many *services*. For example, an enterprise management application has many services: inventory management services, employee management services, and more. In a Dockerized environment, these services are shipped as containers. This choice offers many advantages, like scaling.

Docker has a great tool, called Docker Compose, that's used to define containers with great features like advanced networking and storage options. Docker Compose is very useful for local development.

Create the First docker-compose.yml File

The input of Docker Compose is a `docker-compose.yml` file, which is a plain YAML file that describes the design of the Docker Containers, along with many options such as allocated resources, networking, storage, and so on. See Listing 1-2.

Listing 1-2. Example of a docker-compose.yml File

```
version: "3"
services:
  web:
    image: nebrass/sample-jvm:1.0.0-Final
    deploy:
      replicas: 5
      restart_policy:
        condition: on-failure
    ports:
      - "8080:8080"
    networks:
      - webnetwork
networks:
  webnetwork:
```

This `docker-compose.yml` file will download the `nebrass/sample-jvm:1.0.0-Final` image from the Docker Hub and make five instances from this image. It will map the port 8080 to 8080. In case of failure, these containers will restart. These containers will be available inside the `webnetwork` network.

Achieving More with Docker

Docker optimizes the developer experience and boosts productivity in many ways. For example, you can use Docker containers to:

- Get the needed software and tools very quickly. For example, you can use Docker to get a local database or SonarQube instance.

- Build, debug, and run the source code, even if you don't have the right environment. For example, if you don't have JDK installed locally, or even if you don't have the same required version as a project, you can run it and test it inside containers.

- Resolve some technical requirements. For example, if you have an application that can be executed only on a specific port that's already used on your machine, you can use the container ports mapping feature to use the same application containerized with a different exposed port.

- And more! ☺

Get the Needed Tools Quickly

You can get a Database instance in seconds without any installations, and without touching the local environment or even modifying a local file. You don't have to worry that a MySQL daemon will keep using port 3306 even after uninstall. 😬

Get a Dockerized PostgreSQL Instance

For example, to have a local PostgreSQL instance, run the following:

```
docker run -d --name demo-postgres \           ①
      -e POSTGRES_USER=developer \              ②
      -e POSTGRES_PASSWORD=someCrazyPassword \  ②
      -e POSTGRES_DB=demo \                     ②
      -p 5432:5432 postgres:13                  ③
```

① You run the container called `demo-postgres` in detached mode (as a daemon in the background).

② You define the environment variables:

- Postgres user: `developer`

- Postgres password: `someCrazyPassword`

- Postgres database: `demo`

③ You forward the port 5432 → 5432 and use the official PostgreSQL Image v13.

You can use these credentials in your Java application like any other standalone PostgreSQL.

Unfortunately, the data will be stored exclusively inside the container. If it crashes or is deleted, all the data will be lost.

If you want to persist data available inside the container, you need to map a local mount point as a Docker data volume to a path inside the container.

I create a `volumes` folder (you can give the folder any name you like) in my home directory and then create subfolders for each of the applications I need to create data volume mount points.

Let's start by creating a folder that will be used to store the data in the host machine:

```
mkdir -p $HOME/docker-volumes/postgres
```

This `$HOME/docker-volumes/postgres` folder will be mapped to the `/var/lib/postgresql/data` folder of the PostgreSQL container, where PostgreSQL stores the physical data files.

The Docker command that runs a persistent PostgreSQL container will now be:

```
docker run -d --name demo-postgres \
        -e POSTGRES_USER=developer \
        -e POSTGRES_PASSWORD=someCrazyPassword \
        -e POSTGRES_DB=demo \
        -p 5432:5432 \
        -v $HOME/docker/volumes/postgres:/var/lib/postgresql/data \
        postgres:13
```

Let's move on to another use case that I love to talk about while discussing Docker benefits: having a local SonarQube server. 😊

Get a Dockerized SonarQube Instance

You can easily have a SonarQube instance, using just one Docker command:

```
docker run -d --name sonarqube \
        -p 9000:9000 \
        -p 9092:9092 \
        sonarqube:8.4.1-community
```

This command will run a container base on the Docker image `sonarqube:8.4.1-community` and expose the two SonarQube ports, 9000 and 9092.

If you are used to SonarQube, you can have your local instance, and you can import all the quality profiles (aka *gates*) that your team is using.

Unleash the Requirements Chains

We will not go far here while searching for a use case. We can take as an example the Quarkus requirements as a use case: one of the prerequisites is having GraalVM. If you don't have it installed locally, you can use a GraalVM Docker image to have a container that lets you do GraalVM-based builds.

Let's go back to the `sample-app` that we generated before. If we want to build a GraalVM-based JAR file without having GraalVM installed locally, we can use this example of Dockerfile, which we save as `src/main/docker/Dockerfile.multistage`. See Listing 1-3.

Listing 1-3. src/main/docker/Dockerfile.multistage

```
1 ## Stage 1 : build with maven builder image with native capabilities
2 FROM quay.io/quarkus/centos-quarkus-maven:20.1.0-java11 AS build
3 COPY pom.xml /usr/src/app/
4 RUN mvn -f /usr/src/app/pom.xml -B de.qaware.maven:go-offline-maven-
  plugin:1.2.5:resolve-dependencies
5 COPY src /usr/src/app/src
6 USER root
7 RUN chown -R quarkus /usr/src/app
8 USER quarkus
9 RUN mvn -f /usr/src/app/pom.xml -Pnative clean package
```

```
10
11 ## Stage 2 : create the docker final image
12 FROM registry.access.redhat.com/ubi8/ubi-minimal
13 WORKDIR /work/
14 COPY --from=build /usr/src/app/target/*-runner /work/application
15
16 # set up permissions for user `1001`
17 RUN chmod 775 /work /work/application \
18    && chown -R 1001 /work \
19    && chmod -R "g+rwX" /work \
20    && chown -R 1001:root /work
21
22 EXPOSE 8080
23 USER 1001
24
25 CMD ["./application", "-Dquarkus.http.host=0.0.0.0"]
```

This Dockerfile contains two embedded Dockerfiles. Note there are already two FROM instructions. Each part of this Dockerfile is called a *stage*, which is why we gave the Dockerfile the extension `multistage`.

In the first stage, we generate the native Quarkus executables using Maven, and in the second stage, we use the built JAR file to create the Docker runtime image. We did this using the installed Maven and Docker runtimes.

Traditionally, we have two Dockerfiles. The first one is dedicated to the Development and the second one to Production. The Development Dockerfile brings the JDK and the build tools, while the second one holds only the application binaries along with the runtime. This approach improves productivity, but not by much. We still need to manage two Dockerfiles, which will be painful if we have many applications.

Here comes the multistage builds. We have only one Dockerfile, which has a special name: `Dockerfile.multistage`. Inside, we will have two (or more) FROM instructions to define the base image for each stage. We can have different base images for Development and Production environments. We can have interaction between stages. For example, we can move files that were built in the Development stage to Production.

We build the multistaged Dockerfile the same way we do the regular (one stage) Dockerfile:

```
docker build -f Dockerfile.multistage -t nebrass/sample-app-multistaged .
```

If you run it, it's the same Docker image that we built in the previous steps, but smaller:

```
$ docker images | grep nebrass
```

```
REPOSITORY                       TAG       IMAGE ID       CREATED          SIZE
nebrass/sample-app-jvm           latest    5e1111eeae2b   13 minutes ago   501MB
nebrass/quarkus-multistaged      latest    50591fb707e7   58 minutes ago   199MB
```

The same application is packaged in both images, so why are they different sizes?

Before the multistage builds era, we used to write the instructions that will be executed, and every instruction in the Dockerfile added a layer to the image. So even if we had some cleaning instructions, they had a dedicated weight. In some cases, like many Red Hat Docker images, we used to create scripts that we run in just one instruction in the Dockerfile.

After the multistage builds became available, when we are building across different stages, the final image won't have any unnecessary content except the required artifact.

BUILDING THE NATIVE EXECUTABLE WITHOUT GRAALVM

Quarkus has a great feature that enables developers to build a native executable without having to install GraalVM. You need to have Docker installed, as in the previous steps, but don't have to spend effort on Dockerfiles. The command is just a Maven build:

```
$ mvn package -Pnative -Dquarkus.native.container-build=true
```

The build uses Docker. You can already notice the steps being logged:

```
[INFO] --- quarkus-maven-plugin:1.13.2.Final:build (default) @ example ---
...
[INFO] [io.quarkus.deployment.pkg.steps.NativeImageBuildContainerRunner]
Using docker to run the native image builder
[INFO] [io.quarkus.deployment.pkg.steps.NativeImageBuildContainerRunner]
Checking image status quay.io/quarkus/ubi-quarkus-native-image:21.0-java11
21.0-java11: Pulling from quarkus/ubi-quarkus-native-image
57de4da701b5: Pull complete
...
```

```
Status: Downloaded newer image for quay.io/quarkus/ubi-quarkus-native-
image:21.0-java11
...
[INFO] [io.quarkus.deployment.pkg.steps.NativeImageBuildStep] Running Quarkus
native-image plugin..
[INFO] [io.quarkus.deployment.pkg.steps.NativeImageBuildRunner] docker run
--env LANG=C --rm -v ..
[example-1.0.0-SNAPSHOT-runner:26]    classlist:    5 267,45 ms,   0,96 GB
[example-1.0.0-SNAPSHOT-runner:26]        (cap):      446,08 ms,   0,94 GB
[example-1.0.0-SNAPSHOT-runner:26]        setup:    2 105,02 ms,   0,94 GB

...
[example-1.0.0-SNAPSHOT-runner:26]      compile:   30 414,02 ms,   2,10 GB
[example-1.0.0-SNAPSHOT-runner:26]        image:    2 805,44 ms,   2,09 GB
[example-1.0.0-SNAPSHOT-runner:26]        write:    1 604,06 ms,   2,09 GB
[example-1.0.0-SNAPSHOT-runner:26]      [total]:   72 346,32 ms,   2,09 GB

...
[INFO] [io.quarkus.deployment.QuarkusAugmentor] Quarkus augmentation
completed in 117871ms
```

Containerization Is Not Docker Only

Docker is not the only available containerization solution on the market. Many alternatives are now available. Many of them resolve certain Docker limitations, such as Podman and Buildah.

What Are Docker's Limitations?

After installing Docker, we have a docker.service system that will remain running. To check its status, just type this command:

```
$ sudo service docker status
```

```
● docker.service - Docker Application Container Engine
     Loaded: loaded (/lib/systemd/system/docker.service; enabled; vendor
     preset: enabled)
     Active: active (running) since Thu 2020-08-06 09:23:19 CEST; 8h ago
TriggeredBy: ● docker.socket
```

```
     Docs: https://docs.docker.com
 Main PID: 1659 (dockerd)
    Tasks: 30
   Memory: 3.5G
   CGroup: /system.slice/docker.service
           └─1659 /usr/bin/dockerd -H fd://
--containerd=/run/containerd/containerd.sock
...
```

💡 You can also use operating system utilities, such as `sudo systemctl is-active docker` or `sudo status docker`, or check the service status using Windows Task Manager for example.

This permanently running daemon is the only way to communicate with the Docker Engine. Unfortunately, this is a *single point of failure*. This same daemon will be the parent process for all the running container processes. So, if this daemon is killed or corrupted, we will lose the communication with the engine and the running containers processes will remain orphans. Even more, if this process is greedy with resources, we cannot complain. 😩😩

This same daemon requires root access to be able to do its job, which can be annoying when developers are not granted full root rights to their workstations.

These limitations created the opportunity for other tools to start gaining popularity. We'll discuss two such tools next.

Meet Podman and Buildah

Podman is an alternative to Docker that offers an easier way to do all the containerization tasks that we usually do with Docker, but without the dependency of having a daemon process. The images and containers handled and made by Podman are compliant with the *Open Containers Initiative*.

Podman directly interacts with the image registry, with the container and image storage, and with the Linux kernel through the runC container runtime process (which is not a daemon).

WHAT IS RUNC?

runC (https://github.com/opencontainers/runc) is the Docker's container format and runtime, which Docker donated to the Open Containers Initiative.

WHAT IS THE OPEN CONTAINERS INITIATIVE?

The *Open Containers Initiative* (OCI) is a project hosted by the Linux Foundation to define all the standards and specifications for containers. It was initially launched in 2015 by many containerization-leading companies like Docker.

The project had two main branches. *Image Specification* defines all the standards and requirements for the images. *Runtime Specification* defines all the standards and requirements for the container runtimes.

Any solution seeking to be OCI-compliant needs to be compliant with its two branches of specifications.

With Podman, you can do all what yo are doing with Docker. You can use the same Docker commands with Podman, just by changing the word docker to podman. You can even create a docker alias for podman and everything will work like a charm! 😊

Users without privileges can finally run containers using Podman, with absolute need for the root user.

You can do builds with Podman like you are used to doing with Docker. Podman uses the same code as Buildah for the build process.

With *Buildah*, you can:

- Create an image from a Dockerfile.

- Create an image from an existing container. You can even do modifications on the container and publish them as a new image.

Buildah is the wrapper of the code that creates and manages container images with an advanced management of images.

Buildah's benefits include:

- Powerful control over creating image layers. You can even commit many changes to a single layer, instead of an instruction per layer with the classic Docker world.

- The Buildah CLI is used to write image instructions the same way you create Linux scripts. If you check the Buildah CLI help, you will find that the CLI commands are ones that you have in any Dockerfile instruction:

```
add             Add content to the container
commit          Create an image from a working container
copy            Copy content into the container
from            Create a working container based on an image
images          List images in local storage
info            Display Buildah system information
mount           Mount a working container's root filesystem
pull            Pull an image from the specified location
push            Push an image to a specified destination
rename          Rename a container
run             Run a command inside of the container
tag             Add an additional name to a local image
umount          Unmount the root file system of the specified
                working containers
unshare         Run a command in a modified user namespace
```

Podman gained popularity for two main reasons:

- It uses the same commands used with Docker.

- It uses the same tools used with Docker, such as Image Registries and container hosting solutions.

So every Docker user can switch to Podman. We can keep everything we are doing with Docker. There are cases where you cannot use Podman as an alternative to Docker. For example, in my case, I'm using TestContainers to get lightweight instances of databases for my JUnit tests. This great library has a strong dependency to Docker for provisioning databases for tests, and unfortunately, there are no active tasks for migrating it to Podman. 😩😖 You can check out this issue at testcontainers-java#2088.

Conclusion

Containerization is one of the most powerful technologies that came into the developers' world. 🎉 Many other technologies were born and based on containers, such as Podman, Buildah, and many others. 😄 For sure, you will not use them all, but you can pick the suitable ones that will help you do your job.

CHAPTER 2

Introduction to the Monolithic Architecture

Introduction to an Actual Situation

Nowadays, we use many methods to access online applications. For example, we can use a browser or client apps to access Facebook or Twitter. This is possible through their exposed Application Programming Interfaces (APIs). An API is a software boundary that allows two applications to communicate with each other using a specific protocol (HTTP, for example). In the Facebook context, when people use the mobile app while sending a message, the app uses the Facebook APIs to make the request. Next, the application uses its business logic and makes all the necessary databases queries and finalizes the request by returning HTTP responses.

This is the case with Amazon, eBay, and AliExpress: our main competitors. 😩 Yes! You will be using your Java skills in this book to develop an ecommerce application that will beat them all! 😄

 Yes! This book covers an Online Shop use case. 😄

This ecommerce application will have many components to manage customers, orders, products, reviews, carts, authentication, etc.

We are recruiting many developers for different teams. Every team will be dedicated to a specific business domain and every business domain will have its dedicated code. We have an architect who will be responsible for packaging and building the application.

© Nebrass Lamouchi 2021
N. Lamouchi, *Pro Java Microservices with Quarkus and Kubernetes*,
https://doi.org/10.1007/978-1-4842-7170-4_2

The Java application will be deployed as a huge WAR file that wraps all the code from the different teams and all the external dependencies of the project, such as frameworks and libraries. To deliver this application to the production team, the project manager has to be sure that all the software teams deliver their code on time. If one of the teams has a delay for any reason, the application will be delayed for sure, because it cannot be delivered with unfinished parts.

→ How can we solve this? 😫

We are hearing about Agility as well. Can our project adopt Agility? Can we benefit from an Agile process?

→ How can we solve this? 😫

We know that there are many periods during which our ecommerce site will be bombarded by customers, such as on Black Friday, the days before Christmas, Valentine's day, etc. We asked our production team to provide high-availability for this application. The solution is to have many running instances of the application to be sure it can handle the load. But is this solution the best one? Does our current architecture have benefits in the matter of high availability?

→ How can we solve this? 😫

Presenting the Context

The actual architecture of this application is *monolithic*, which means it consists of a single application that is:

- **Simple to design**: We can easily design and refactor the components, as we have a full view of the full ecosystem.

- **Simple to develop**: The goal of current development tools and IDEs is to support the development of monolithic applications.

- **Simple to deploy**: We need to deploy the WAR file (or directory hierarchy) to the appropriate runtime.

- **Simple to scale**: We can scale the application by running multiple copies of the application behind a load balancer.

However, once the application becomes large and the team grows in size, this approach has a number of drawbacks that become increasingly significant:

- **Increasing complexity**: A large monolithic codebase intimidates developers, especially new ones. The source code can be difficult to read/understand and refactor. As a result, development typically will slow down. It will be difficult to understand how to correctly implement a change, which will decrease the quality of the code.

- **Overloaded development machines**: A large application will cause heavy load on the development machines, which decreases productivity.

- **Overloaded servers**: A large application is hard to monitor and needs huge server resources, which impacts productivity.

- **Continuous deployment is difficult**: A large, monolithic application is also hard to deploy, as it will need strong synchronization between teams working on different services. Moreover, to update one component, you have to redeploy the entire application. The risk associated with redeployment increases, which discourages frequent updates. This is especially problematic for user interface developers, since they usually need to iterative rapidly and redeploy frequently.

- **Scaling the application can be difficult**: A monolithic architecture can only scale in one dimension: just by creating copies of the monolith. Each copy of application instance will access all the data, which makes caching less effective and increases memory consumption and I/O traffic. Also, different application components have different resource requirements. One might be CPU intensive and another might be memory intensive. With a monolithic architecture, we cannot scale each component independently.

- **Obstacle to a scaling development**: A monolithic application is also an obstacle to a scaling development. Once the application gets to a certain size, it's useful to divide the engineering organization into teams that focus on specific functional areas. The trouble with a monolithic application is that it prevents the teams from working independently. The teams must coordinate their development and deployment efforts. It is much more difficult for a team to make a change and update production.

Solving These Issues

To solve these issues, we will be talking about *microservices*: the main subject of this book and one of the trendiest words of nowadays, as I am writing this book. This is what we cover in the next few chapters. Stay tuned! 😈

I wish you happy reading. 😊 Good luck!😄

CHAPTER 3

Coding a Monolithic Application

Presenting the Domain

From the online shop, registered customers can purchase products that they find in the catalog. Customers can also read and post reviews about articles that they purchased. To simplify the use case for payments, we will be using Stripe or PayPal as a payment gateway.

---

❶ We will not be covering payment transactions in this book.

Use Case Diagram

The following functionalities are offered by the application:

- For the Customer: Search and Browse Product, Browse and Write Reviews, Create, View and Update Cart, Update Profile, and Checkout and pay.

- For the Shop Manager: Add Product, Update Product, and Remove Product.

© Nebrass Lamouchi 2021
N. Lamouchi, *Pro Java Microservices with Quarkus and Kubernetes*,
https://doi.org/10.1007/978-1-4842-7170-4_3

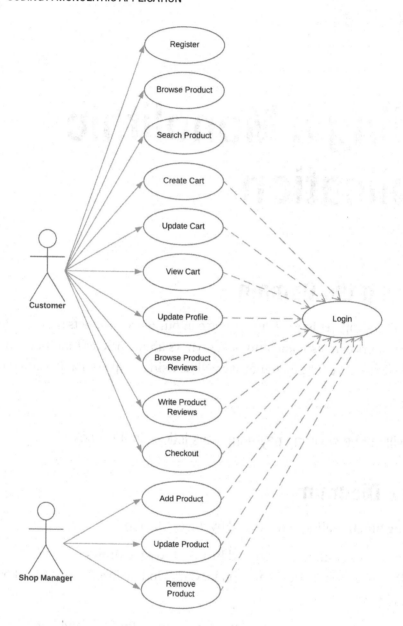

Class Diagram

The class diagram will look like this:

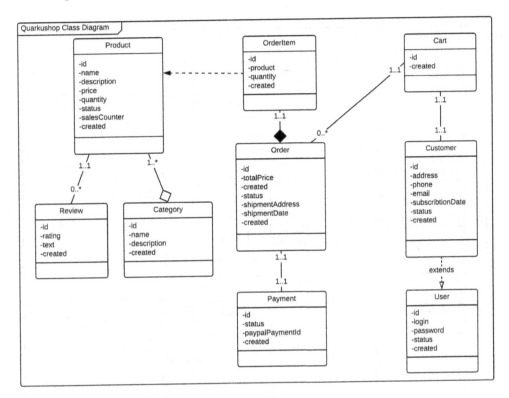

Sequence Diagram

The sequence diagram for a classic shopping trip will look like this:

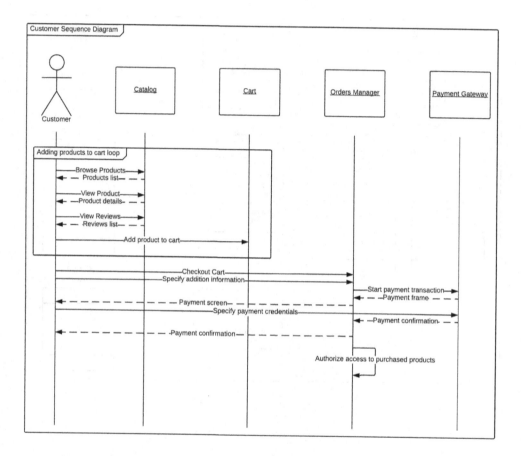

Coding the Application

It's almost time to start coding the application. Before attacking the code, let's look at the technical stack that we will be using.

Presenting the Technology Stack

In this book, we are implementing the backend of an ecommerce application, so our stack will be:

- 🛢 PostgreSQL 13

- ☕ Java 11 with GraalVM 21.0.x

- Maven 3.6.2+

- Quarkus 1.13+

- The latest version of 🐳 Docker

The PostgreSQL Database

As a requirement, you need to have a 🛢 PostgreSQL instance. You can use your 🐳 Docker skills to create it quickly, simply by typing:

```
docker run -d --name demo-postgres \          ①
        -e POSTGRES_USER=developer \          ②
        -e POSTGRES_PASSWORD=p4SSWOrd \       ③
        -e POSTGRES_DB=demo \                 ④
        -p 5432:5432 postgres:13              ⑤
```

① Run the container called demo-postgres in detached mode (as a daemon in the background).

② Define the environment variables:

- Postgres user: developer

- Postgres password: p4SSWOrd

- Postgres database: demo

③ Forward the port 5432 → 5432 and use the official PostgreSQL Image v13.

Java 11

Java Standard Edition 11 is a major feature edition, released on September 25th, 2018.

ℹ️   You can check out the Java 11 new features at `https://openjdk.java.net/projects/jdk/11/`.

Can you see why we used Java 11 and not 16 (the latest while writing this book) 😬? It's because Java 11 is the maximum version available for GraalVM.

⚠️   The Quarkus Team highly recommends using Java 11, as Quarkus 2.x does not support Java 8.

Maven

Here's the official introduction of Maven from its website:

> *Maven,* a Yiddish word meaning accumulator of knowledge, was originally started as an attempt to simplify the build processes in the Jakarta Turbine project. There were several projects, each with their own Ant build files that were all slightly different and JARs were checked into CVS. We wanted a standard way to build the projects, a clear definition of what the project consisted of, an easy way to publish project information, and a way to share JARs across several projects.
>
> The result is a tool that can now be used for building and managing any Java-based project. We hope that we have created something that will make the day-to-day work of Java developers easier and generally help with the comprehension of any Java-based project.

Maven's primary goal is to allow developers to comprehend the complete state of a development effort in the shortest period. In order to attain this goal, there are several areas of concern that Maven attempts to deal with:

- Making the build process easy

- Providing a uniform build system

- Providing quality project information

- Providing guidelines for best practices development

- Allowing transparent migration to new features

The Quarkus Framework

Quarkus is a full-stack, cloud-native Java framework made for JVMs and native compilation, optimizing Java specifically for containers and enabling it to become an effective platform for serverless, cloud, and Kubernetes environments.

Quarkus is designed to work with popular Java standards, frameworks, and libraries, such as Eclipse MicroProfile and Spring, as well as Apache Kafka, RESTEasy (JAX-RS), Hibernate ORM (JPA), Spring, Infinispan, and many more.

The dependency injection mechanism in Quarkus is based on CDI (contexts and dependency injection) and includes an extension framework to expand functionality and to configure, boot, and integrate a framework into your application. Adding an extension is as easy as adding a Maven dependency.

It also configures GraalVM with the necessary metadata needed to build the native binary.

Quarkus was designed to be easy to use right from the start, with features that work well with little to no configuration.

Developers can choose the Java frameworks they want for their applications, which can be run in JVM mode or compiled and run in Native mode.

Quarkus also includes the following capabilities:

- Live coding so that developers can immediately check the effect of code changes and quickly troubleshoot them

- Unified imperative and reactive programming with an embedded managed event bus

- Unified configuration

- Easy native executable generation

JetBrains IntelliJ IDEA

IntelliJ IDEA, the flagship JetBrains IDE for JVM languages, is designed to maximize developer productivity.

IntelliJ IDEA helps you stay productive with a suite of features for efficient development, such as intelligent coding assistance, reliable refactorings, on-the-fly code analysis, smart code navigation, built-in developer tools, web and enterprise development support, and much more.

IntelliJ IDEA Ultimate provides first-class support for microservices frameworks and technologies, including Quarkus, Micronaut, Spring, Helidon, and OpenAPI.

Specifically for Quarkus, IntelliJ IDEA includes the Quarkus Project Wizard, which will walk you through the initial configuration of a new project and allow you to specify its name, Java version, build tool, extensions, and more. The IDE provides intelligent code insight for Quarkus .properties and YAML configuration files. It also allows you to create a Quarkus Run Configuration. You can run and debug configurations, application servers, database sessions, Docker connections, and more all from one place—the Services tool window.

IntelliJ IDEA Ultimate provides an aggregated view of the client and server APIs used in your project for HTTP and WebSocket protocols in the Endpoints tool window.

With the integrated editor-based HTTP client, you can compose, edit, and execute HTTP requests right in the editor while testing your web service.

IntelliJ IDEA lets you connect to locally running Docker machines to manage images, containers, and Docker Compose services. What's more, the IDE provides support for Kubernetes resource configuration files.

🔥   JetBrains is offering to all my readers an extended trial license for IntelliJ IDEA Ultimate, which is valid for three months instead of the regular one-month trial license. ☺

You can redeem your extended trial license by using this coupon code **IJBOOK202**. Go to `https://www.jetbrains.com/store/redeem/` to redeem it.

Thank you JetBrains for your support!

⚠   The coupon code is valid only for new users. ☺

Implementing the QuarkuShop

Now we will start the implementation of this application. We will split the implementation using the layers composing a typical Java EE Application. For this split, I use an old architectural pattern called Entity Control Boundary, initially published by Ivar Jacobson in 1992. This pattern aims to classify each software component based on its responsibility.

- **Entity → Persistence Layer** holds the entities, JPA repositories, and related classes.

- **Control → Services Layer** holds the services, configuration, batches, etc.

- **Boundary → Web Layer** holds the web services endpoints.

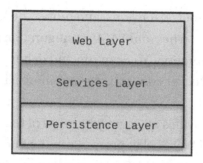

Generating the Project Skull

Here we go! In this section, you will start discovering and using the great features and options offered by the Quarkus Framework.

To avoid the hard parts when creating a new project and getting it started, the Quarkus Team has created the *Code Quarkus Project*. This is an online tool for easily generating a Quarkus application structure. It offers the ability to choose the build tool (Maven or Gradle) and to pick the extensions that you want to add to your project.

QUARKUS EXTENSION

Think of Quarkus *extensions* as project dependencies. Extensions configure, boot, and integrate a framework or technology into your Quarkus application. They also do all of the heavy lifting of providing the right information to GraalVM for your application to compile natively.

ℹ   If you are used to the Spring Boot ecosystem, the Code Quarkus is the equivalent of the Spring Initializr and the Quarkus extension is roughly similar to the Spring Boot Starters.

You can generate a Quarkus-based application in several ways:

- Using a web-based interface code.quarkus.io

- Using the Quarkus Maven archetype, for example:

```
mvn io.quarkus:quarkus-maven-plugin:1.13.2.Final:create \
    -DprojectGroupId=org.acme \
```

```
    -DprojectArtifactId=getting-started \
    -DclassName="org.acme.getting.started.GreetingResource" \
    -Dpath="/hello"
```

To run the generated application, just run mvn quarkus:dev, as follows:

```
$ mvn quarkus:dev
...
[INFO] Scanning for projects...
[INFO]
[INFO] ---------------------< org.acme:getting-started >------------------
[INFO] Building getting-started 1.0.0-SNAPSHOT
[INFO] --------------------------------[ jar ]---------------------------
[INFO]
[INFO] --- quarkus-maven-plugin:1.13.2.Final:dev (default-cli) @ getting-
        started ---
[INFO] Using 'UTF-8' encoding to copy filtered resources.
[INFO] Copying 2 resources
[INFO] Nothing to compile - all classes are up to date
Listening for transport dt_socket at address: 5005

 __  ____  __  ____   ____  __ ___  _____
 --/ __ \/ / / / _ | / _ \/ //_/ / / / __/
 -/ /_/ / /_/ / __ |/ , _/ ,< / /_/ /\ \
--_____/_/ |_/_/|_/_/|_|\____/___/
2021-04-24 17:07:20,323 INFO  [io.quarkus] (Quarkus Main Thread) getting-
started 1.0.0-SNAPSHOT on JVM (powered by Quarkus 1.13.2.Final) started in
1.476s. Listening on: http://localhost:8080
2021-04-24 17:07:20,336 INFO  [io.quarkus] (Quarkus Main Thread) Profile
dev activated. Live Coding activated.
2021-04-24 17:07:20,336 INFO  [io.quarkus] (Quarkus Main Thread) Installed
features: [cdi, resteasy]
```

WHAT IS THE ROLE OF MVN QUARKUS:DEV?

You can run it using `mvn quarkus:dev`, which enables hot deployment with background compilation, which means that when you modify your Java files or your resource files and refresh your browser, these changes will automatically take effect.

This also works for resource files like the configuration property file.

The act of refreshing the browser triggers a scan of the workspace, and if any changes are detected, the Java files are compiled, and the application is redeployed. Your request is then serviced by the redeployed application. If there are any issues with compilation or deployment, an error page will let you know.

Starting from Quarkus 1.11, the `mvn quarkus:dev` will enable the Quarkus Dev UI, which is a developer's console that visualizes all the extensions currently loaded along with their status and a direct link to their documentation. The Dev UI looks like this:

For example, we can see the Beans listed by the Arc Extension available at
`http://localhost:8080/q/dev/io.quarkus.quarkus-arc/beans`:

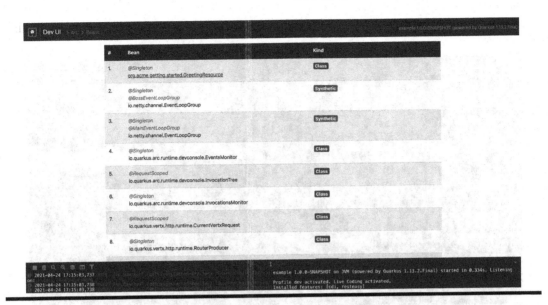

When you go to `http://localhost:8080/index.html`:

Your new Cloud-Native application is ready!

Congratulations, you have created a new Quarkus application.

Why do you see this?

This page is served by Quarkus. The source is in `src/main/resources/META-INF/resources/index.html`.

What can I do from here?

If not already done, run the application in *dev mode* using: `mvn compile quarkus:dev`.

- Add REST resources, Servlets, functions and other services in `src/main/java`.
- Your static assets are located in `src/main/resources/META-INF/resources`.
- Configure your application in `src/main/resources/application.properties`.

Do you like Quarkus?

Go give it a star on GitHub.

How do I get rid of this page?

Just delete the `src/main/resources/META-INF/resources/index.html` file.

Application

GroupId: org.acme
ArtifactId: getting-started
Version: 1.0-SNAPSHOT
Quarkus Version: 1.6.1.Final

Next steps

Setup your IDE
Getting started
Quarkus Web Site

For this Quarkus project, you will use the web interface to generate the project skull:

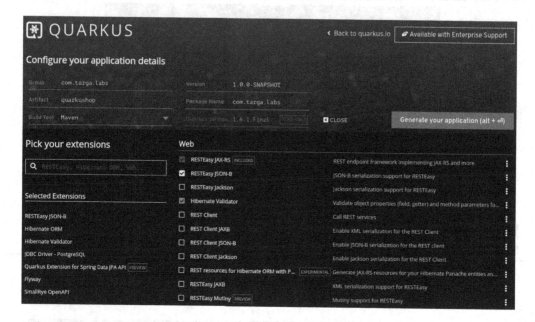

Pick these extensions:

- **RESTEasy JSON-B**: Adds the JSON-B serialization library support for RESTEasy.

- **SmallRye OpenAPI**: Documents your REST APIs based on the OpenAPI specification and comes with Swagger UI.

- **Hibernate ORM**: Adds all the requirements to define the persistent model with Hibernate ORM as JPA Implementation.

- **Hibernate Validator**: Adds the mechanisms for validating the input/output of the REST APIs and/or the parameters and return values of the methods of your business services.

- **JDBC Driver - PostgreSQL**: Adds the requirements to help you connect to the PostgreSQL database via JDBC.

- **Quarkus Extension for Spring Data JPA API**: Brings the Spring Data JPA to Quarkus to create your Data Access Layer, as you are used to in Spring Boot.

- **Flyway**: Handles the database schema migrations.

You need to add Lombok to the pom.xml file. Project Lombok is a Java library that automatically plugs into your editor and build tools, spicing up your Java. Lombok saves the time and effort of writing boilerplate code like getters/setters/constructors/etc.

Here's the Lombok Maven dependency:

```
<dependency>
    <groupId>org.projectlombok</groupId>
    <artifactId>lombok</artifactId>
    <version>1.18.16</version>
</dependency>
```

ℹ️   We will add more dependencies to this example as we need them.

Once you create the blank project, you can start building the monolithic layers. Let's begin with the persistence layer.

Creating the Persistence Layer

If you look back at the class diagram, you'll see these Entity classes:

- Address
- Cart
- Category
- Customer
- Order
- OrderItem
- Payment
- Product
- Review

Here are some of the enumerations:

- CartStatus
- OrderStatus

- ProductStatus

- PaymentStatus

This diagram illustrates the relationship between the classes:

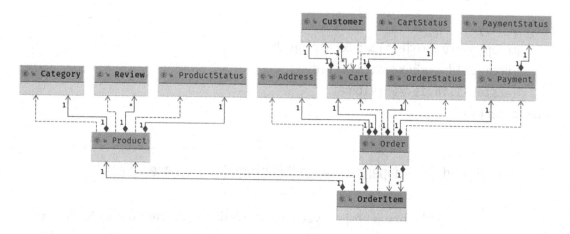

For every entity of the list, you will create:

- A JPA entity

- A Spring Data JPA repository

These entities will share some attributes that are always commonly used, like id, created date, etc. These attributes will be located in the AbstractEntity class that will be extended by our entities.

The AbstractEntity looks like this:

```
@Getter ①
@Setter ①
@MappedSuperclass ②
@EntityListeners(AuditingEntityListener.class) ③
public abstract class AbstractEntity {

    @Id
    @GeneratedValue(strategy = GenerationType.AUTO)
    private Long id;

    @Column(name = "created_date", nullable = false)
    private Instant createdDate;
```

```
@Column(name = "last_modified_date")
private Instant lastModifiedDate;
}
```

① The Lombok annotations generate getters and setters for the AbstractEntity class.

② Declares this class as JPA base class, which holds properties that will be inherited by the subclasses entities[1].

③ Activates auditing the entity using the AuditingEntityListener class[2]:

```
public class AuditingEntityListener {
    @PrePersist ①
    void preCreate(AbstractEntity auditable) {
        Instant now = Instant.now();
        auditable.setCreatedDate(now);
        auditable.setLastModifiedDate(now);
    }

    @PreUpdate ②
    void preUpdate(AbstractEntity auditable) {
        Instant now = Instant.now();
        auditable.setLastModifiedDate(now);
    }
}
```

① Specifies that the annotated method will be invoked before persisting the entity in the database.

② Specifies that the annotated method will be invoked before updating the entity in the database.

Cart

The class Cart entity looks like this:

```
@Getter ①
@Setter ①
```

```java
@NoArgsConstructor ②
@ToString(callSuper = true) ③
@Entity ④
@Table(name = "carts") ④
public class Cart extends AbstractEntity {

    @ManyToOne
    private final Customer customer;

    @NotNull ⑤
    @Column(nullable = false) ⑥
    @Enumerated(EnumType.STRING)
    private final CartStatus status;

    public Cart(Customer customer, @NotNull CartStatus status) {
        this.customer = customer;
        this.status = status;
    }

    @Override
    public boolean equals(Object o) {
        if (this == o) return true;
        if (o == null || getClass() != o.getClass()) return false;
        Cart cart = (Cart) o;
        return Objects.equals(customer, cart.customer) &&
                status == cart.status;
    }

    @Override
    public int hashCode() {
        return Objects.hash(customer, status);
    }
}
```

① This Lombok annotation generates getters/setters for all fields.

② This Lombok annotation generates a no-args constructor, which is **required by JPA**.

③ This Lombok annotation generates the toString() method based on the current class fields and including the superclass fields.

④ This is an @Entity and its corresponding @Table will be named carts.

⑤ Validation annotation used to control the integrity of the data. If the status is null, a Validation Exception will be thrown.[3]

⑥ Column definition: name, length, and a definition of a nullability constraint.

♀   The difference between the validation annotations and constraints defined in the @Column is that the validation annotations are application-scoped and the constraints are DB scoped.

The CartRepository looks like this:

```
@Repository ①
public interface CartRepository extends JpaRepository<Cart, Long> { ②

    List<Cart> findByStatus(CartStatus status); ③

    List<Cart> findByStatusAndCustomerId(CartStatus status, Long customerId); ③
}
```

① Indicates that an annotated class is a repository, as originally defined by *Domain-Driven Design* (Eric Evans, 2003) as "a mechanism for encapsulating storage, retrieval, and search behavior which emulates a collection of objects."

② JPA specific extension of a repository in Spring Data JPA. This will enable Spring Data to find this interface and automatically create an implementation for it.

③ These methods implement queries automatically using the Spring Data Query Methods Builder Mechanism.

WHAT IS A SPRING DATA JPAREPOSITORY?

`JpaRepository` extends `PagingAndSortingRepository`, which in turn extends `CrudRepository`. Their main functions are:

- `CrudRepository` mainly provides CRUD functions.

- `PagingAndSortingRepository` provides methods to do pagination and sorting records.

- `JpaRepository` provides some JPA-related method such as flushing the persistence context and delete record in a batch.

Because of the inheritance mentioned here, `JpaRepository` will have all the functions of `CrudRepository` and `PagingAndSortingRepository`. So if you don't need the repository to have the functions provided by `JpaRepository` and `PagingAndSortingRepository`, use `CrudRepository`.

WHAT IS THE SPRING DATA QUERY METHODS BUILDER MECHANISM?

The query builder mechanism built into the Spring Data repository infrastructure is useful for building constraining queries over entities of the repository. The mechanism strips the prefixes find…By, read…By, query…By, count…By, and get…By from the method and starts parsing the rest of it. The introducing clause can contain further expressions, such as a `Distinct` to set a distinct flag on the query to be created. However, the first By acts as a delimiter to indicate the start of the actual criteria. At a very basic level, you can define conditions on entity properties and concatenate them with And and Or.

❗ No need to write custom JPQL queries. This is why I use the Quarkus Extension for Spring Data JPA API to enjoy these powerful features of Spring Data JPA.

CartStatus

The CartStatus enumeration class looks like this:

```
public enum CartStatus {
    NEW, CANCELED, CONFIRMED
}
```

Address

The Address class looks like this:

```
@Getter
@NoArgsConstructor
@AllArgsConstructor
@ToString
@Embeddable
public class Address {

    @Column(name = "address_1")
    private String address1;

    @Column(name = "address_2")
    private String address2;

    @Column(name = "city")
    private String city;

    @NotNull
    @Size(max = 10)
    @Column(name = "postcode", length = 10, nullable = false)
    private String postcode;

    @NotNull
    @Size(max = 2)
    @Column(name = "country", length = 2, nullable = false)
    private String country;

    @Override
    public boolean equals(Object o) {
```

```
        if (this == o) return true;
        if (o == null || getClass() != o.getClass()) return false;
        Address address = (Address) o;
        return Objects.equals(address1, address.address1) &&
                Objects.equals(address2, address.address2) &&
                Objects.equals(city, address.city) &&
                Objects.equals(postcode, address.postcode) &&
                Objects.equals(country, address.country);
    }

    @Override
    public int hashCode() {
        return Objects.hash(address1, address2, city, postcode, country);
    }
}
```

The Address class will be used as an embeddable class. Embeddable classes are used to represent the state of an entity but don't have a persistent identity of their own, unlike entity classes. Instances of an embeddable class share the identity of the entity that owns it. Embeddable classes exist only as the state of another entity.

Category

The Category entity looks like this:

```
@Getter
@NoArgsConstructor
@ToString(callSuper = true)
@Entity
@Table(name = "categories")
public class Category extends AbstractEntity {

    @NotNull
    @Column(name = "name", nullable = false)
    private String name;

    @NotNull
    @Column(name = "description", nullable = false)
```

```java
    private String description;

    public Category(@NotNull String name, @NotNull String description) {
        this.name = name;
        this.description = description;
    }

    @Override
    public boolean equals(Object o) {
        if (this == o) return true;
        if (o == null || getClass() != o.getClass()) return false;
        Category category = (Category) o;
        return Objects.equals(name, category.name) &&
                Objects.equals(description, category.description);
    }

    @Override
    public int hashCode() {
        return Objects.hash(name, description);
    }
}
```

The CategoryRepository looks as follows:

```java
@Repository
public interface CategoryRepository extends JpaRepository<Category, Long> {
}
```

Customer

The Customer entity is as follows:

```java
@Getter @Setter
@NoArgsConstructor
@ToString(callSuper = true)
@Entity
@Table(name = "customers")
public class Customer extends AbstractEntity {
```

```java
@Column(name = "first_name")
private String firstName;

@Column(name = "last_name")
private String lastName;

@Email
@Column(name = "email")
private String email;

@Column(name = "telephone")
private String telephone;

@OneToMany(mappedBy = "customer")
private Set<Cart> carts;

@Column(name = "enabled", nullable = false)
private Boolean enabled;

public Customer(String firstName, String lastName, @Email String email,
                String telephone, Set<Cart> carts, Boolean enabled) {
    this.firstName = firstName;
    this.lastName = lastName;
    this.email = email;
    this.telephone = telephone;
    this.carts = carts;
    this.enabled = enabled;
}

@Override
public boolean equals(Object o) {
    if (this == o) return true;
    if (o == null || getClass() != o.getClass()) return false;
    Customer customer = (Customer) o;
    return Objects.equals(firstName, customer.firstName) &&
            Objects.equals(lastName, customer.lastName) &&
            Objects.equals(email, customer.email) &&
            Objects.equals(telephone, customer.telephone) &&
```

```
                Objects.equals(carts, customer.carts) &&
                Objects.equals(enabled, customer.enabled);
    }

    @Override
    public int hashCode() {
        return Objects.hash(firstName, lastName, email, telephone,
        enabled);
    }
}
```

The CustomerRepository is as follows:

```
@Repository
public interface CustomerRepository extends JpaRepository<Customer, Long> {
    List<Customer> findAllByEnabled(Boolean enabled);
}
```

Order

The Order entity is as follows:

```
@Getter
@Setter
@NoArgsConstructor
@ToString(callSuper = true)
@Entity
@Table(name = "orders")
public class Order extends AbstractEntity {

    @NotNull
    @Column(name = "total_price", precision = 10, scale = 2, nullable = false)
    private BigDecimal price;

    @NotNull
    @Enumerated(EnumType.STRING)
    @Column(name = "status", nullable = false)
    private OrderStatus status;
```

```java
@Column(name = "shipped")
private ZonedDateTime shipped;

@OneToOne(cascade = CascadeType.REMOVE)
@JoinColumn(unique = true)
private Payment payment;

@Embedded
private Address shipmentAddress;

@OneToMany(mappedBy = "order", fetch = FetchType.LAZY, cascade =
CascadeType.REMOVE)
private Set<OrderItem> orderItems;

@OneToOne
private Cart cart;

public Order(@NotNull BigDecimal price, @NotNull OrderStatus status,
            ZonedDateTime shipped, Payment payment, Address
            shipmentAddress,
            Set<OrderItem> orderItems, Cart cart) {
    this.price = price;
    this.status = status;
    this.shipped = shipped;
    this.payment = payment;
    this.shipmentAddress = shipmentAddress;
    this.orderItems = orderItems;
    this.cart = cart;
}

@Override
public boolean equals(Object o) {
    if (this == o) return true;
    if (o == null || getClass() != o.getClass()) return false;
    Order order = (Order) o;
    return Objects.equals(price, order.price) && status == order.status &&
            Objects.equals(shipped, order.shipped) &&
            Objects.equals(payment, order.payment) &&
```

```
            Objects.equals(shipmentAddress, order.shipmentAddress) &&
            Objects.equals(orderItems, order.orderItems) &&
            Objects.equals(cart, order.cart);
    }

    @Override
    public int hashCode() {
        return Objects.hash(price, status, shipped, payment,
        shipmentAddress, cart);
    }
}
```

The OrderRepository is as follows:

```
@Repository
public interface OrderRepository extends JpaRepository<Order, Long> {
    List<Order> findByCartCustomerId(Long customerId);
    Optional<Order> findByPaymentId(Long id);
}
```

OrderItem

The OrderItem entity is as follows:

```
@Getter @NoArgsConstructor
@ToString(callSuper = true)
@Entity @Table(name = "order_items")
public class OrderItem extends AbstractEntity {

    @NotNull
    @Column(name = "quantity", nullable = false)
    private Long quantity;

    @ManyToOne(fetch = FetchType.LAZY)
    private Product product;

    @ManyToOne(fetch = FetchType.LAZY)
    private Order order;
```

```
    public OrderItem(@NotNull Long quantity, Product product, Order order) {
        this.quantity = quantity;
        this.product = product;
        this.order = order;
    }

    @Override
    public boolean equals(Object o) {
        if (this == o) return true;
        if (o == null || getClass() != o.getClass()) return false;
        OrderItem orderItem = (OrderItem) o;
        return Objects.equals(quantity, orderItem.quantity) &&
                Objects.equals(product, orderItem.product) &&
                Objects.equals(order, orderItem.order);
    }

    @Override
    public int hashCode() { return Objects.hash(quantity, product, order); }
}
```

The OrderItemRepository is as follows:

```
@Repository
public interface OrderItemRepository extends JpaRepository<OrderItem, Long> {
    List<OrderItem> findAllByOrderId(Long id);
}
```

Payment

The Payment entity is as follows:

```
@Getter @NoArgsConstructor
@ToString(callSuper = true)
@Entity @Table(name = "payments")
public class Payment extends AbstractEntity {
```

```java
@Column(name = "paypal_payment_id")
private String paypalPaymentId;

@NotNull
@Enumerated(EnumType.STRING)
@Column(name = "status", nullable = false)
private PaymentStatus status;

@NotNull
@Column(name = "amount", nullable = false)
private BigDecimal amount;

public Payment(String paypalPaymentId, @NotNull PaymentStatus status,
@NotNull BigDecimal amount) {
    this.paypalPaymentId = paypalPaymentId;
    this.status = status;
    this.amount = amount;
}

@Override
public boolean equals(Object o) {
    if (this == o) return true;
    if (o == null || getClass() != o.getClass()) return false;
    Payment payment = (Payment) o;
    return Objects.equals(paypalPaymentId, payment.paypalPaymentId);
}

@Override
public int hashCode() { return Objects.hash(paypalPaymentId); }
}
```

The PaymentRepository is as follows:

```java
@Repository
public interface PaymentRepository extends JpaRepository<Payment, Long> {
    List<Payment> findAllByAmountBetween(BigDecimal min, BigDecimal max);
}
```

The PaymentStatus is as follows:

```
public enum PaymentStatus {
    ACCEPTED, PENDING, REFUSED, ERROR
}
```

Product

The Product entity is as follows:

```
@Getter
@NoArgsConstructor
@ToString(callSuper = true)
@Entity
@Table(name = "products")
public class Product extends AbstractEntity {

    @NotNull
    @Column(name = "name", nullable = false)
    private String name;

    @NotNull
    @Column(name = "description", nullable = false)
    private String description;

    @NotNull
    @Column(name = "price", precision = 10, scale = 2, nullable = false)
    private BigDecimal price;

    @NotNull
    @Enumerated(EnumType.STRING)
    @Column(name = "status", nullable = false)
    private ProductStatus status;

    @Column(name = "sales_counter")
    private Integer salesCounter;

    @OneToMany(fetch = FetchType.LAZY, cascade = CascadeType.REMOVE)
    @JoinTable(name = "products_reviews",
            joinColumns = @JoinColumn(name = "product_id"),
```

```java
                inverseJoinColumns = @JoinColumn(name = "reviews_id"))
    private Set<Review> reviews = new HashSet<>();

    @ManyToOne
    @JoinColumn(name = "category_id")
    private Category category;

    public Product(@NotNull String name, @NotNull String description,
                    @NotNull BigDecimal price, @NotNull ProductStatus status,
                    Integer salesCounter, Set<Review> reviews, Category category) {
        this.name = name;
        this.description = description;
        this.price = price;
        this.status = status;
        this.salesCounter = salesCounter;
        this.reviews = reviews;
        this.category = category;
    }

    @Override
    public boolean equals(Object o) {
        if (this == o) return true;
        if (o == null || getClass() != o.getClass()) return false;
        Product product = (Product) o;
        return Objects.equals(name, product.name) &&
                Objects.equals(description, product.description) &&
                Objects.equals(price, product.price) && status == product.
                status &&
                Objects.equals(salesCounter, product.salesCounter) &&
                Objects.equals(reviews, product.reviews) &&
                Objects.equals(category, product.category);
    }

    @Override
    public int hashCode() {
        return Objects.hash(name, description, price, category);
    }
}
```

The ProductRepository is as follows:

```
@Repository
public interface ProductRepository extends JpaRepository<Product, Long> {
    List<Product> findByCategoryId(Long categoryId);

    Long countAllByCategoryId(Long categoryId);

    @Query("select p from Product p JOIN p.reviews r WHERE r.id = ?1")
    Product findProductByReviewId(Long reviewId);

    void deleteAllByCategoryId(Long id);

    List<Product> findAllByCategoryId(Long id);
}
```

ProductStatus

The ProductStatus enumeration class looks as follows:

```
public enum ProductStatus {
    AVAILABLE, DISCONTINUED
}
```

Review

The Review entity is as follows:

```
@Getter
@NoArgsConstructor
@ToString(callSuper = true)
@Entity
@Table(name = "reviews")
public class Review extends AbstractEntity {

    @NotNull
    @Column(name = "title", nullable = false)
    private String title;
```

```java
@NotNull
@Column(name = "description", nullable = false)
private String description;

@NotNull
@Column(name = "rating", nullable = false)
private Long rating;

public Review(@NotNull String title, @NotNull String description,
@NotNull Long rating) {
    this.title = title;
    this.description = description;
    this.rating = rating;
}

@Override
public boolean equals(Object o) {
    if (this == o) return true;
    if (o == null || getClass() != o.getClass()) return false;
    Review review = (Review) o;
    return Objects.equals(title, review.title) &&
            Objects.equals(description, review.description) &&
            Objects.equals(rating, review.rating);
}

@Override
public int hashCode() {
    return Objects.hash(title, description, rating);
}
}
```

The ReviewRepository is as follows:

```java
@Repository
public interface ReviewRepository extends JpaRepository<Review, Long> {

    @Query("select p.reviews from Product p where p.id = ?1")
    List<Review> findReviewsByProductId(Long id);

}
```

At this stage, you have finished creating the entities and repositories. The entities diagram now looks like this:

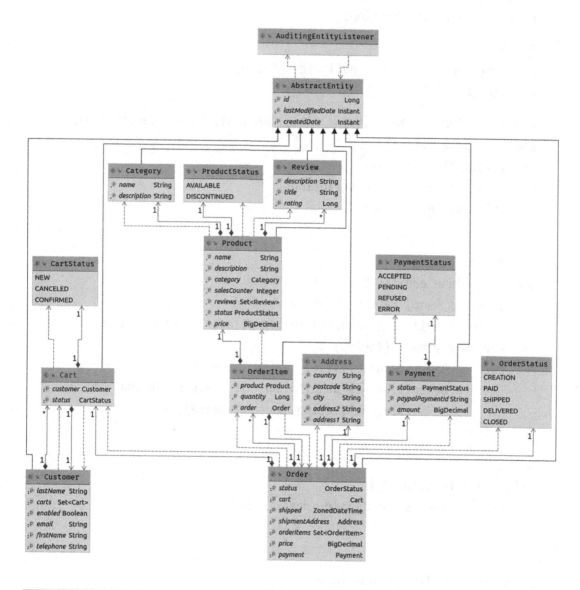

💡 I generated this diagram using IntelliJ IDEA. To generate one, just right-click the package containing the targeted classes and choose Diagrams ➤ Show Diagram. Next, in the list that opens, select Java Class Diagram:

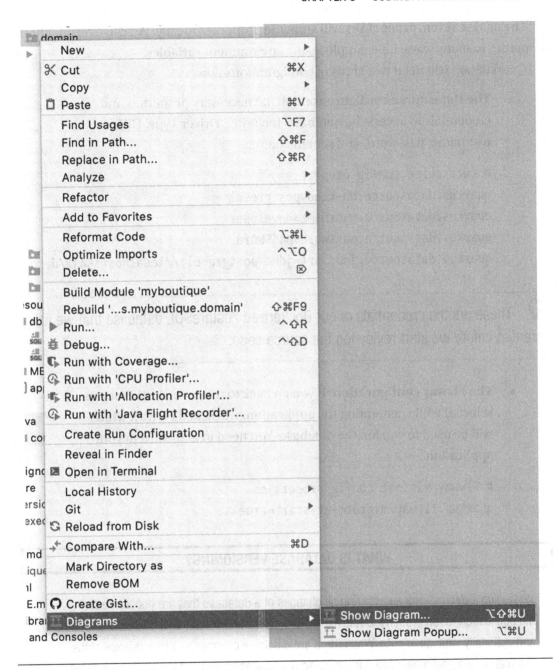

Now you need to provide the Quarkus application with a Hibernate/JPA configuration and the database credentials.

Just like with Spring Boot, Quarkus stores its configurations and properties inside an application.properties file located in src/main/resources.

The `application.properties` will store the properties locally. We can override these properties in many ways, for example, using environment variables.

QuarkuShop will need two kinds of configurations now:

- **The Datasource configuration**: All the necessary properties and credentials to access the database, including Driver Type, URL, username, password, and schema name:

```
# Datasource config properties
quarkus.datasource.db-kind=postgresql
quarkus.datasource.username=developer
quarkus.datasource.password=p4SSWOrd
quarkus.datasource.jdbc.url=jdbc:postgresql://localhost:5432/demo
```

💡   These are the credentials of our Dockerized PostgreSQL database that we just created before we start reviewing the source code. ☻

- **The Flyway configuration**: If you go back to the extensions that you selected while generating the application, we picked Flyway, which will be used to version the database. You need to activate it in your application.

```
# Flyway minimal config properties
quarkus.flyway.migrate-at-start=true
```

WHAT IS DATABASE VERSIONING?

Versioning a database means sharing all changes of a database that are necessary for the application to run properly. Database versioning starts with an initial database schema and optionally with some data. When there are database changes in a new release of the application, we ship a new patch file to perform changes on an existing database instead of starting from scratch with an updated dump, so when deploying the new version, the application will run properly. A patch file describes how to transform an existing database into a new state and how to revert it in order to get back to the old state.

In this case, we will have two Flyway scripts and they must be located in the default Flyway folder `src/main/resources/db/migration`:

- `src/main/resources/db/migration/V1.0__Init_app.sql`: The initial skeleton creation script that contains the SQL queries to create the tables and their constraints that we defined in the source code, such as primary keys, foreign keys between entities, and non-nullable columns. This Flyway script will also bring the Hibernate SQL sequence needed by the ORM to provide IDs for entities while persisted.

- `src/main/resources/db/migration/V1.1__Insert_samples.sql`: The initial sample data insertion script, which contains the sample data that we will insert into the database in order to have sample data during the execution.

ⓘ   Notice the versioning used here—V1.0 and V1.1—this is used to guarantee the execution order of the Flyway scripts.

Now we can move to the next layer: the Service layer.

Creating the Service Layer

Now that you've created the entities, it's time to create the services.

A *service* is a component that wraps the business logic. At this point, we haven't discussed business logic, we just have CRUD operations. You will implement these CRUD operations in your services.

You need a separate service for each entity in order to apply the single responsibility practice to your services.

The Service layer is the glue between the Persistence and Web layers. A service will grab the data from the repositories and apply its business logic to the loaded data. It will encapsulate the calculated data into a wrapper used to transfer the data between the Service and the Web layers. This wrapper is called a Data Transfer Object (DTO).

```
┌──────────────────────────────────────────────────────────────────┐
│                    DO YOU REALLY NEED DTOS?                         │
└──────────────────────────────────────────────────────────────────┘
```

In fact, in many cases, you do really need DTOs in your applications.

Let's imagine a case where you have a service that lists the users available on a database. If you don't use the DTOs and instead send back the User class, you will transfer to the web services, and to the caller behind them, the credentials of your users as the password in an encapsulated field of the User entity.

Typical Service: CartService

The CartService looks like this:

```
@Slf4j ①
@ApplicationScoped ②
@Transactional ③
public class CartService {

    @Inject ④
    CartRepository cartRepository;

    @Inject ④
    CustomerRepository customerRepository;

    public List<CartDto> findAll() {
        log.debug("Request to get all Carts");
        return this.cartRepository.findAll()
                .stream()
                .map(CartService::mapToDto)
                .collect(Collectors.toList());
    }

    public List<CartDto> findAllActiveCarts() {
        return this.cartRepository.findByStatus(CartStatus.NEW)
                .stream()
                .map(CartService::mapToDto)
                .collect(Collectors.toList());
    }
```

```java
public Cart create(Long customerId) {
    if (this.getActiveCart(customerId) == null) {
        var customer =
                this.customerRepository.findById(customerId).
                orElseThrow(() ->
                        new IllegalStateException("The Customer does
                        not exist!"));

        var cart = new Cart(customer, CartStatus.NEW);

        return this.cartRepository.save(cart);
    } else {
        throw new IllegalStateException("There is already an active cart");
    }
}

public CartDto createDto(Long customerId) {
    return mapToDto(this.create(customerId));
}

@Transactional(SUPPORTS)
public CartDto findById(Long id) {
    log.debug("Request to get Cart : {}", id);
    return this.cartRepository.findById(id).map(CartService::mapToDto).
    orElse(null);
}

public void delete(Long id) {
    log.debug("Request to delete Cart : {}", id);
    Cart cart = this.cartRepository.findById(id)
            .orElseThrow(() -> new IllegalStateException("Cannot find
            cart with id " + id));

    cart.setStatus(CartStatus.CANCELED);

    this.cartRepository.save(cart);
}
```

```java
public CartDto getActiveCart(Long customerId) {
    List<Cart> carts = this.cartRepository
            .findByStatusAndCustomerId(CartStatus.NEW, customerId);
    if (carts != null) {

        if (carts.size() == 1) {
            return mapToDto(carts.get(0));
        }
        if (carts.size() > 1) {
            throw new IllegalStateException("Many active carts
            detected !!!");
        }
    }
    return null;
}

public static CartDto mapToDto(Cart cart) {
    return new CartDto(
            cart.getId(),
            CustomerService.mapToDto(cart.getCustomer()),
            cart.getStatus().name()
    );
}
}
```

① The Lombok annotation used to generate a logger in the class. When used, you have a static final log field, initialized to the name of your class, which you can then use to write log statements.

② Specifies that this class is application scoped.

③ @Transactional annotation provides the application the ability to declaratively control transaction boundaries.

④ The most famous annotation in the Java EE world! It's used to request an instance of the annotated field type.

WHAT IS @APPLICATIONSCOPED?

An object annotated with @ApplicationScoped is created once during the application lifecycle.

Quarkus supports all the built-in scopes defined in the JSR 365: Contexts and Dependency Injection for Java 2.0, except for @ConversationScoped:

- @ApplicationScoped
- @Singleton
- @RequestScoped
- @Dependent
- @SessionScoped

To learn more about CDI scopes and the differences between them, you can check out the Quarkus CDI Guide at https://quarkus.io/guides/cdi.

The CartDto class looks like this:

```
@Data
@NoArgsConstructor
@AllArgsConstructor
public class CartDto {
    private Long id;
    private CustomerDto customer;
    private String status;
}
```

AddressService

The AddressService class looks like this:

```
@ApplicationScoped
public class AddressService {

    public static Address createFromDto(AddressDto addressDto) {
        return new Address(
```

```java
                addressDto.getAddress1(),
                addressDto.getAddress2(),
                addressDto.getCity(),
                addressDto.getPostcode(),
                addressDto.getCountry()
        );
    }

    public static AddressDto mapToDto(Address address) {
        return new AddressDto(
                address.getAddress1(),
                address.getAddress2(),
                address.getCity(),
                address.getPostcode(),
                address.getCountry()
        );
    }
}
```

The AddressDto class looks like this:

```java
@Data
@NoArgsConstructor
@AllArgsConstructor
public class AddressDto {
    private String address1;
    private String address2;
    private String city;
    private String postcode;
    @Size(min = 2, max = 2)
    private String country;
}
```

CategoryService

The CategoryService class looks like this:

```
@Slf4j
@ApplicationScoped
@Transactional
public class CategoryService {
    @Inject
    CategoryRepository categoryRepository;
    @Inject
    ProductRepository productRepository;

    public static CategoryDto mapToDto(Category category, Long
    productsCount) {
        return new CategoryDto(
                category.getId(),
                category.getName(),
                category.getDescription(),
                productsCount);
    }

    public List<CategoryDto> findAll() {
        log.debug("Request to get all Categories");
        return this.categoryRepository.findAll()
                .stream().map(category ->
                        mapToDto(category,
                                productRepository
                                        .countAllByCategoryId(category.
                                        getId()))))
                .collect(Collectors.toList());
    }

    public CategoryDto findById(Long id) {
        log.debug("Request to get Category : {}", id);
        return this.categoryRepository.findById(id).map(category ->
                        mapToDto(category,
                                productRepository
```

```
                                        .countAllByCategoryId(category.
                                    getId())))
                .orElse(null);
    }

    public CategoryDto create(CategoryDto categoryDto) {
        log.debug("Request to create Category : {}", categoryDto);
        return mapToDto(this.categoryRepository
                .save(new Category(
                                categoryDto.getName(),
                                categoryDto.getDescription())
                ), 0L);
    }

    public void delete(Long id) {
        log.debug("Request to delete Category : {}", id);
        log.debug("Deleting all products for the Category : {}", id);
        this.productRepository.deleteAllByCategoryId(id);
        log.debug("Deleting Category : {}", id);
        this.categoryRepository.deleteById(id);
    }

    public List<ProductDto> findProductsByCategoryId(Long id) {
        return this.productRepository.findAllByCategoryId(id)
                .stream()
                .map(ProductService::mapToDto)
                .collect(Collectors.toList());
    }
}
}
```

The CategoryDto class looks like this:

```
@Data
@NoArgsConstructor
@AllArgsConstructor
public class CategoryDto {
    private Long id;
    private String name;
```

```
    private String description;
    private Long products;
}
```

CustomerService

The CustomerService class looks like this:

```
@Slf4j
@ApplicationScoped
@Transactional
public class CustomerService {

    @Inject
    CustomerRepository customerRepository;

    public CustomerDto create(CustomerDto customerDto) {
        log.debug("Request to create Customer : {}", customerDto);
        return mapToDto(this.customerRepository.save(
                        new Customer(customerDto.getFirstName(),
                                customerDto.getLastName(),
                                customerDto.getEmail(),
                                customerDto.getTelephone(),
                                Collections.emptySet(),
                                Boolean.TRUE)
                ));
    }

    public List<CustomerDto> findAll() {
        log.debug("Request to get all Customers");
        return this.customerRepository.findAll()
                .stream()
                .map(CustomerService::mapToDto)
                .collect(Collectors.toList());
    }

    @Transactional
    public CustomerDto findById(Long id) {
        log.debug("Request to get Customer : {}", id);
```

```
        return this.customerRepository.findById(id)
                .map(CustomerService::mapToDto).orElse(null);
    }

    public List<CustomerDto> findAllActive() {
        log.debug("Request to get all active customers");
        return this.customerRepository.findAllByEnabled(true)
                .stream().map(CustomerService::mapToDto)
                .collect(Collectors.toList());
    }

    public List<CustomerDto> findAllInactive() {
        log.debug("Request to get all inactive customers");
        return this.customerRepository.findAllByEnabled(false)
                .stream().map(CustomerService::mapToDto)
                .collect(Collectors.toList());
    }

    public void delete(Long id) {
        log.debug("Request to delete Customer : {}", id);

        Customer customer = this.customerRepository.findById(id)
                .orElseThrow(() ->
                        new IllegalStateException("Cannot find Customer
                        with id " + id));

        customer.setEnabled(false);
        this.customerRepository.save(customer);
    }

    public static CustomerDto mapToDto(Customer customer) {
        return new CustomerDto(customer.getId(),
                customer.getFirstName(),
                customer.getLastName(),
                customer.getEmail(),
                customer.getTelephone()
        );
    }
}
```

The CustomerDto class looks like this:

```
@Data
@NoArgsConstructor
@AllArgsConstructor
public class CustomerDto {
    private Long id;
    private String firstName;
    private String lastName;
    private String email;
    private String telephone;
}
```

OrderItemService

The OrderItemService class looks like this:

```
@Slf4j
@ApplicationScoped
@Transactional
public class OrderItemService {

    @Inject
    OrderItemRepository orderItemRepository;
    @Inject
    OrderRepository orderRepository;
    @Inject
    ProductRepository productRepository;

    public static OrderItemDto mapToDto(OrderItem orderItem) {
        return new OrderItemDto(
                orderItem.getId(),
                orderItem.getQuantity(),
                orderItem.getProduct().getId(),
                orderItem.getOrder().getId()
        );
    }
```

```java
public OrderItemDto findById(Long id) {
    log.debug("Request to get OrderItem : {}", id);
    return this.orderItemRepository.findById(id)
            .map(OrderItemService::mapToDto).orElse(null);
}

public OrderItemDto create(OrderItemDto orderItemDto) {
    log.debug("Request to create OrderItem : {}", orderItemDto);
    var order =
            this.orderRepository
                    .findById(orderItemDto.getOrderId())
                    .orElseThrow(() ->
                        new IllegalStateException("The Order does not
                        exist!"));

    var product =
            this.productRepository
                    .findById(orderItemDto.getProductId())
                    .orElseThrow(() ->
                        new IllegalStateException("The Product does not
                        exist!"));

    var orderItem = this.orderItemRepository.save(
            new OrderItem(
                    orderItemDto.getQuantity(),
                    product,
                    order
            ));
    order.setPrice(order.getPrice().add(orderItem.getProduct().getPrice()));
    this.orderRepository.save(order);

    return mapToDto(orderItem);
}

public void delete(Long id) {
    log.debug("Request to delete OrderItem : {}", id);

    var orderItem = this.orderItemRepository.findById(id)
```

```
        .orElseThrow(() ->
                new IllegalStateException("The OrderItem does not
                exist!"));

    var order = orderItem.getOrder();
    order.setPrice(order.getPrice().subtract(orderItem.getProduct().
    getPrice()));

    this.orderItemRepository.deleteById(id);

    order.getOrderItems().remove(orderItem);

    this.orderRepository.save(order);
    }

    public List<OrderItemDto> findByOrderId(Long id) {
        log.debug("Request to get all OrderItems of OrderId {}", id);
        return this.orderItemRepository.findAllByOrderId(id)
                .stream()
                .map(OrderItemService::mapToDto)
                .collect(Collectors.toList());
    }
}
```

The OrderItemDto class looks like this:

```
@Data @NoArgsConstructor @AllArgsConstructor
public class OrderItemDto {
    private Long id;
    private Long quantity;
    private Long productId;
    private Long orderId;
}
```

OrderService

The OrderService class looks like this:

```
@Slf4j
@ApplicationScoped @Transactional
```

```java
public class OrderService {

    @Inject OrderRepository orderRepository;
    @Inject PaymentRepository paymentRepository;
    @Inject CartRepository cartRepository;

    public List<OrderDto> findAll() {
        log.debug("Request to get all Orders");
        return this.orderRepository.findAll().stream().
        map(OrderService::mapToDto)
                .collect(Collectors.toList());
    }

    public OrderDto findById(Long id) {
        log.debug("Request to get Order : {}", id);
        return this.orderRepository.findById(id)
                .map(OrderService::mapToDto).orElse(null);
    }

    public List<OrderDto> findAllByUser(Long id) {
        return this.orderRepository.findByCartCustomerId(id)
                .stream().map(OrderService::mapToDto).collect(Collectors.
                toList());
    }

    public OrderDto create(OrderDto orderDto) {
        log.debug("Request to create Order : {}", orderDto);

        Long cartId = orderDto.getCart().getId();
        Cart cart = this.cartRepository.findById(cartId)
                .orElseThrow(() -> new IllegalStateException(
                        "The Cart with ID[" + cartId + "] was not found !"));

        return mapToDto(this.orderRepository.save(new Order(BigDecimal.ZERO,
                        OrderStatus.CREATION, null, null,
                        AddressService.createFromDto(orderDto.
                        getShipmentAddress()),
                        Collections.emptySet(), cart)));
    }
```

```
@Transactional
public void delete(Long id) {
    log.debug("Request to delete Order : {}", id);

    Order order = this.orderRepository.findById(id)
            .orElseThrow(() ->
                new IllegalStateException(
                    "Order with ID[" + id + "] cannot be found!"));

    Optional.ofNullable(order.getPayment())
            .ifPresent(paymentRepository::delete);

    orderRepository.delete(order);
}

public boolean existsById(Long id) {
    return this.orderRepository.existsById(id);
}

public static OrderDto mapToDto(Order order) {
    Set<OrderItemDto> orderItems = order.getOrderItems()
            .stream().map(OrderItemService::mapToDto).
            collect(Collectors.toSet());

    return new OrderDto(
            order.getId(),
            order.getPrice(),
            order.getStatus().name(),
            order.getShipped(),
            order.getPayment() != null ? order.getPayment().getId() : null,
            AddressService.mapToDto(order.getShipmentAddress()),
            orderItems,
            CartService.mapToDto(order.getCart())
    );
}
}
```

The OrderDto class looks like this:

```
@Data
@NoArgsConstructor
@AllArgsConstructor
public class OrderDto {
    private Long id;
    private BigDecimal totalPrice;
    private String status;
    private ZonedDateTime shipped;
    private Long paymentId;
    private AddressDto shipmentAddress;
    private Set<OrderItemDto> orderItems;
    private CartDto cart;
}
```

PaymentService

The PaymentService class looks like this:

```
@Slf4j
@ApplicationScoped @Transactional
public class PaymentService {

    @Inject
    PaymentRepository paymentRepository;
    @Inject
    OrderRepository orderRepository;

    public List<PaymentDto> findByPriceRange(Double max) {
        return this.paymentRepository
                .findAllByAmountBetween(BigDecimal.ZERO, BigDecimal.
                valueOf(max))
                .stream().map(payment -> mapToDto(payment,
                                findOrderByPaymentId(payment.getId()).
                                getId()))
                .collect(Collectors.toList());
    }
```

```java
public List<PaymentDto> findAll() {
    return this.paymentRepository.findAll().stream()
            .map(payment -> findById(payment.getId())).
            collect(Collectors.toList());
}

public PaymentDto findById(Long id) {
    log.debug("Request to get Payment : {}", id);
    Order order = findOrderByPaymentId(id).orElseThrow(() ->
                        new IllegalStateException("The Order does not
                        exist!"));

    return this.paymentRepository.findById(id)
            .map(payment -> mapToDto(payment, order.getId())).
            orElse(null);
}

public PaymentDto create(PaymentDto paymentDto) {
    log.debug("Request to create Payment : {}", paymentDto);

    Order order = this.orderRepository.findById(paymentDto.getOrderId())
                    .orElseThrow(() ->
                        new IllegalStateException("The Order does not
                        exist!"));
    order.setStatus(OrderStatus.PAID);

    Payment payment = this.paymentRepository.saveAndFlush(new Payment(
            paymentDto.getPaypalPaymentId(),
            PaymentStatus.valueOf(paymentDto.getStatus()),
            order.getPrice()
    ));

    this.orderRepository.saveAndFlush(order);

    return mapToDto(payment, order.getId());
}
```

```java
    private Order findOrderByPaymentId(Long id) {
        return this.orderRepository.findByPaymentId(id).orElseThrow(() ->
            new IllegalStateException("No Order exists for the
            Payment ID " + id));
    }

    public void delete(Long id) {
        log.debug("Request to delete Payment : {}", id);
        this.paymentRepository.deleteById(id);
    }

    public static PaymentDto mapToDto(Payment payment, Long orderId) {
        if (payment != null) {
            return new PaymentDto(
                    payment.getId(),
                    payment.getPaypalPaymentId(),
                    payment.getStatus().name(),
                    orderId);
        }
        return null;
    }
}
```

The PaymentDto class looks like this:

```java
@Data
@NoArgsConstructor
@AllArgsConstructor
public class PaymentDto {
    private Long id;
    private String paypalPaymentId;
    private String status;
    private Long orderId;
}
```

Product Service

The ProductService class looks like this:

```
@Slf4j
@ApplicationScoped
@Transactional
public class ProductService {

    @Inject
    ProductRepository productRepository;
    @Inject
    CategoryRepository categoryRepository;

    public List<ProductDto> findAll() {
        log.debug("Request to get all Products");
        return this.productRepository.findAll()
                .stream().map(ProductService::mapToDto)
                .collect(Collectors.toList());
    }

    public ProductDto findById(Long id) {
        log.debug("Request to get Product : {}", id);
        return this.productRepository.findById(id)
                .map(ProductService::mapToDto).orElse(null);
    }

    public Long countAll() {
        return this.productRepository.count();
    }

    public Long countByCategoryId(Long id) {
        return this.productRepository.countAllByCategoryId(id);
    }

    public ProductDto create(ProductDto productDto) {
        log.debug("Request to create Product : {}", productDto);

        return mapToDto(this.productRepository.save(
                new Product(
```

```
                        productDto.getName(),
                        productDto.getDescription(),
                        productDto.getPrice(),
                        ProductStatus.valueOf(productDto.getStatus()),
                        productDto.getSalesCounter(),
                        Collections.emptySet(),
                      categoryRepository.findById(productDto.getCategoryId())
                                        .orElse(null)
            )));
    }

    public void delete(Long id) {
        log.debug("Request to delete Product : {}", id);
        this.productRepository.deleteById(id);
    }

    public List<ProductDto> findByCategoryId(Long id) {
        return this.productRepository.findByCategoryId(id).stream()
                .map(ProductService::mapToDto).collect(Collectors.toList());
    }

    public static ProductDto mapToDto(Product product) {
        return new ProductDto(
                product.getId(),
                product.getName(),
                product.getDescription(),
                product.getPrice(),
                product.getStatus().name(),
                product.getSalesCounter(),
                product.getReviews().stream().map(ReviewService::mapToDto)
                            .collect(Collectors.toSet()),
                product.getCategory().getId()
        );
    }
}
```

The ProductDto class looks like this:

```
@Data
@NoArgsConstructor
@AllArgsConstructor
public class ProductDto {
    private Long id;
    private String name;
    private String description;
    private BigDecimal price;
    private String status;
    private Integer salesCounter;
    private Set<ReviewDto> reviews;
    private Long categoryId;
}
```

ReviewService

The ReviewService class looks like this:

```
@Slf4j
@ApplicationScoped
@Transactional
public class ReviewService {

    @Inject
    ReviewRepository reviewRepository;

    @Inject
    ProductRepository productRepository;

    public List<ReviewDto> findReviewsByProductId(Long id) {
        log.debug("Request to get all Reviews");
        return this.reviewRepository.findReviewsByProductId(id)
                .stream()
                .map(ReviewService::mapToDto)
                .collect(Collectors.toList());
    }
```

```java
public ReviewDto findById(Long id) {
    log.debug("Request to get Review : {}", id);
    return this.reviewRepository
                .findById(id)
                .map(ReviewService::mapToDto)
                .orElse(null);
}

public ReviewDto create(ReviewDto reviewDto, Long productId) {
    log.debug("Request to create Review : {} ofr the Product {}",
            reviewDto, productId);

    Product product = this.productRepository.findById(productId)
            .orElseThrow(() ->
                new IllegalStateException(
                    "Product with ID:" + productId + " was not found !"));

    Review savedReview = this.reviewRepository.saveAndFlush(
            new Review(
                    reviewDto.getTitle(),
                    reviewDto.getDescription(),
                    reviewDto.getRating()));

    product.getReviews().add(savedReview);
    this.productRepository.saveAndFlush(product);

    return mapToDto(savedReview);
}

public void delete(Long reviewId) {
    log.debug("Request to delete Review : {}", reviewId);

    Review review = this.reviewRepository.findById(reviewId)
            .orElseThrow(() ->
                new IllegalStateException(
                    "Product with ID:" + reviewId + " was not found !"));

    Product product = this.productRepository.findProductByReviewId
    (reviewId);
```

```
        product.getReviews().remove(review);

        this.productRepository.saveAndFlush(product);
        this.reviewRepository.delete(review);
    }

    public static ReviewDto mapToDto(Review review) {
        return new ReviewDto(
                review.getId(),
                review.getTitle(),
                review.getDescription(),
                review.getRating()
        );
    }
}
```

The ReviewDto class looks like this:

```
@Data
@NoArgsConstructor
@AllArgsConstructor
public class ReviewDto {
    private Long id;
    private String title;
    private String description;
    private Long rating;
}
```

Creating the Web Layer

This section exposes the operations that we implemented in the Service classes as REST web services.

In the Spring Framework, a REST web service can be implemented using a RestController.

ℹ️   *REST API Base Path*

We want our RESTful web services to be accessed via /api/carts, /api/ orders, etc., so we need to define the base path /api as a root path, to be reused by all the REST web services.

This is can be configured in Quarkus using the following property:

quarkus.http.root-path=/api

Typical RestController: CartResource

The CartResource looks like this:

```
@Path("/carts") ①
public class CartResource { ②

    @Inject CartService cartService;

    @GET
    public List<CartDto> findAll() {
        return this.cartService.findAll();
    }

    @GET @Path("/active")
    public List<CartDto> findAllActiveCarts() {
        return this.cartService.findAllActiveCarts();
    }

    @GET @Path("/customer/{id}")
    public CartDto getActiveCartForCustomer(@PathParam("id") Long customerId) {
        return this.cartService.getActiveCart(customerId);
    }

    @GET @Path("/{id}")
    public CartDto findById(@PathParam("id") Long id) {
        return this.cartService.findById(id);
    }
```

```
@POST @Path("/customer/{id}")
public CartDto create(@PathParam("id") Long customerId) {
    return this.cartService.createDto(customerId);
}

@DELETE @Path("/{id}")
public void delete(@PathParam("id") Long id) {
    this.cartService.delete(id);
}
}
```

① Identifies the URI path that a resource class or class method will use to serve requests.

② By default, all produced content of all the methods will be in JSON. If you want to change this, or if you want to add another serialization format, use the @Produces annotation.

In this REST web service, we are:

- Listing all carts: HTTP GET on /api/carts.

- Listing active carts: HTTP GET on `/api/carts/active.

- Listing active carts for a customer: HTTP GET on /api/carts/customer/{id} with {id}, which holds the customer's ID.

- Listing all details of a cart: HTTP GET on api/carts/{id} with {id}, which holds the cart's ID.

- Creating a new cart for a given customer: HTTP POST on /api/carts/customer/{id} with {id}, which holds the customer's ID.

- Deleting a cart: HTTP DELETE on /api/carts/{id} with {id}.

These operations are described using the OpenAPI specification to facilitate the consumption of the REST web services by external callers. The API description is generated automatically. 😄

CategoryResource

The CategoryResource class looks like this:

```
@Path("/categories")
public class CategoryResource {
    @Inject CategoryService categoryService;
    @GET
    public List<CategoryDto> findAll() {
        return this.categoryService.findAll();
    }

    @GET @Path("/{id}")
    public CategoryDto findById(@PathParam("id") Long id) {
        return this.categoryService.findById(id);
    }

    @GET @Path("/{id}/products")
    public List<ProductDto> findProductsByCategoryId(@PathParam("id") Long id) {
        return this.categoryService.findProductsByCategoryId(id);
    }

    @POST    public CategoryDto create(CategoryDto categoryDto) {
        return this.categoryService.create(categoryDto);
    }

    @DELETE @Path("/{id}")
    public void delete(@PathParam("id") Long id) {
        this.categoryService.delete(id);
    }
}
```

CustomerResource

The CustomerResource class looks like this:

```
@Path("/customers")
public class CustomerResource {

    @Inject
```

```java
CustomerService customerService;

@GET
public List<CustomerDto> findAll() {
    return this.customerService.findAll();
}

@GET
@Path("/{id}")
public CustomerDto findById(@PathParam("id") Long id) {
    return this.customerService.findById(id);
}

@GET
@Path("/active")
public List<CustomerDto> findAllActive() {
    return this.customerService.findAllActive();
}

@GET
@Path("/inactive")
public List<CustomerDto> findAllInactive() {
    return this.customerService.findAllInactive();
}

@POST
    public CustomerDto create(CustomerDto customerDto) {
    return this.customerService.create(customerDto);
}

@DELETE
@Path("/{id}")
public void delete(@PathParam("id") Long id) {
    this.customerService.delete(id);
}
}
```

OrderItemResource

The OrderItemResource class looks like this:

```
@Path("/order-items")
public class OrderItemResource {

    @Inject
    OrderItemService itemService;

    @GET
    @Path("/order/{id}")
    public List<OrderItemDto> findByOrderId(@PathParam("id") Long id) {
        return this.itemService.findByOrderId(id);
    }

    @GET
    @Path("/{id}")
    public OrderItemDto findById(@PathParam("id") Long id) {
        return this.itemService.findById(id);
    }

    @POST
        public OrderItemDto create(OrderItemDto orderItemDto) {
        return this.itemService.create(orderItemDto);
    }

    @DELETE
    @Path("/{id}")
    public void delete(@PathParam("id") Long id) {
        this.itemService.delete(id);
    }
}
```

OrderResource

The OrderResource class looks like this:

```
@Path("/orders")
public class OrderResource {
```

```java
@Inject
OrderService orderService;

@GET
public List<OrderDto> findAll() {
    return this.orderService.findAll();
}

@GET
@Path("/customer/{id}")
public List<OrderDto> findAllByUser(@PathParam("id") Long id) {
    return this.orderService.findAllByUser(id);
}

@GET
@Path("/{id}")
public OrderDto findById(@PathParam("id") Long id) {
    return this.orderService.findById(id);
}

@POST
    public OrderDto create(OrderDto orderDto) {
    return this.orderService.create(orderDto);
}

@DELETE
@Path("/{id}")
public void delete(@PathParam("id") Long id) {
    this.orderService.delete(id);
}

@GET
@Path("/exists/{id}")
public boolean existsById(@PathParam("id") Long id) {
    return this.orderService.existsById(id);
}
}
```

PaymentResource

The PaymentResource class looks like this:

```
@Path("/payments")
public class PaymentResource {

    @Inject
    PaymentService paymentService;

    @GET
    public List<PaymentDto> findAll() {
        return this.paymentService.findAll();
    }

    @GET
    @Path("/{id}")
    public PaymentDto findById(@PathParam("id") Long id) {
        return this.paymentService.findById(id);
    }

    @POST
        public PaymentDto create(PaymentDto orderItemDto) {
        return this.paymentService.create(orderItemDto);
    }

    @DELETE
    @Path("/{id}")
    public void delete(@PathParam("id") Long id) {
        this.paymentService.delete(id);
    }

    @GET
    @Path("/price/{max}")
    public List<PaymentDto> findPaymentsByAmountRangeMax(@PathParam("max")
    double max) {
        return this.paymentService.findByPriceRange(max);
    }
}
```

ProductResource

The ProductResource class looks like this:

```java
@Path("/products")
public class ProductResource {

    @Inject ProductService productService;

    @GET
    public List<ProductDto> findAll() {
        return this.productService.findAll();
    }

    @GET @Path("/count")
    public Long countAllProducts() {
        return this.productService.countAll();
    }

    @GET @Path("/{id}")
    public ProductDto findById(@PathParam("id") Long id) {
        return this.productService.findById(id);
    }

    @POST    public ProductDto create(ProductDto productDto) {
        return this.productService.create(productDto);
    }

    @DELETE @Path("/{id}")
    public void delete(@PathParam("id") Long id) {
        this.productService.delete(id);
    }

    @GET @Path("/category/{id}")
    public List<ProductDto> findByCategoryId(@PathParam("id") Long id) {
        return this.productService.findByCategoryId(id);
    }
```

```
@GET @Path("/count/category/{id}")
public Long countByCategoryId(@PathParam("id") Long id) {
    return this.productService.countByCategoryId(id);
}
}
```

ReviewResource

The ReviewResource class looks like this:

```
@Path("/reviews")
public class ReviewResource {

    @Inject ReviewService reviewService;

    @GET @Path("/product/{id}")
    public List<ReviewDto> findAllByProduct(@PathParam("id") Long id) {
        return this.reviewService.findReviewsByProductId(id);
    }

    @GET @Path("/{id}")
    public ReviewDto findById(@PathParam("id") Long id) {
        return this.reviewService.findById(id);
    }

    @POST @Path("/product/{id}")
        public ReviewDto create(ReviewDto reviewDto, @PathParam("id") Long id) {
        return this.reviewService.create(reviewDto, id);
    }

    @DELETE @Path("/{id}")
    public void delete(@PathParam("id") Long id) {
        this.reviewService.delete(id);
    }
}
```

Automated API Documentation

Swagger 2 is an open-source project used to describe and document RESTful APIs. It's language-agnostic and is extensible into new technologies and protocols beyond HTTP. The current version defines set HTML, JavaScript, and CSS assets to dynamically generate documentation from a Swagger-compliant API. These files are bundled by the Swagger UI project to display the API on browser. Besides rendering documentation, Swagger UI allows other API developers and consumers to interact with the API's resources without having any of the implementation logic in place.

The Swagger 2 specification, which is also known as the OpenAPI specification, has several implementations. We will be using the SmallRye OpenAPI implementation in this project.

SmallRye OpenAPI automatically generates the API documentation. SmallRye OpenAPI works by examining an application once, at build time, to infer API semantics based on the Quarkus configurations, class structure, and various compile-time Java annotations.

You already added the `quarkus-smallrye-openapi` dependency to your project. There is no need to make any additional configurations or developments. This extension will easily generate the OpenAPI descriptors and the Swagger UI!

Hello World Swagger!

To run the Quarkus application, just run the `mvn quarkus:dev` command.

The application will run on the 8080 port. To access the Swagger UI, go to `http://localhost:8080/api/swagger-ui/`.

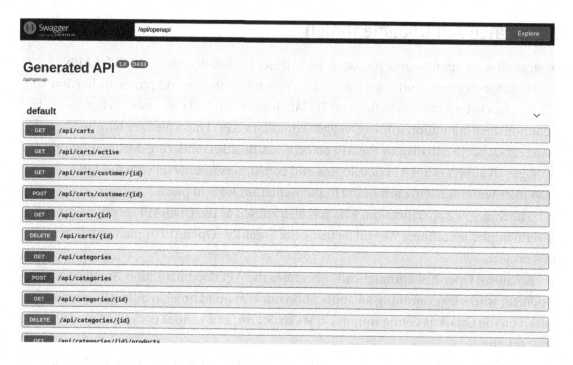

You can also check the generated OpenAPI descriptor, which is available at
http://localhost:8080/api/openapi:

```
---
openapi: 3.0.1
info:
  title: Generated API
  version: "1.0"
paths:
  /api/carts:
    get:
      responses:
        "200":
          description: OK
          content:
            application/json:
              schema:
                $ref: '#/components/schemas/ListCartDto'
  /api/carts/active:
```

```yaml
get:
  responses:
    "200":
      description: OK
      content:
        application/json:
          schema:
            $ref: '#/components/schemas/ListCartDto'
...
```

The Swagger UI is available only in the non-production environment. To enable it permanently, you need to add one parameter to the `application.properties`:

```properties
# Swagger UI
quarkus.swagger-ui.always-include=true
```

Finally, for better code organization, add an OpenAPI @Tag annotation to all your REST APIs classes, in order to describe each class. This is useful to regroup all the methods that belong to the same REST API into one section. Consider the example of the CartResource:

```java
@Path("/carts")
@Tag(name = "cart", description = "All the cart methods")
public class CartResource {

...

}
```

---

❶   Don't forget to add @Tag to each class.

When you restart the application and access the Swagger UI again, you can see that the description appears for each REST API and the methods are grouped together under the same tag name:

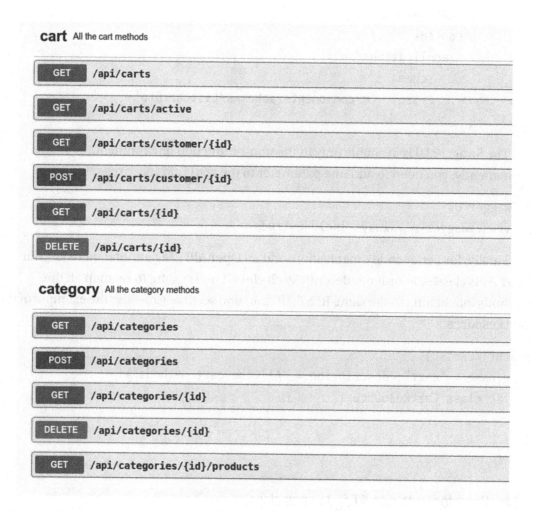

Customize the Quarkus Banner

The last part of this chapter shows you how to customize the application banner, as is done in Spring Boot. This operation is very easy in Quarkus. First of all, you need to create a banner.txt file in src/main/resources, as shown in Listing 3-1.

Listing 3-1. src/main/resources/banner.txt

```
 __  ___                               _         ___   __
 _ _/ _ \ _  _ __  ___ / /__ _ _/ _/ / /_  ___   ___
 --/ / / // / / // _ \ / __// //_// / / /\_ \ /  _ \ /  _ \ /  __ \
 -/ /_/ // /_/ // /_/ // /  /  / ,< / / / /__/ / / / // /_/ // /_/ /
 --\___\_\\___/ \_,_//_/   /_/|_| \___//___// /_/ /_/ \___// ,___/
                                                      /_/ Part of the
#PlayingWith Series
```

Then, you simply need to tell the application that you have a custom banner in the banner.txt file:

```
# Define the custom banner
quarkus.banner.path=banner.txt
```

Conclusion

You now have all the essential components of your project—the source code, the API documentation, and the database.☺

In the next chapter, you'll create the necessary tests to protect your code against future modifications or refactoring. The chapter also digs into building and deploying your application using the best CI/CD pipelines.

[1] Learn more about @MappedSuperclass at https://docs.jboss.org/hibernate/orm/5.4/userguide/html_single/Hibernate_User_Guide.html#entity-inheritance-mapped-superclass

[2] Learn more about @EntityListeners at https://docs.jboss.org/hibernate/stable/entitymanager/reference/en/html/listeners.html

[3] Learn more about validation constraints at https://docs.jboss.org/hibernate/validator/7.0/reference/en-US/html_single/#_validating_constraints

## CHAPTER 4

Upgrading a Monolithic Application

Writing source code and running it is not the real win! The real win is writing code covered with tests that guarantee that the business logic is correctly implemented.

Tests coverage is a very important metric that shows the dark side of the code. The bigger the coverage is, the more insurance we have that our code is protected against any hasty or dirty updates or refactoring.

In this example case, the tests will be the protective shield against problems that occur while splitting this monolithic application into microservices.

Implementing QuarkuShop Tests

Introducing Tests Libraries in Quarkus

In the Java ecosystem, JUnit is the most common testing framework. This is why Quarkus provides it automatically as a test dependency when generating a new project:

```
<dependencies>
...
    <!-- Test dependencies -->
    <dependency>
        <groupId>io.quarkus</groupId>
        <artifactId>quarkus-junit5</artifactId>
        <scope>test</scope>
    </dependency>
    <dependency>
        <groupId>io.rest-assured</groupId>
```

© Nebrass Lamouchi 2021
N. Lamouchi, *Pro Java Microservices with Quarkus and Kubernetes*,
https://doi.org/10.1007/978-1-4842-7170-4_4

```
        <artifactId>rest-assured</artifactId>
        <scope>test</scope>
    </dependency>
</dependencies>
```

Note the Rest Assured library, which is pulled along with JUnit 5.

WHAT IS REST ASSURED?

Rest Assured is a library used for testing and validating REST web services in Java very easily. It simply makes HTTP requests and validates the HTTP responses. It has a very rich set of matchers and methods to fetch data and to parse requests/responses. It has a very good integration with build tools (such as Maven) and IDEs.

The Rest Assured Framework makes API automation testing very simple using core Java knowledge, which is a very desirable thing to do.

We need another library for these tests: AssertJ.

WHAT IS ASSERTJ?

AssertJ an open-source community-driven library that provides a rich set of assertions and truly helpful error messages. It improves test code readability and is designed to be super easy to use within any IDE or build tool.

Here is the AssertJ Maven dependency to add to your pom.xml file:

```
<dependency>
    <groupId>org.assertj</groupId>
    <artifactId>assertj-core</artifactId>
    <scope>test</scope>
</dependency>
```

To run the tests using Maven, just type mvn verify. The application will execute the tests under the test profile. To define test configuration properties, such as the database that will be used for the tests, you need to add these properties to the application.properties with a %test prefix. This prefix informs the application that these properties are for the test profile.

WHAT IS AN APPLICATION PROFILE?

The development lifecycle of an application has different stages; the most common ones are *development*, *testing*, and *production*. Quarkus profiles group parts of the application configuration and make them available only in certain environments.

A *profile* is a set of configuration settings. Quarkus allows you to define profile-specific properties using the %profile prefix of the property. Then, it automatically loads the properties based on the activated profile. See Listing 4-1.

ℹ   When no %profile is present, the property is associated with all the profiles.

⚠   While testing the proof-of-concept for the book, I found an issue with having multiple application.properties, as we used to have with Spring Boot. I opened an issue in the Quarkus GitHub #11072. Georgios Andrianakis, one of the Quarkus Team leaders, informed me that it's strongly recommended to have only one application.properties file.

Listing 4-1. src/main/resources/application.properties

```
...=
# Test Datasource config properties
%test.quarkus.datasource.db-kind=postgresql        ①
%test.quarkus.datasource.username=developer
%test.quarkus.datasource.password=p4SSWOrd
%test.quarkus.datasource.jdbc.url=jdbc:postgresql://localhost:5432/test
# Test Flyway minimal config properties
%test.quarkus.flyway.migrate-at-start=true         ②
```

① You need to define the parameters and the credentials of the dedicated test database instance.

② You need to activate Flyway for the tests.

ℹ️   There's no need to copy the Flyway migration scripts in the `src/test` folder. Flyway will find them in `src/main/resources` before checking in `src/test/resources`.

Talking about databases, we need a database dedicated to tests. We will use TestContainers to provide lightweight instances of common databases as Docker containers. We don't need thousands of words to define TestContainers. You will discover it and love it through practical exercise.

Start by adding the TestContainers Maven dependencies, as follows:

```
<dependency>
    <groupId>org.testcontainers</groupId>
    <artifactId>junit-jupiter</artifactId>
    <version>1.15.3</version>
    <scope>test</scope>
</dependency>
<dependency>
    <groupId>org.testcontainers</groupId>
    <artifactId>postgresql</artifactId>
    <version>1.15.3</version>
    <scope>test</scope>
</dependency>
```

Next, you'll create the Glue class that will bring TestContainers to Quarkus. This is a test utility class only. Under the test code, inside the `com.targa.labs.quarkushop.utils` package, you need to create the TestContainerResource class, as shown in Listing 4-2.

Listing 4-2. src/test/com.targa.labs.quarkushop.utils.TestContainerResource

```
public class TestContainerResource implements
QuarkusTestResourceLifecycleManager { ①

    private static final PostgreSQLContainer<?> DATABASE =
                                new PostgreSQLContainer<>
                                ("postgres:13");    ②
```

```
@Override
public Map<String, String> start() {

    DATABASE.start();    ③

    Map<String, String> confMap = new HashMap<>();    ④

    confMap.put("quarkus.datasource.jdbc.url", DATABASE.getJdbcUrl());    ④
    confMap.put("quarkus.datasource.username", DATABASE.getUsername());    ④
    confMap.put("quarkus.datasource.password", DATABASE.getPassword());    ④

    return confMap;    ④
}

@Override
public void stop() {
    DATABASE.close();    ⑤
}
}
```

① TestContainerResource will implement
QuarkusTestResourceLifecycleManager, which manages the
lifecycle of a test resource. These resources are started before
the first test runs and are closed at the end of the test suite. This
resource is brought to the test class using the @QuarkusTest
Resource(TestContainerResource.class) annotation.

② This is the core element of this custom test resource. The
postgres:13 parameter is the name of the PostgreSQL Docker
image that you will use.

③ When the start() method is called, you begin by starting the
DATABASE container.

④ Next, you collect the Datasource credentials generated
dynamically by TestContainers inside a confMap. When the
confMap is returned, these credentials are applied instead of
those available in the application.properties.

⑤ When the close() method is called, you close the DATABASE
container.

ⓘ   Starting with Quarkus 1.13, `TestContainers` are no longer required, with the new feature called DevServices.

DevServices provides you with a zero config database out-of-the-box. Depending on your database type, you may need to have Docker installed in order to use this feature. DevServices is supported by many databases, such as PostgreSQL, MySQL, etc.

If you want to use DevServices, all you need to do is include the relevant extension for the type of database you want (reactive or JDBC, or both), and don't configure a database URL, username, and password. Quarkus will provide the database and you can just start coding without worrying about the config.

To learn more about the DevServices, take a look here: `https://quarkus.io/guides/datasource#dev-services`.

While Quarkus will listen on port 8080 by default, when running tests, it defaults to 8081. This allows you to run tests while running the application in parallel. This HTTP test port can be changed, to 9999 for example, in the `application.properties` using the `quarkus.http.test-port=9999` property.

🔥   What if you inserted `quarkus.http.test-port=8888` and `%test.quarkus.http.test-port=9999` into `application.properties`?

Easy! Here, you are dealing with the HTTP port for the `test` profile. So the property with the `%test` will override any value defined before it. When running the tests, you will see the tests' runtime exposing the 9999 port.

A final configuration you need to have is to measure the test coverage, a very important metric for code quality. We will be using JaCoCo to generate code coverage reports.

First of all, you need to add the JaCoCo Quarkus extension to the pom.xml file:

```
<dependency>
    <groupId>io.quarkus</groupId>
    <artifactId>quarkus-jacoco</artifactId>
    <scope>test</scope>
</dependency>
```

No more Maven configuration is needed! The JaCoCo Quarkus extension will do all the magic! 😁

You will use this JaCoCo reporting later to see how much coverage you have in your tests.

Writing the First Tests

Let's start by testing the first REST API: the Cart REST API. 😁

Based on the CartResource or the Swagger UI, note that there are six services:

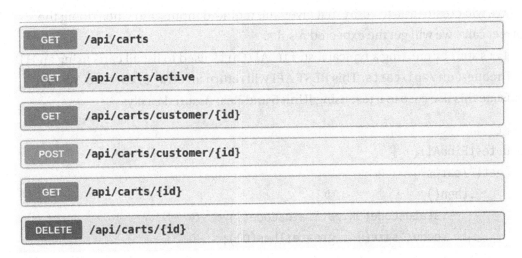

So you will have at least six tests, one test per service.

Before you start the tests, Listing 4-3 shows how a typical test class looks in the Quarkus world.

Listing 4-3. src/test/java/com/targa/labs/quarkushop/web

```
@QuarkusTest                                              ①
@QuarkusTestResource(TestContainerResource.class)        ②
class CartResourceTest {

    @Test                                                 ③
    void testSomeOperationOrFeature() {

    }
}
```

① Annotation that controls the JUnit 5 testing framework in
  Quarkus.

② Annotation that makes the TestContainerResource available to
  your CartResourceTest.

③ Used to signal that the annotated method is a test.

We will create tests to verify that given the required inputs and when doing the
correct calls, we will get the expected results.

Let's start by creating a typical test: findAllCarts used to list all carts using an HTTP
GET request on /api/carts. This REST API will return an array of CartDto. We can
translate this use case to a test using JUnit 5 and Rest Assured easily:

```
@Test
void testFindAll() {
    get("/carts")         ①
        .then()                     ②
            .statusCode(OK.getStatusCode())        ③
            .body("size()", greaterThan(0));       ④
}
```

① Starts a Rest Assured test case for sending an HTTP GET request
  to the /carts REST API.

② Extracts a Rest Assured ValidatableResponse of the request
  made in the previous line.

③ Validates that the Response Status Code matches 200 OK, which
   is returned by OK.getStatusCode() from the Response.Status
   enumeration coming from Rest Assured.

④ Validates that the JSON or XML response body element size()
   conforms to the Hamcrest matcher greaterThan(0).

To summarize, this test will verify that doing an HTTP GET on /cart will return the following:

- A header containing 200 as the status code

- A body with a non-empty array of elements

ℹ   In the previous call, we called the /carts path and not /api/carts because
the /api root base is added by the quarkus.http.root-path=/api property,
which we added previously to application.properties.

You use the same style for testing the findAllActiveCarts() and
getActiveCartForCustomer() methods, findById() and deleteById():

```
@Test ①
void testFindAllActiveCarts() {
    get("/carts/active").then()
            .statusCode(OK.getStatusCode());
}

@Test ②
void testGetActiveCartForCustomer() {
    get("/carts/customer/3").then()
            .contentType(ContentType.JSON)
            .statusCode(OK.getStatusCode())
            .body(containsString("Peter"));
}

@Test ③
void testFindById() {
    get("/carts/3").then()
            .statusCode(OK.getStatusCode())
```

```
                .body(containsString("status"))
                .body(containsString("NEW"));

    get("/carts/100").then()
                .statusCode(NO_CONTENT.getStatusCode());
}

@Test ④
void testDelete() {
    get("/carts/active").then()
                .statusCode(OK.getStatusCode())
                .body(containsString("Jason"))
                .body(containsString("NEW"));

    delete("/carts/1").then()
                .statusCode(NO_CONTENT.getStatusCode());

    get("/carts/1").then()
                .statusCode(OK.getStatusCode())
                .body(containsString("Jason"))
                .body(containsString("CANCELED"));
}
```

In these tests, we verify that:

① The response of the HTTP GET request on /carts/active has 200 as its status code.

② The response of the HTTP GET request on /carts/customer/3 has 200 as its status code and the body contains "Peter". Peter Quinn is the customer with ID 3 and has an active cart. This value is from the sample data that we imported using Flyway in the V1.1__Insert_samples.sql script.

③ The response of the HTTP GET request on /carts/3 has 200 as its status code and the body contains "NEW" as the cart status. The response of the HTTP GET request on /carts/100 has 404 as its status code and its body is empty, because we don't have a cart with ID 100.

④ For a given active cart with ID 1 that's owned by the customer
Jason, after we execute an HTTP DELETE on /carts/1, the cart
status will change from "NEW" to "CANCELED".

Now we will go into deeper test cases. We will verify an incorrect situation. In our
business logic, a customer cannot have more than one active cart at any moment. So
we will create a test to verify that the application will throw an error when there are two
active carts for a given customer.

We need to insert a record of an extra active cart for the customer with ID 3. Keep
calm! ☺ We will delete this record at the end of the test to keep the database clean. To do
these insertion and deletion SQL queries, we need to access the database from the tests
context. To make this interaction possible, we need to get a datasource in the test.
Quarkus supports this by allowing you to inject CDI beans into your tests via the @Inject
annotation. As the datasource is a CDI bean, we can inject it in our test.

ℹ   Tests in Quarkus are full CDI beans, so you can enjoy all the CDI features. ☻

The test looks like this:

```
@QuarkusTest
@QuarkusTestResource(TestContainerResource.class)
class CartResourceTest {

    private static final String INSERT_WRONG_CART_IN_DB =
      "insert into carts values (999, current_timestamp, current_timestamp,
      'NEW', 3)";

    private static final String DELETE_WRONG_CART_IN_DB =
            "delete from carts where id = 999";
    @Inject
    Datasource datasource;

...

    @Test
    void testGetActiveCartForCustomerWhenThereAreTwoCartsInDB() {
        executeSql(INSERT_WRONG_CART_IN_DB);
```

```
        get("/carts/customer/3").then()
                .statusCode(INTERNAL_SERVER_ERROR.getStatusCode())
                .body(containsString(INTERNAL_SERVER_ERROR.
                getReasonPhrase()))
                .body(containsString("Many active carts detected !!!"));
        executeSql(DELETE_WRONG_CART_IN_DB);
    }

    private void executeSql(String query) {
        try (var connection = dataSource.getConnection()) {
            var statement = connection.createStatement();
            statement.executeUpdate(query);
        } catch (SQLException e) {
            throw new IllegalStateException("Error has occurred while
            trying to execute SQL Query: " + e.getMessage());
        }
    }
...
}
```

The test will verify that an HTTP GET request on /carts/customer/3 will have the following:

- Status code is 500, which means an internal server error

- The Body contains "Internal Server Error"

The next test will be about creating a new cart.

To create a cart, we need to create a customer. Then, based on its ID, we can create the cart. This test will have calls to the Customer API for customer creation, and to the Cart API to create a cart. For database consistency, at the end of the test, we will delete the created records:

```
@Test
void testCreateCart() {
    var requestParams = Map.of("firstName", "Saul", "lastName", "Berenson",
    "email", "call.saul@mail.com"); ①

    var newCustomerId = given()
            .header(HttpHeaders.CONTENT_TYPE, MediaType.APPLICATION_JSON)
```

```
        .body(requestParams).post("/customers").then()
        .statusCode(OK.getStatusCode())
        .extract()              ②
        .jsonPath()             ②
        .getInt("id");          ②

var response = post("/carts/customer/" + newCustomerId).then()
        .statusCode(OK.getStatusCode())
        .extract()              ③
        .jsonPath()             ③
        .getMap("$");           ③

assertThat(response.get("id")).isNotNull();
assertThat(response).containsEntry("status", CartStatus.NEW.name());

delete("/carts/" + response.get("id")).then()
        .statusCode(NO_CONTENT.getStatusCode());

delete("/customers/" + newCustomerId).then()
        .statusCode(NO_CONTENT.getStatusCode());
}
```

① You are packaging the request parameters into a `Map` that will be serialized to JSON by REST Assured.

② The `extract().jsonPath().getInt("id")` is used to extract the value for the `"id"` attribute in the response JSON body.

③ The `extract().jsonPath().getMap("$")` is used to extract all the JSON body and deserialize it into a `Map`.

The last test for the Cart API is to verify that the API will refuse to create another cart for the same customer when that customer already has an active cart:

```
@Test
void testFailCreateCartWhileHavingAlreadyActiveCart() {

    var requestParams = Map.of("firstName", "Saul", "lastName", "Berenson",
    "email", "call.saul@mail.com");
```

```
var newCustomerId = given()
        .header(HttpHeaders.CONTENT_TYPE, MediaType.APPLICATION_JSON)
        .body(requestParams)
        .post("/customers").then()
        .statusCode(OK.getStatusCode())
        .extract()
        .jsonPath()
        .getLong("id");

var newCartId = post("/carts/customer/" + newCustomerId).then()
        .statusCode(OK.getStatusCode())
        .extract()
        .jsonPath()
        .getLong("id");

post("/carts/customer/" + newCustomerId).then()
        .statusCode(INTERNAL_SERVER_ERROR.getStatusCode())
        .body(containsString(INTERNAL_SERVER_ERROR.getReasonPhrase()))
        .body(containsString("There is already an active cart"));

assertThat(newCartId).isNotNull();

delete("/carts/" + newCartId).then()
        .statusCode(NO_CONTENT.getStatusCode());

delete("/customers/" + newCustomerId).then()
        .statusCode(NO_CONTENT.getStatusCode());
}
```

In this test, we verify that, other than Status Code 500 and the infamous Internal Server Error, the response body contains the message "There is already an active cart".

ℹ️   I cover only the CartResourceTest, as it's the most panoramic test in the eight test classes. You will find all the code on my ○ GitHub repository. ☺

We will use SonarQube to check the coverage of the tests and to analyze the quality of the code.

Discovering SonarQube

SonarQube is an open-source platform developed by SonarSource for continuous inspection of code quality. You can perform automatic reviews with static analysis of code to detect bugs, code smells, and security vulnerabilities on 20+ programming languages. SonarQube offers reports about duplicated code, coding standards, unit tests, code coverage, code complexity, comments, bugs, and security vulnerabilities.

SonarQube can record metrics history and provides evolution graphs. SonarQube provides fully automated analysis and integration with Maven, Ant, Gradle, MSBuild and continuous integration tools (Atlassian Bamboo, Jenkins, Hudson, etc.).

You need to install SonarQube locally on your machine or use a hosted version. For example, you can use SonarCloud, where you have the possibility to analyze the project for free.

WHAT IS SONARCLOUD?

SonarCloud is the leading online service to catch bugs and security vulnerabilities in your pull requests and throughout your code repositories.

SonarCloud is a cloud-based code quality and security service of SonarQube. The main features of SonarCloud are:

- Supports 23 languages, including Java, JS, C#, C/C++, Objective-C, TypeScript, Python, ABAP, PLSQL, T-SQL, and more.

- Thousands of rules to track down hard-to-find bugs and quality issues, thanks to its powerful static code analyzers.

- Cloud CI integrations with Travis, Azure DevOps, BitBucket, AppVeyor, and more.

- Deep code analysis to explore all source files, whether in branches or pull requests, to reach a green Quality Gate and promote the build.

- Fast and scalable.

You can create a free account in SonarCloud.

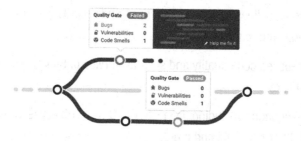

Maximize your throughput and only release clean code
SonarCloud automatically analyzes branches and decorates pull requests

Next, choose to start with SonarCloud using a GitHub or Azure DevOps or even a BitBucket or GitLab account. I use GitHub in this case.

Next, click Create Projects Manually:

Welcome to SonarCloud

Let us help you get started in your journey to code quality

 Analyze your first projects

Grant access to the SonarCloud application in your GitHub organization or user account. You will then be able to select which repositories you want to analyze.

Just testing? You can create projects manually.

 Join an organization

Now that you have an account on SonarCloud, just ask the Organization Administrator to add you manually. Learn More

Next, click Choose an Organization on GitHub to import your organization into GitHub:

Create an organization

An organization is a space where a team or a whole company can collaborate accross many projects.

You will be asked to grant access to the SonarCloud application on your organization or user account, which will allow you to choose which repositories you want to analyze.

Choose an organization on GitHub

Just testing? You can create manually.

Next, choose the organization where you are storing your project source code:

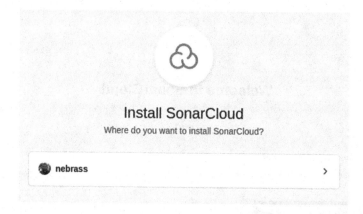

Next, choose the project from the list:

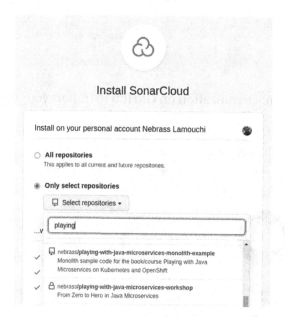

Next, you need to define the organization name:

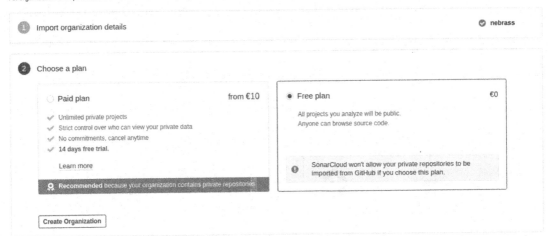

You can choose the free plan, which is suitable for all public repositories and projects:

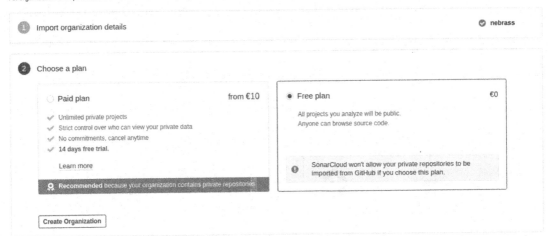

Now, you can select the public repositories that you want to analyze. Click Set Up:

Analyze projects - Select repositories

Organization*

◯ Nebrass Lamouchi nebrass   ▼   Import another organization

☐ Select all available repositories   🔍 Playing   ✕

☐ ◯ playing-with-cqrs-and-event-sourcing-in-spring-boot-and-axon

☐ ◯ playing-with-java-microservices-book-code

☐ ◯ playing-with-java-microservices-monolith-example

☐ ◯ playing-with-reactive-spring-boot

☐ ◯ playing-with-spring-boot-and-kafka-on-azure-event-hub

☐ ◯ playing-with-spring-boot-on-k8s

Don't see your repo? Check your GitHub app configuration.

Analyze private projects with our Paid Plan   from €10

✓ Unlimited private projects
✓ Strict control over who can view your private data
✓ No commitments, cancel anytime
✓ **14 days free trial.**

[Upgrade] Learn more

Just testing? You can create manually.
Setup a monorepo.

You will land next to the Project Configuration screen:

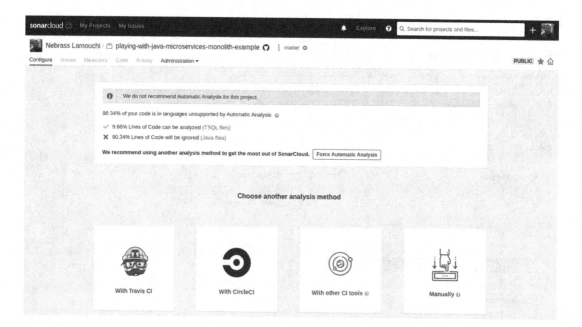

Choose the Manual Analysis Method and pick Maven as the build tool:

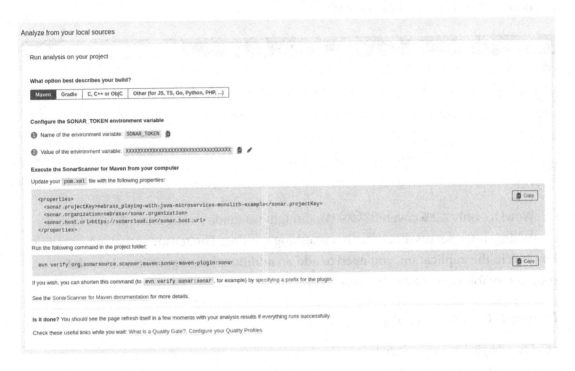

You will get the custom configuration that you will use to analyze your project on SonarCloud. There are some properties you need to add to the pom.xml file:

```
<properties>
  <sonar.projectKey>nebrass_quarkushop</sonar.projectKey>
  <sonar.organization>nebrass</sonar.organization>
  <sonar.host.url>https://sonarcloud.io</sonar.host.url>
</properties>
```

You need to define an environment variable called SONAR_TOKEN with the value generated here. This token is used to authenticate the SonarQube Maven plugin to the SonarCloud.

Now, the project is configured to be analyzed on SonarCloud, which you can do just by running mvn verify sonar:sonar:

Wow! It's only 2.2% covered? 😵😵 We thought we made strong enough tests to test everything, but it seems that there is something missing. The reason is that, when using Lombok in the application, you need to add an additional configuration file to the project root folder, as shown in Listing 4-4.

Listing 4-4. lombok.config

```
config.stopBubbling = true                          ①
lombok.addLombokGeneratedAnnotation = true          ②
```

① Tells Lombok that this is your root directory. You can then create
   lombok.config files in any subdirectories (generally representing
   projects or source packages) with different settings.

② Lombok can be configured to add @lombok.Generated annotations
   to all generated nodes, which is so useful for JaCoCo (which has
   built-in support) or other style checkers and code coverage tools.

Run the Sonar Analyzer again by typing mvn clean verify sonar:sonar:

Yippee! 😄 Now Sonar is aware of the Lombok-generated code and the analysis results are more acceptable. 😎

Building and Running QuarkuShop

Building the QuarkuShop

Packaging Modes in Quarkus

The QuarkuShop uses Maven as a build tool, so you can use the `mvn package` to build it. This command will build the following:

- The `quarkushop-1.0.0-SNAPSHOT.jar` file in the `target/` directory, which is not a runnable JAR. It contains the project classes and resources.

- The `quarkus-run.jar` file in the `target/quarkus-app` directory, which is a runnable JAR. But this JAR file cannot be executed anywhere without the `target/quarkus-app/lib/` folder, which is where all the required libraries are copied. So if you want to distribute the `quarkus-run.jar`, you need to distribute the whole `quarkus-app` directory.

To have a standalone JAR file that packages the QuarkuShop with all the necessary files, you can create a Fat JAR (aka an UberJAR).

WHAT ARE FAT OR UBER JARS?

Maven (especially Spring Boot) popularized this well-known approach to packaging, which includes everything needed to run the whole app in a standard Java runtime environment (i.e., you can run the app with `java -jar myapp.jar`).

To build the UberJAR for QuarkuShop, just type this command:

```
mvn clean package -Dquarkus.package.type=uber-jar
```

So easy and so simple! Nothing to configure or to add to your project. Quarkus natively supports this creation.

⚠ The major drawback of the UberJAR is that it cannot be layered during images builds, which can considerably increase the build time and image size.

Quarkus also supports native mode, which is the best and most promoted feature of this great framework.

Meeting the Quarkus Native

Quarkus makes it very easy to create a native binary by integrating deeply with GraalVM. These binaries are also called *native images*. GraalVM can compile Java bytecode into native images to get faster startups and smaller footprints for your applications.

The native-image feature is not available by default while installing GraalVM. To install native image with GraalVM, run the following command:

```
gu install native-image
```

❗ Make sure to have the GRAALVM_HOME environment variable configured and pointing to your GraalVM install directory.

To build the native QuarkuShop binary, run this command:

```
./mvnw clean package -Pnative
```

To build the native executable, we are using the native maven profile in the pom.xml file. The Maven profile is added when the project is generated:

```
<profiles>
    <profile>
        <id>native</id>
        <activation>
            <property><name>native</name></property>
        </activation>
        <build>
            <plugins>
                <plugin>
```

```xml
                <artifactId>maven-failsafe-plugin</artifactId>
                <version>${surefire-plugin.version}</version>
                <executions>
                    <execution>
                        <goals>
                            <goal>integration-test</goal>
                            <goal>verify</goal>
                        </goals>
                        <configuration>
                            <systemProperties>
                                <native.image.path>
${project.build.directory}/${project.build.finalName}-runner
                                </native.image.path>
                                <java.util.logging.manager>
                                    org.jboss.logmanager.LogManager
                                </java.util.logging.manager>
                                <maven.home>${maven.home}</maven.home>
                            </systemProperties>
                        </configuration>
                    </execution>
                </executions>
            </plugin>
        </plugins>
    </build>
    <properties>
        <quarkus.package.type>native</quarkus.package.type>
    </properties>
</profile>
</profiles>
```

Running the Tests in Native Mode

Note that there are the two goals configured: `integration-test` and `verify`. These are used to execute the tests that run for the native version of the application. You can reuse the tests that you have in the classic JAR and bring them to the native image. This is can be done by creating new Java classes that inherit from each `@QuarkusTest` class. The inheriting class needs to be annotated by `@NativeImageTest`, which indicates that this test should be run using a native image, rather than in the JVM.

⚠ `@NativeImageTest` will execute the tests against an existing native binary. The native binary path is defined in the Maven failsafe plugin `configuration` block:

```
<systemProperties>
    <native.image.path>
        ${project.build.directory}/${project.build.finalName}-runner
    </native.image.path>
...
</systemProperties>
```

To learn more about native tests, see this guide: `https://quarkus.io/guides/building-native-image#testing-the-native-executable`.

For example, for `CartResourceTest`:

```
@QuarkusTest
@QuarkusTestResource(TestContainerResource.class)
class CartResourceTest {
    ...
}
```

You create the `CartResourceIT` that will run the test in the native image:

```
@NativeImageTest
class CartResourceIT extends CartResourceTest {
}
```

🔥   I'm using the same naming conventions as the official Quarkus documentation. I use the `Test` suffix for JVM integration tests and use the `IT` suffix for the native image tests.

After creating the native image tests, try to run the tests using the native image:

```
mvn verify -Pnative
```

All the tests pass except the native test class that inherits from `CartResourceTest`. 😵😵 The error message is very clear:

```
[ERROR] Errors:
[ERROR]   CartResourceIT » JUnit @Inject is not supported in
NativeImageTest tests. Offe...
[INFO]
[ERROR] Tests run: 39, Failures: 0, Errors: 1, Skipped: 0
[INFO]
```

This is due to lack of support for injecting into Native mode. Although, in the `CartResourceTest`, you are injecting the `DataSource` into the test for database interaction. This is possible in JVM mode, but not in native mode. Let's delete `CartResourceIT`, as it will be useless to keep it disabled.

ℹ️   To disable a specific parent test class in native mode, just annotate that class using `@DisabledOnNativeImage`.

Now if you run the mvn verify -Pnative command again, you will skip the disabled tests and all the remaining tests will pass:

```
[INFO] Results:
[INFO]
[WARNING] Tests run: 39, Failures: 0, Errors: 0, Skipped: 1
```

Packaging and Running the Native QuarkuShop

The native binary build using the mvn verify -Pnative command cannot be distributed and cannot be executed in other machines. The native executable is specific to your operating system, where it was compiled. 😟

Keep calm! There is a solution for this, brought to you by the wonderful containerization and the fabulous Quarkus team! 😁 The solution is to build the native binary inside a Docker container so it will be isolated from the host OS. You can do this using the following command:

```
$ mvn package -Pnative -Dquarkus.native.container-build=true

...
[INFO] --- quarkus-maven-plugin:1.13.3.Final:build (default) @ quarkushop ---
[INFO] [org.jboss.threads] JBoss Threads version 3.2.0.Final
[INFO] [io.quarkus.flyway.FlywayProcessor] Adding application migrations in
path 'file:/home/nebrass/java/playing-with-java-microservices-monolith-example/
target/quarkushop-1.0.0-SNAPSHOT.jar!/db/migration' using protocol 'jar'
[INFO] [org.hibernate.Version] HHH000412: Hibernate ORM core version
5.4.29.Final
[INFO] [io.quarkus.deployment.pkg.steps.JarResultBuildStep] Building native
image source jar: ...quarkushop-1.0.0-SNAPSHOT-runner.jar
[INFO] [io.quarkus.deployment.pkg.steps.NativeImageBuildStep] Building
native image from ...quarkushop-1.0.0-SNAPSHOT-runner.jar
[INFO] [io.quarkus.deployment.pkg.steps.NativeImageBuildStep] Checking
image status quay.io/quarkus/ubi-quarkus-native-image:21.0-java11
21.0-java11: Pulling from quarkus/ubi-quarkus-native-image
57de4da701b5: Pull complete
cf0f3ebe9f53: Pull complete
6d14943d1530: Pull complete
```

```
Digest: sha256:176e619ad7cc2881477d04a2b2681fae41db08a92be06cddffd698f
9c9546388
Status: Downloaded newer image for quay.io/quarkus/ubi-quarkus-native-
image:21.0-java11
quay.io/quarkus/ubi-quarkus-native-image:21.0-java11
[INFO] [io.quarkus.deployment.pkg.steps.NativeImageBuildStep] Running
Quarkus native-image plugin on GraalVM Version 21.0.0.2 (Java Version
11.0.10+8-jvmci-21.0-b06)
[INFO] [io.quarkus.deployment.pkg.steps.NativeImageBuildStep] docker run \
    -v /home/nebrass/java/playing-with-java-microservices-monolith-example/
target/quarkushop-1.0.0-SNAPSHOT-native-image-source-jar:/project:z \
    --env LANG=C \
    --user 1000:1000 \
    --rm \
    quay.io/quarkus/ubi-quarkus-native-image:21.0-java11 \
    -J-Dsun.nio.ch.maxUpdateArraySize=100 \
    -J-DCoordinatorEnvironmentBean.transactionStatusManagerEnable=false \
    -J-Djava.util.logging.manager=org.jboss.logmanager.LogManager \
    -J-Dvertx.logger-delegate-factory-class-name=io.quarkus.vertx.core.
runtime.VertxLogDelegateFactory \
    -J-Dvertx.disableDnsResolver=true \
    -J-Dio.netty.leakDetection.level=DISABLED \
    -J-Dio.netty.allocator.maxOrder=1 \
    -J-Duser.language=en \
    -J-Dfile.encoding=UTF-8 \
    --initialize-at-build-time= \
    -H:InitialCollectionPolicy=com.oracle.svm.core.genscavenge.
CollectionPolicy$BySpaceAndTime \
    -H:+JNI -jar quarkushop-1.0.0-SNAPSHOT-runner.jar \
    -H:FallbackThreshold=0 \
    -H:+ReportExceptionStackTraces \
    -H:-AddAllCharsets \
    -H:EnableURLProtocols=http,https \
    --enable-all-security-services \
    --no-server \
```

```
   -H:-UseServiceLoaderFeature \
   -H:+StackTrace quarkushop-1.0.0-SNAPSHOT-runner
```

[quarkushop-1.0.0-SNAPSHOT-runner:25]   classlist: 12 734,03 ms, 1,15 GB
[quarkushop-1.0.0-SNAPSHOT-runner:25]   (cap):   786,61 ms, 1,15 GB
[quarkushop-1.0.0-SNAPSHOT-runner:25]   setup: 2 837,21 ms, 1,15 GB
18:02:44,230 INFO [org.hib.Version] HHH000412: Hibernate ORM core version
5.4.29.Final
18:02:44,258 INFO [org.hib.ann.com.Version] HCANN000001: Hibernate Commons
Annotations {5.1.2.Final}
18:02:44,357 INFO [org.hib.dia.Dialect] HHH000400: Using dialect:
io.quarkus.hibernate.orm.runtime.dialect.QuarkusPostgreSQL10Dialect
18:02:44,526 INFO [org.hib.val.int.uti.Version] HV000001: Hibernate
Validator 6.2.0.Final
18:03:20,036 INFO [org.jbo.threads] JBoss Threads version 3.2.0.Final
[quarkushop-1.0.0-SNAPSHOT-runner:25]   (clinit):   2 685,63 ms, 3,98 GB
[quarkushop-1.0.0-SNAPSHOT-runner:25]   (typeflow): 53 377,69 ms, 3,98 GB
[quarkushop-1.0.0-SNAPSHOT-runner:25]   (objects): 54 520,56 ms, 3,98 GB
[quarkushop-1.0.0-SNAPSHOT-runner:25]   (features):   2 615,98 ms, 3,98 GB
[quarkushop-1.0.0-SNAPSHOT-runner:25]   analysis: 118 704,92 ms, 3,98 GB
[quarkushop-1.0.0-SNAPSHOT-runner:25]   universe: 4 451,62 ms, 3,93 GB
[quarkushop-1.0.0-SNAPSHOT-runner:25]   (parse): 21 315,61 ms, 4,98 GB
[quarkushop-1.0.0-SNAPSHOT-runner:25]   (inline): 11 952,68 ms, 6,25 GB
[quarkushop-1.0.0-SNAPSHOT-runner:25]   (compile): 40 647,63 ms, 6,54 GB
[quarkushop-1.0.0-SNAPSHOT-runner:25]   compile: 79 193,30 ms, 6,54 GB
[quarkushop-1.0.0-SNAPSHOT-runner:25]   image: 13 638,67 ms, 6,29 GB
[quarkushop-1.0.0-SNAPSHOT-runner:25]   write: 4 589,92 ms, 6,29 GB
[quarkushop-1.0.0-SNAPSHOT-runner:25]   [total]: 236 996,22 ms, 6,29 GB
[WARNING] [io.quarkus.deployment.pkg.steps.NativeImageBuildStep] objcopy
executable not found in PATH. Debug symbols will not be separated from executable.
[WARNING] [io.quarkus.deployment.pkg.steps.NativeImageBuildStep] That will
result in a larger native image with debug symbols embedded in it.
[INFO] [io.quarkus.deployment.QuarkusAugmentor] Quarkus augmentation
completed in 254801ms

```
[INFO] ------------------------------------------------------------------------
[INFO] BUILD SUCCESS
[INFO] ------------------------------------------------------------------------
[INFO] Total time:  04:42 min
[INFO] Finished at: 2021-05-01T20:06:24+02:00
[INFO] ------------------------------------------------------------------------
```

In the previous Maven log, a very long Docker command is listed:

```
docker run \
-v /home/nebrass/java/playing-with-java-microservices-monolith-example/
target/quarkushop-1.0.0-SNAPSHOT-native-image-source-jar:/project:z \
--env LANG=C \
--user 1000:1000 \
--rm \
quay.io/quarkus/ubi-quarkus-native-image:21.0-java11 \
-J-Dsun.nio.ch.maxUpdateArraySize=100 \
-J-DCoordinatorEnvironmentBean.transactionStatusManagerEnable=false \
-J-Djava.util.logging.manager=org.jboss.logmanager.LogManager \
-J-Dvertx.logger-delegate-factory-class-name=io.quarkus.vertx.core.runtime.
VertxLogDelegateFactory \
-J-Dvertx.disableDnsResolver=true \
-J-Dio.netty.leakDetection.level=DISABLED \
-J-Dio.netty.allocator.maxOrder=1 \
-J-Duser.language=en \
-J-Dfile.encoding=UTF-8 \
--initialize-at-build-time= \
-H:InitialCollectionPolicy=com.oracle.svm.core.genscavenge.
CollectionPolicy$BySpaceAndTime \
-H:+JNI -jar quarkushop-1.0.0-SNAPSHOT-runner.jar \
-H:FallbackThreshold=0 \
-H:+ReportExceptionStackTraces \
-H:-AddAllCharsets \
-H:EnableURLProtocols=http,https \
--enable-all-security-services \
--no-server \
```

```
-H:-UseServiceLoaderFeature \
-H:+StackTrace quarkushop-1.0.0-SNAPSHOT-runner
```

This very long command is executed to build the native executable inside a Docker container based on the quay.io/quarkus/ubi-quarkus-native-image:21.0-java11 image, which has GraalVM support. So, even if you don't have GraalVM installed locally, you can build the native executable without any problem. 😊

 You can select the containerization engine explicitly using these commands:

```
# To select Docker

mvn package -Pnative -Dquarkus.native.container-runtime=docker

# To select Podman

mvn package -Pnative -Dquarkus.native.container-runtime=podman
```

The produced executable will be a 64-bit Linux executable, which you can run in a Docker container. When we generated QuarkuShop, we got a default Dockerfile.native file available in the src/main/docker directory, with the contents shown in Listing 4-5.

Listing 4-5. src/main/docker/Dockerfile.native

```
FROM registry.access.redhat.com/ubi8/ubi-minimal
WORKDIR /work/
COPY target/*-runner /work/application
RUN chmod 775 /work
EXPOSE 8080
CMD ["./application", "-Dquarkus.http.host=0.0.0.0"]
```

Let's build and run the Dockerfile.native. Before running the container, be sure that your PostgreSQL container is running. 😊

```
$ docker build -f src/main/docker/Dockerfile.native -t nebrass/
quarkushop-native .
...
Successfully built b14f563446d1
```

```
Successfully tagged nebrass/quarkushop-native:latest

$ docker run --network host --name quarkushop-native -p 8080:8080 nebrass/
quarkushop-native
WARNING: Published ports are discarded when using host network mode


 __   ___                                __           ____  __
_ __/ __ \ _  __ ___   ___ / /_  _  __/ __/ / /_   ___    ___
  --/ / / // / / / // __ \ / __// //_// / / /\_  \ / _ \ / _ \ / _  \
  -/ /_/ // /_/ // /_/ // /   / ,<  / /_/ /__/ / // / / // /_/ // /_/ /
 --\___\_\\___/ \_,_//_/   /_/|_| \___//___//_/ /_/ \___// ,___/
/_/ Part of the #PlayingWith Series
Powered by Quarkus 1.13.3.Final
2020-08-08 13:42:37,722 INFO  [org.fly.cor.int.lic.VersionPrinter] (main)
Flyway Community Edition 6.5.3 by Redgate
2020-08-08 13:42:37,725 INFO  [org.fly.cor.int.dat.DatabaseFactory] (main)
Database: jdbc:postgresql://localhost:5432/demo (PostgreSQL 9.6)
2020-08-08 13:42:37,729 INFO  [org.fly.cor.int.com.DbMigrate] (main)
Current version of schema "public": 1.1
2020-08-08 13:42:37,729 INFO  [org.fly.cor.int.com.DbMigrate] (main)
Schema "public" is up to date. No migration necessary.
2020-08-08 13:42:37,799 INFO  [io.quarkus] (main) quarkushop 1.0.0-SNAPSHOT
native (powered by Quarkus 1.13.3.Final) started in 0.085s. Listening on:
http://0.0.0.0:8080
2020-08-08 13:42:37,799 INFO  [io.quarkus] (main) Profile prod activated.
...
```

Hakuna Matata! ☺ All is good! The application is running and available on port 8080.

⚠ You might be asking yourself, why there is (main) Profile prod activated? 😵 Don't we build the application using the native profile? 😕 Why there is prod here? 😵

This profile is the application runtime profile: prod. As mentioned, the Quarkus application has three predefined profiles: dev, test, and prod. When we run a packaged application, we are in the prod profile, although when we run the source code using mvn quarkus:dev, we are obviously in dev mode.

The Maven native profile is for building the source code, whereas the prod is the runtime profile. 😇

Good! We built this Docker image based on the native binary of QuarkuShop: the *supersonic subatomic* Java binary build with Quarkus. But how performant is Quarkus? Does it really produce better results than Spring Boot? Does the native image really optimize the startup time and is it reducing the memory footprint?

ℹ Quarkus has a great extension called container-image-docker that deals with Docker and the Dockerfiles in the src/main/docker folder.

Differences Between the JVM and Native Modes

We need to do scientific checks to see if Quarkus is really so performant. 😊 Performance is the first selling point of Quarkus. You will find endless comparison reports that showcase the differences between Quarkus JVM, Quarkus Native, and many other frameworks like Spring Boot.

Let's start by reviewing the most famous metrics graphic made by the Quarkus Team. It compares the Quarkus JVM and native modes to a traditional cloud-native stack (which I think is Spring Boot 😊):

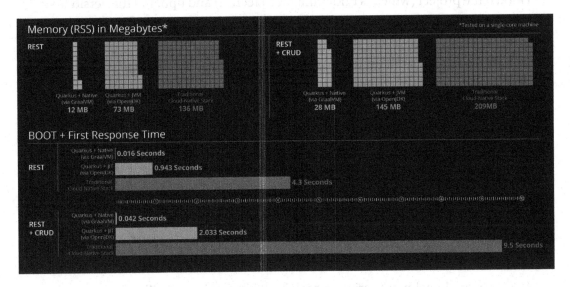

ⓘ   Memory RSS (which stands for resident set size) is the amount of physical memory currently allocated and used by a process (without swapped out pages). It includes the code, data, and shared libraries (which are counted in every process that uses them).

But we all know that this stuff is purely a marketing tool. ☺ Why don't we try this ourselves! 😊

I first considered creating a full environment with some Hello World REST APIs using Spring Boot, Quarkus JVM and Quarkus Native. Before starting the task, I searched in ☉ GitHub to see if there were similar projects. Fortunately, I found an excellent lab made by Harald Reinmüller (https://github.com/rmh78/quarkus-performance). The lab makes a benchmarking and metrics collection for sample REST and REST plus CRUD applications featuring many frameworks:

- Payara Micro
- Spring Boot

- Quarkus JVM and Native

- And even Python, which I will omit as out of scope 😃

I forked the project (which is under the MIT License) and updated the versions so the benchmarking was more efficient. You can find the project on my ⬡ GitHub repository at nebrass/quarkus-performance.

I do not explain in detail what the lab does, but I will list the basic steps:

1. All the tasks are executed inside a Docker container based on CentOs 8.

2. The first step is to install all the required software, such as Maven, GraalVM 21.1.0 CE, and Enterprise Edition, Python and the tests tools like Jabba (Java versions manager similar to NVM), etc.

3. Build the Docker image and run it, and while accessing its bash, build the source code for all the sample applications (all Java variants and Python).

4. Apply a benchmark script on each built binary via a specific runtime. The benchmark script is a load test based on the Apache Benchmarking tool.

5. A Python MatplotLib (plotting library for Python) figure is generated for each case. These figures contain a visualization of the metrics for the CPU and memory utilization.

WHAT IS THE DIFFERENCE BETWEEN GRAALVM CE AND EE?

GraalVM is distributed in Community and Enterprise editions.

The GraalVM Community edition is open-source software built from the sources available on GitHub and distributed under version 2 of the GNU General Public License with the "classpath" exception, which is the same terms as for Java.

GraalVM Community is free to use for any purpose and comes with no strings attached, but also no guarantees or support.

Oracle GraalVM Enterprise Edition is licensed under either the GraalVM OTN License Agreement, which is free for testing, evaluation, or for developing non-production applications, or under the terms of the Oracle Master License Agreement for customers.

— Official GraalVM Documentation from Oracle www.graalvm.org/docs/why-graal/

The benchmark results:

- Quarkus via GraalVM native image

REST Only   **REST + CRUD**

- Quarkus via Java runtime

REST Only

REST plus CRUD

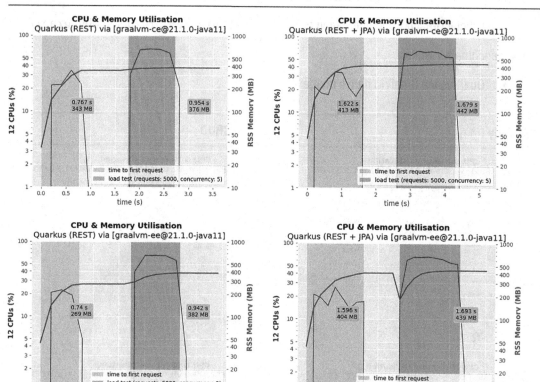

- Payara Micro via Java runtime

REST Only   **REST plus CRUD**

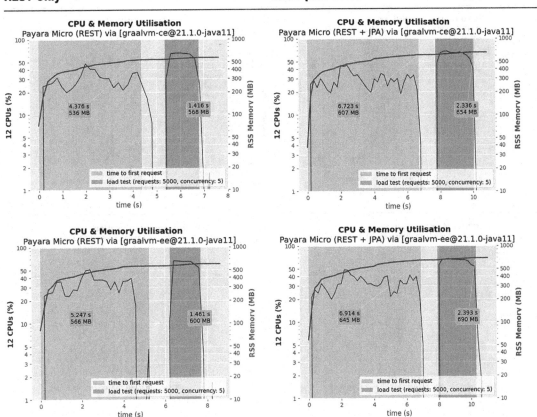

- Spring Boot via Java runtime

REST Only   **REST plus CRUD**

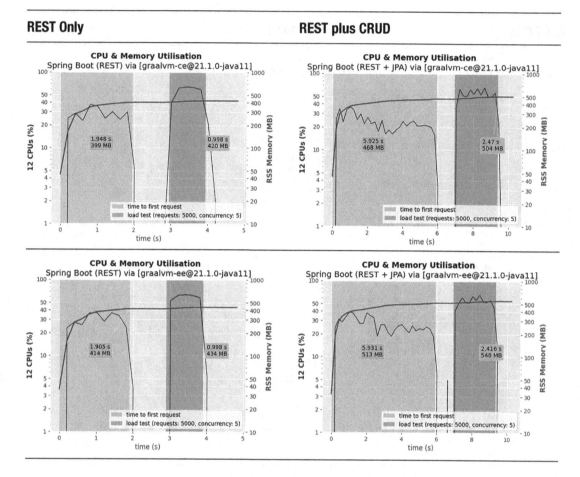

For a REST plus CRUD app like QuarkuShop, you have for the first request:

- **Quarkus Native**: Response time 0.054s and Memory RSS 48MB.

- **Quarkus JVM:** Response time 1.622s and Memory RSS 413MB. Quarkus native is 30 times faster and 8 times lighter.

- **Spring Boot:** Response time 5.925s and Memory RSS 468MB. Quarkus native is 109 times faster and 9 times lighter.

- **Payara Micro:** Response time 6.723s and Memory RSS 607 MB. Quarkus native is 124 times faster and 12 times lighter.

You can see that there really is a huge difference in the performance; Quarkus native is the champion! 🏆 😄

Note also the difference between Quarkus JVM and Spring Boot; Quarkus is faster than Spring Boot. 🏆 😄

The Magic Behind GraalVM's Power

Running your application inside a Java VM comes with startup and footprint costs.

The image-generation process employs static analysis to find any code reachable from the `main()` Java method and then performs full ahead-of-time (AOT) compilation.

This powerful combination is making the magic! The *supersonic subatomic* Java story is made here! 😊

Conclusion

QuarkuShop is ready to be tested, built, and distributed. You can enjoy the power of GraalVM to produce a powerful and blazing fast native binary.

As we are using Maven as a build tool, this application can be built and deployed easily to production using CI/CD pipelines—through Jenkins or Azure DevOps, for example.

## CHAPTER 5

Building and Deploying a Monolithic Application

Introduction

In QuarkuShop, we are using Maven as a build tool. This application can be built and deployed easily to production using CI/CD pipelines—thru Jenkins or Azure DevOps, for example.

Importing the Project into Azure DevOps

First of all, you need to create a project in Azure DevOps. Okay, but what is Azure DevOps? 😊

Azure DevOps is a Software as a Service (SaaS) product from ▦ Microsoft that provides many great features for software teams. These features cover the lifecycle of a typical application:

- **Azure pipelines**: CI/CD that works with any language, platform, and cloud (not only Azure 😜).

- **Azure boards**: Powerful work tracking with Kanban boards, backlogs, team dashboards, and custom reporting.

- **Azure artifacts**: Maven, npm, and NuGet package feeds from public and private sources.

© Nebrass Lamouchi 2021
N. Lamouchi, *Pro Java Microservices with Quarkus and Kubernetes*,
https://doi.org/10.1007/978-1-4842-7170-4_5

- **Azure Repos**: Unlimited cloud-hosted private Git repos for your project. Collaborative pull requests, advanced file management, and more.

- **Azure Test Plans**: An all-in-one planned and exploratory testing solution.

For ☕ Java developers, Azure DevOps (also known as ADO) is a great alternative to Jenkins/Hudson or GitHub Actions. This chapter showcases how to easily create a full CI/CD pipeline for this project.

First of all, go to the Azure DevOps portal and click Start Free to create an account:

Azure DevOps

Plan smarter, collaborate better, and ship faster with a set of modern dev services.

Already have an account?

Sign in to Azure DevOps >

Next, authenticate to your Outlook/Hotmail/Live account (or create a new one 😵)
and then confirm enrollment:

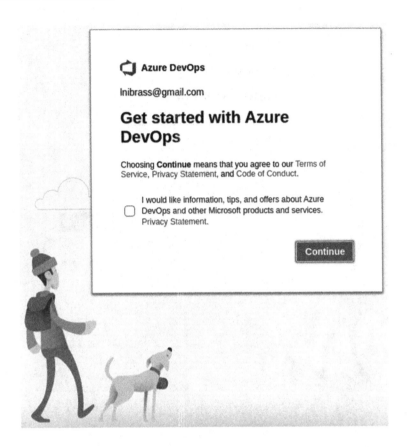

Next, you need to create an Azure DevOps organization:

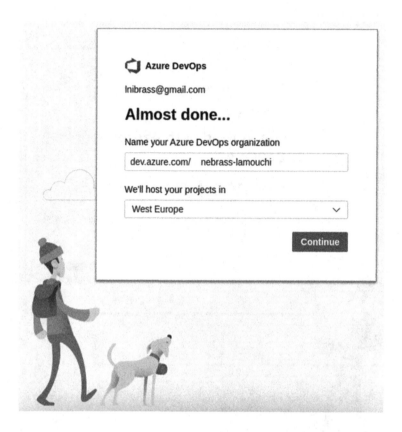

Next, create your first Azure DevOps project:

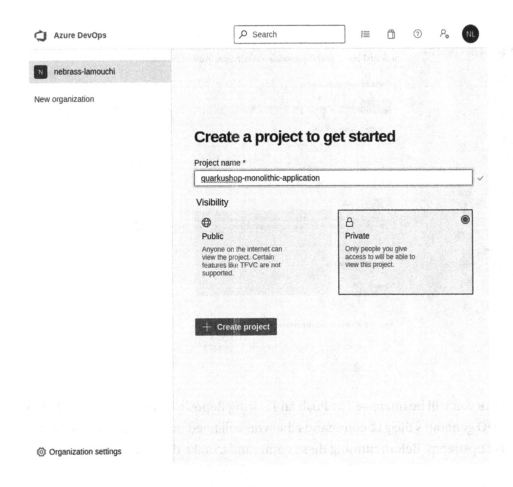

Next, go to Repos ➤ Files:

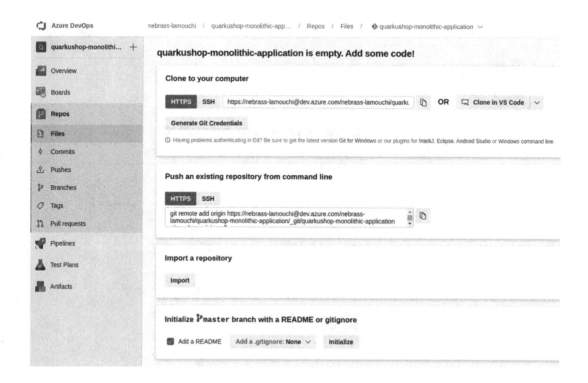

Here you will be interested in Push an Existing Repository From Command Line.

ADO generates the `git` commands that you will need in order to push the local project upstream. Before running these commands, make the local project a *git-enabled project*.

To do this, just run these commands, which will initiate and add all the files, then make the first commit:

```
git init
git add .
git commit -m "first commit"
```

Next, you should run the `git` commands that will push the full project to ADO:

```
1 git remote add origin https://nebrass-lamouchi@dev.azure.com/nebrass-
lamouchi/quarkushop-monolithic-application/_git/quarkushop-monolithic-
application
2 git push -u origin --all
```

The source code is now hosted in the ADO repositories. Now you'll create the CI/CD pipelines. 😎

Creating the CI/CD Pipelines

The next step is to configure the Continuous Integration pipeline, which will run each time there is new code on the main development branch (the master branch in our case).

Creating the Continuous Integration Pipeline

To create your first CI pipeline, go to the Pipelines section and click Create Pipeline:

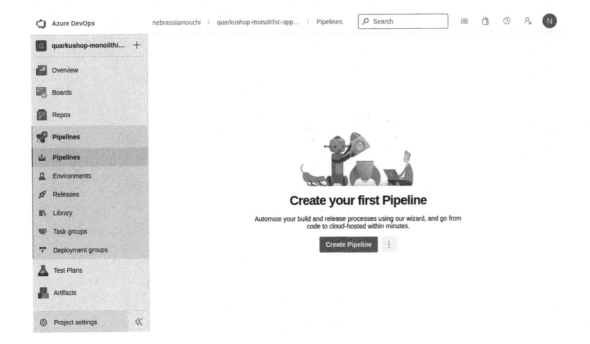

Next, choose where the source code is stored. Click Use the Classic Editor:

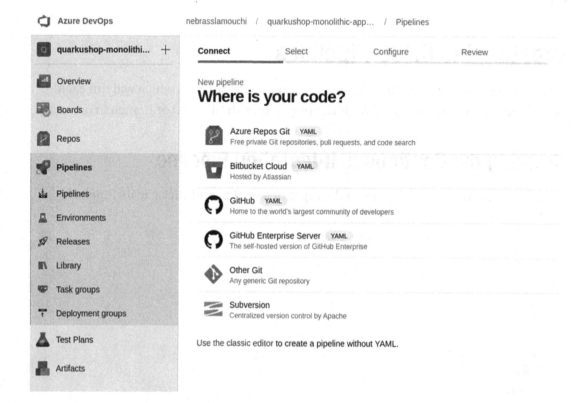

Next, select AzureRepos Git and choose the QuarkuShop repository that you just created:

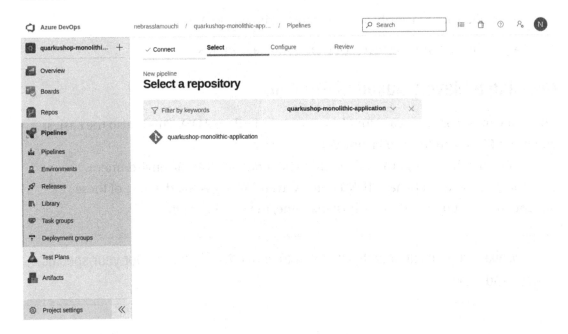

The Pipeline Configuration screen will appear. Choose the Maven pipeline:

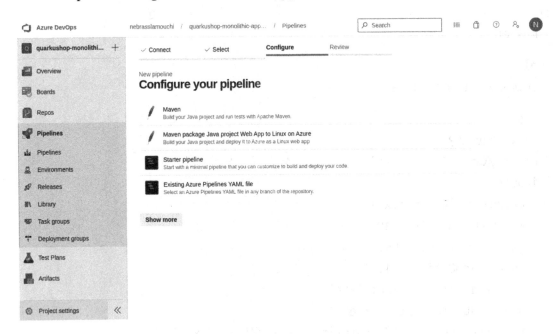

Then insert the most important part, defining the pipeline configuration using a definition YAML file. You have two choices:

- Build your Maven-based Java project directly in ADO

- Build your project using Docker multistage builds

Creating a Maven-Based CI Pipeline

This is the most common case for Maven projects built in ADO. This is also the easiest choice for Maven builds. See Listing 5-1.

Unfortunately, this approach has strong dependencies to the environment. For example, you need to have JDK 11 and Maven 3.6.2+ installed. If one of these dependencies is not found in the host machine, the build will fail.

---

❶   While using this approach, you need to adopt the CI platform for your specific needs and tools.

Listing 5-1. azure-pipelines.yml

```
trigger:                                                    ①
- master

pool:
  vmImage: 'ubuntu-latest'                                  ②

steps:
- task: Maven@3
  displayName: 'Maven verify & Sonar Analysis'             ③
  inputs:
    mavenPomFile: 'pom.xml'
    mavenOptions: '-Xmx3072m'
    javaHomeOption: 'JDKVersion'
    jdkVersionOption: '1.11'
    jdkArchitectureOption: 'x64'
    publishJUnitResults: true
    testResultsFiles: '**/surefire-reports/TEST-*.xml'
    goals: 'verify sonar:sonar'
```

```
- task: CopyFiles@2
  displayName: 'CopyFiles for Target'                    ④
  inputs:
    SourceFolder: 'target'
    Contents: '*.*'
    TargetFolder: '$(Build.ArtifactStagingDirectory)'
- task: PublishBuildArtifacts@1
  displayName: 'Publish Artifact: drop'                  ⑤
  inputs:
    pathtoPublish: '$(Build.ArtifactStagingDirectory)'
    artifactName: drop
```

① This pipeline will be triggered when there is an update on the
   `master` branch.

② Use the latest image of Ubuntu. It's 20.04 as of writing this book.

③ The first task in the CI scenario is to run all the tests and
   generate the Sonar report. Define the runtime to Java 11 and
   allocate 3GB of memory for the Maven task.

④ Copy the contents of the target folder to the predefined
   `$(Build.ArtifactStagingDirectory)`.

⑤ Finally, upload the contents of `$(Build.`
   `ArtifactStagingDirectory)` as an Azure DevOps artifact.

Creating a Docker Multistage Based CI Pipeline

This is the trendy way to build a project. This is the best choice to build a project that
has very specific requirements. As with the QuarkuShop application, you need to have
JDK 11 and GraalVM AND Maven 3.6.2+ installed. This cannot be satisfied even in ADO,
because there is no GraalVM in Azure pipelines (at least, as of now, while I'm writing
these words).

Fortunately, this build approach has no dependencies on the environment. Every
required component will be installed and configured in the different Dockerfile stages.

> ❶   While using this approach, you bring your specific needed tools to the CI
> platform.

Let's look at Stage 1 of the `Dockerfile.multistage` file, shown in Listing 5-2.

Listing 5-2. src/main/docker/Dockerfile.multistage

```
## Stage 1 : build with maven builder image with native capabilities
FROM quay.io/quarkus/centos-quarkus-maven:20.1.0-java11 AS build
```

In the Build stage, we are using the `centos-quarkus-maven:20.1.0-java11` Docker
base image, which comes with Java 11 with GraalVM, Maven, Podman, and Buildah.
These are exactly what we need as tools and versions.

As you might notice, I'm trying to convince you to adopt this approach. 😀 First of all,
it's the only possible one, as ADO doesn't have GraalVM, and moreover, it's the most
suitable approach to avoid any unexpected issues. 😇

The `azure-pipelines.yml` file for the Docker multistage CI pipeline is shown in
Listing 5-3.

Listing 5-3. azure-pipelines.yml

```
trigger:
- master

pool:
  vmImage: 'ubuntu-latest'

steps:
- task: Maven@3
  displayName: 'Maven verify & Sonar Analysis'
  inputs:
    mavenPomFile: 'pom.xml'
    mavenOptions: '-Xmx3072m'
    javaHomeOption: 'JDKVersion'
    jdkVersionOption: '1.11'
    jdkArchitectureOption: 'x64'
    publishJUnitResults: true
```

```
    testResultsFiles: '**/surefire-reports/TEST-*.xml'
    goals: 'verify sonar:sonar'
- task: Docker@2
  displayName: 'Docker Multistage Build'                        ①
  inputs:
    containerRegistry: 'nebrass@DockerHub'                      ③
    repository: 'nebrass/quarkushop-monolithic-application'
    command: 'build'
    Dockerfile: '**/Dockerfile.multistage'
    buildContext: '.'
    tags: |
      $(Build.BuildId)
      latest
- task: Docker@2
  displayName: 'Push Image to DockerHub'                        ②
  inputs:
    containerRegistry: 'nebrass@DockerHub'                      ③
    repository: 'nebrass/quarkushop-monolithic-application'
    command: 'push'
```

① Use the first Docker@2 task to:

- Build the Docker image based on the Dockerfile.multistage file.

- Name the built image nebrass/quarkushop-monolithic-application.

- Tag the built image with $(Build.BuildId), which is an ADO builds variable and with the latest tag.

② Use the second Docker@2 task to push the nebrass/quarkushop-monolithic-application image to the appropriate Docker Hub account.

③ Use an Azure Service connection called nebrass@DockerHub, which stores the appropriate Docker Hub credentials.

♀ The @ in Docker@2 defines the selected version of the Docker task in ADO.

ℹ️   To learn more about creating the Azure Service Connection to SonarCloud, check out this excellent Azure DevOps Labs tutorial at `https://www.azuredevopslabs.com/labs/vstsextend/sonarcloud/`.

Don't be surprised that I didn't delete the Maven verify & Sonar Analysis task. Unfortunately, the `Testcontainers` library that we are using for these integration tests cannot be invoked from inside the Docker context. This is why I decided to run the tests using the Maven command and then complete all the steps inside the Docker containers.

This CI pipeline is missing one requirement: the SONAR_TOKEN environment variable that Maven will use to authenticate to SonarCloud to publish the analysis report generated in the pipeline.

To define an environment variable in an Azure pipeline, go to Pipelines ➤ Choose Your Pipeline ➤ Edit ➤ Variables ➤ New Variable, then define the environment variable as SONAR_TOKEN and give it the SonarCloud token that you got when creating your project.

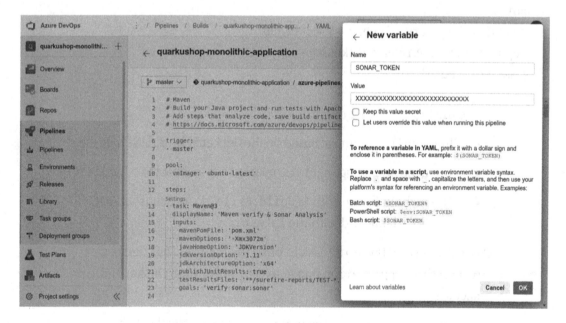

🔥   Without the SONAR_TOKEN environment variable, the `sonar:sonar` fails with an error message: `java.lang.IllegalStateException: You're not authorized to run analysis. Please contact the project administrator.`

At this level, the CI pipeline is ready. You now need to start looking at the continuous deployment pipeline.

Making the Continuous Deployment Pipeline

For the deployment part, the Docker container can be deployed to many products and locations:

- Kubernetes clusters: We are not there yet 😊

- Managed Docker hosting slot: Azure Container Instance, Amazon Container Service, Docker Enterprise, etc.

- Virtual machines

In this case, we will be using an Azure VM to deploy the Docker container. You can follow the same procedure to make the same CD pipeline.

Create the Virtual Machine

The first step is to create an Azure Resource Group, which is a logical group that holds the Azure resource, like the virtual machine that you want to create.

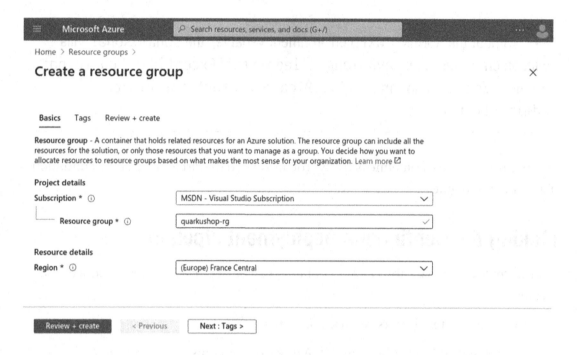

Next, create the VM by defining the following:

- **VM Name**: quarkushop-vm

- **Region**: France Central

- **Image**: Ubuntu Server 18.04 LTS

- **Size**: Standard_B2ms 2 vCPUS plus 8GB of RAM

Next, you need to define the following:

- **Authentication type**: Password

- **Username**: nebrass

- **Password**: Create and confirm it - I will not give you mine 😊

- Be sure to keep the SSH port set to allowed

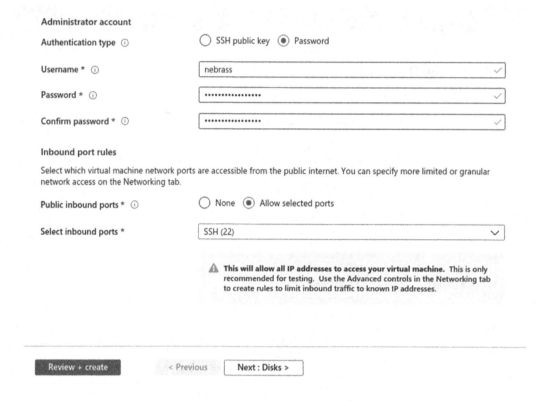

Confirm the creation by clicking Review + Create. Then in the validation screen, click Create.

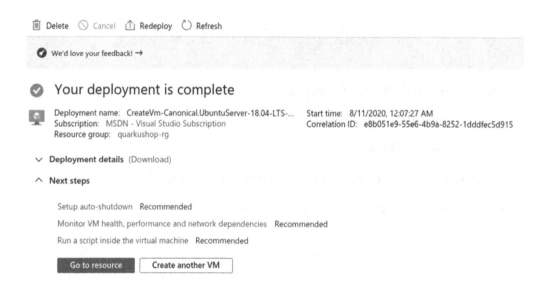

Check the created VM by clicking Go to Resource:

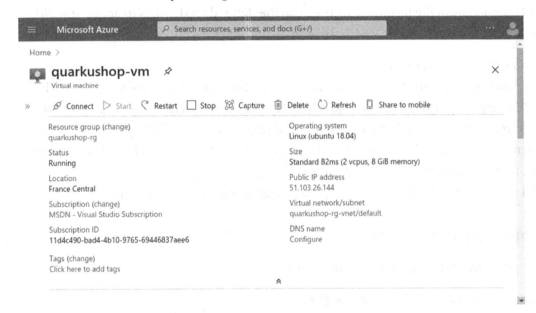

Next, you need to add an exception for the incoming access to the 8080 port (which is the QuarkuShop HTTP port) in the VM networking security rules. To do so, go to the Networking section of the Azure Virtual Machine and choose Add Inbound Port Rule:

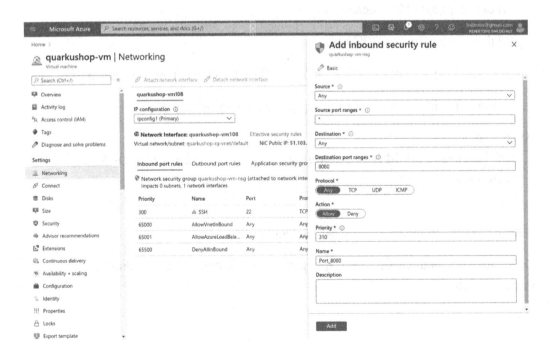

You already have the IP address for the created VM. To access it, just open an SSH session from the terminal. You can use the defined credentials to access the VM instance:

```
$ ssh nebrass@51.103.26.144
The authenticity of host '51.103.26.144 (51.103.26.144)' can't be established.
ECDSA key fingerprint is SHA256:bioO7HNjtKKgy8g7EAgfR+82Pz4gFyEmlOQyMjpLNVk.
Are you sure you want to continue connecting (yes/no/[fingerprint])? yes
Warning: Permanently added '51.103.26.144' (ECDSA) to the list of known hosts.
nebrass@51.103.26.144's password:
Welcome to Ubuntu 18.04.4 LTS (GNU/Linux 5.3.0-1034-azure x86_64)
...
nebrass@quarkushop-vm:~$
```

Begin by updating the virtual machine:

```
sudo apt update && sudo apt upgrade
```

Install the Docker Engine:

```
$ sudo apt-get install apt-transport-https \
    ca-certificates curl gnupg-agent \
    software-properties-common
```

Add the official Docker GPG key:

```
$ curl -fsSL https://download.docker.com/linux/ubuntu/gpg | sudo apt-key add -
```

Use the following command to set up the stable repository:

```
$ sudo add-apt-repository \
    "deb [arch=amd64] https://download.docker.com/linux/ubuntu \
    $(lsb_release -cs) \
    stable"
```

Now, it's time to install (finally 😁) the Docker Engine:

```
$ sudo apt-get update && sudo apt-get install docker-ce docker-ce-cli
containerd.io
```

Next, install Docker Compose:

```
$ sudo curl -L \
  "https://github.com/docker/compose/releases/download/1.26.2/docker-
  compose-$(uname -s)-$(uname -m)" \
    -o /usr/local/bin/docker-compose
```

Apply executable permissions to the binary:

```
$ sudo chmod +x /usr/local/bin/docker-compose
```

Then, create the docker-compose.yml file in the /opt/ folder:

```
version: '3'
services:
  quarkushop:
    image: nebrass/quarkushop-monolithic-application:latest
    environment:
      - QUARKUS_DATASOURCE_JDBC_URL=jdbc:postgresql://postgresql-db:5432/prod
    ports:
      - 8080:8080
  postgresql-db:
    image: postgres:13
    volumes:
      - /opt/postgres-volume:/var/lib/postgresql/data
    environment:
      - POSTGRES_USER=developer
      - POSTGRES_PASSWORD=p4SSW0rd
      - POSTGRES_DB=prod
      - POSTGRES_HOST_AUTH_METHOD=trust
    ports:
      - 5432:5432
```

Next, you need to create a local folder in the Azure VM that will be used as a Docker volume for PostgreSQL:

```
$ sudo mkdir /opt/postgres-volume
$ sudo chmod 777 /opt/postgres-volume
```

The Azure VM is now ready to be used as your production runtime. ☺ Let's move to the CD pipeline.

Create the Continuous Deployment Pipeline

Go back to Azure DevOps, then go to Pipelines ➤ Releases:

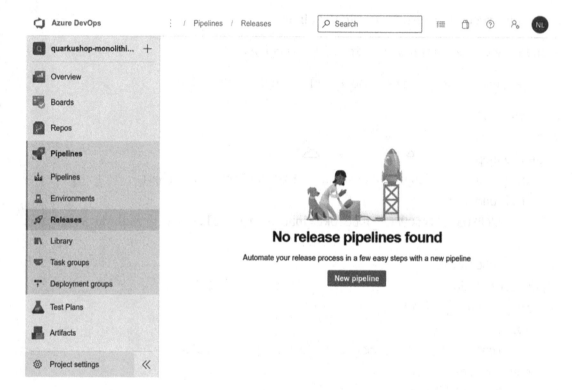

Next, click New Pipeline and then click Empty Job:

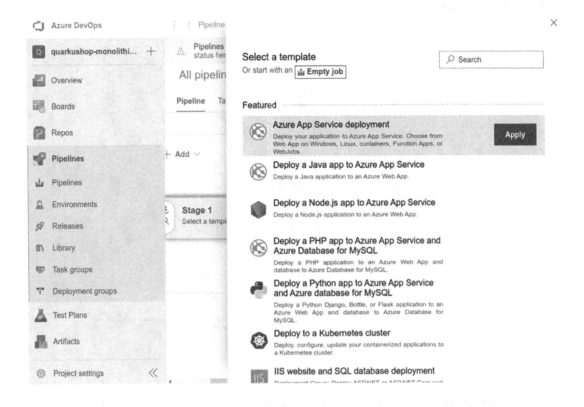

Add an artifact. Choose Build as the source type and select the appropriate project and source from the list:

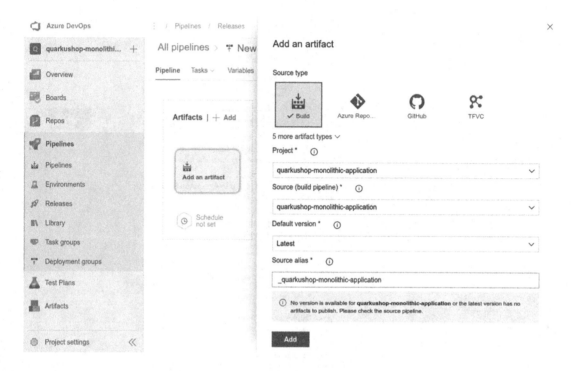

Next, click the available Stage 1 and click the Agent job. Change the Agent Specification to `ubuntu-20.04`.

Add a task to the pipeline:

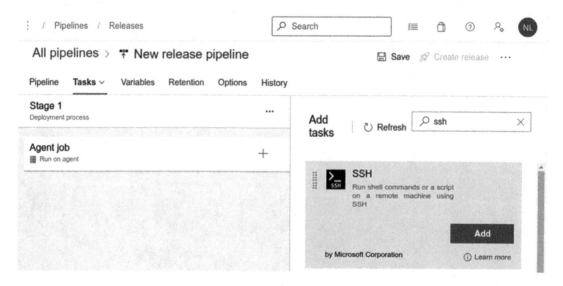

Click the added task and then click Manage near the SSH Service Connection to access the Service Connections manager:

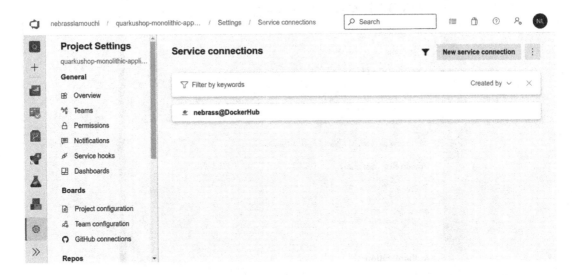

Next, click New Service Connection. Search for SSH and choose it:

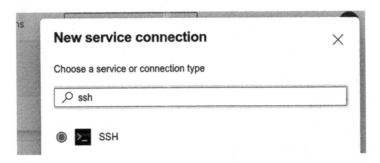

In the next screen, you need to configure access to the Azure VM instance:

Go back to the Release Pipeline screen and click the refresh button for the SSH service connection. Choose the created service connection.

Next, to the `Commands,` add these `docker-compose` instructions:

```
docker login -u $(docker.username) -p $(docker.password)
docker-compose -f /opt/docker-compose.yml stop
docker-compose -f /opt/docker-compose.yml pull
docker-compose -f /opt/docker-compose.yml rm quarkushop
docker-compose -f /opt/docker-compose.yml up -d
```

These commands will stop all the Docker Compose services, pull the latest images, delete the QuarkuShop service, and create it again.

ⓘ `$(docker.username)` and `$(docker.password)` are my Docker Hub credentials. We will define them as environment variables.

Then click Save.

Go to Variables to define the environment variables:

The last step is to activate the trigger:

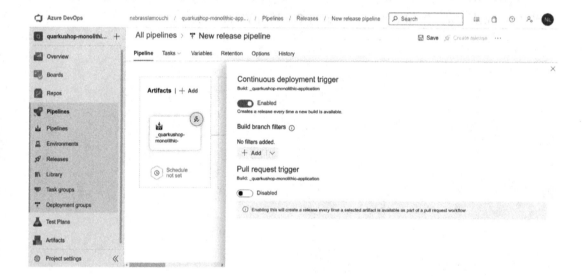

Finally, save the modifications and trigger the release by clicking 🚀 Create Release:

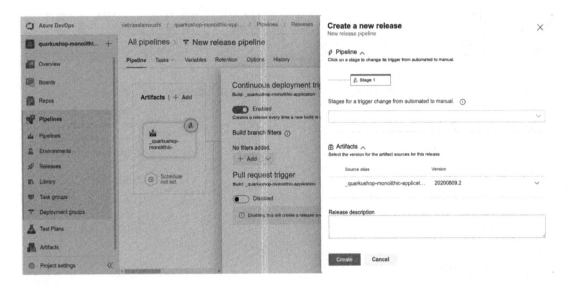

Yippee!! When the release pipeline execution finishes, just open the URL in your browser: IP_ADDRESS:8080.

For example, in my case QuarkuShop is reachable on 51.103.26.144:8080. You will get the default response:

Resource not found

Finally, you can access the predefined Quarkus `index.html` page:

Your new Cloud-Native application is ready!

Congratulations, you have created a new Quarkus application.

Why do you see this?

This page is served by Quarkus. The source is in `src/main/resources/META-INF/resources/index.html`.

What can I do from here?

If not already done, run the application in *dev mode* using: `mvn compile quarkus:dev`.

- Add REST resources, Servlets, functions and other services in `src/main/java`.
- Your static assets are located in `src/main/resources/META-INF/resources`.
- Configure your application in `src/main/resources/application.properties`.

Do you like Quarkus?

Go give it a star on GitHub.

How do I get rid of this page?

Just delete the `src/main/resources/META-INF/resources/index.html` file.

Application

GroupId: com.targa.labs
ArtifactId: quarkushop
Version: 1.0.0-SNAPSHOT
Quarkus Version: 1.6.0.Final

Next steps

Setup your IDE
Getting started
Quarkus Web Site

You also have the Swagger UI in the QuarkuShop production environment reachable on 51.103.26.144:8080/api/swagger-ui/.

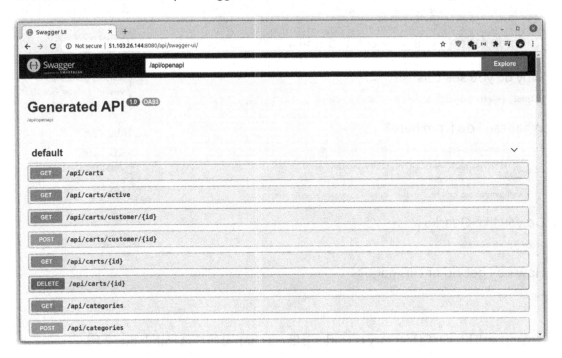

🔥   The Swagger UI can be used for dev/test environments, and it needs to be disabled in the production environment for security purposes.

Good! 😄 Let's now change the version listed in this index page and push the modification, to see if the CI/CD pipeline is working like expected: 😎

Your new Cloud-Native application is ready!

Congratulations, you have created a new Quarkus application.

Why do you see this?

This page is served by Quarkus. The source is in `src/main/resources/META-INF/resources/index.html`.

What can I do from here?

If not already done, run the application in *dev mode* using: `mvn compile quarkus:dev`.

- Add REST resources, Servlets, functions and other services in `src/main/java`.
- Your static assets are located in `src/main/resources/META-INF/resources`.
- Configure your application in `src/main/resources/application.properties`.

Do you like Quarkus?

Go give it a star on GitHub.

How do I get rid of this page?

Just delete the `src/main/resources/META-INF/resources/index.html` file.

Application

GroupId: com.targa.labs
ArtifactId: quarkushop
Version: 1.0.0-SNAPSHOT
Quarkus Version: 1.7.0.Final

Next steps

Setup your IDE
Getting started
Quarkus Web Site

Yippee! This CI/CD factory is working like a charm! ☺ Congratulations! 🥂

Conclusion

QuarkuShop now has a dedicated CI/CD pipeline:

- **The Continuous Integration Pipeline**: On each commit on the `master` branch, the pipeline will run all the tests and build the native binary, which will be packaged inside a Docker image.

- **The Continuous Deployment Pipeline**: When the CI succeeds, the Docker image will be deployed to the Azure VM. ☺

In the next chapter, you will implement more layers:

- **Security**: To prevent unauthenticated visitors from accessing the application.

- **Monitoring**: To ensure that the application is running correctly and to avoid any bad surprises.

Why wait for disaster to happen?☺

CHAPTER 6

Adding Anti-Disaster Layers

Introduction

Writing code, running unit and integration tests, doing code quality analysis, creating CI/CD pipelines—many developers think that the trip ends there, and a new iteration will start again. We forget the application runtime. I don't mean *where* it's to be executed, we already said that we will be running this application in Docker containers. I'm talking about *how* the application will run:

- How will users use QuarkuShop?

- How will user access to the application be controlled?

- Can we handle unauthorized access? Do we know which ones to admit and which ones to reject?

- How is the consumption of CPU and memory resources measured and tracked?

- What will happen if the application runs out of resources?

There are even more questions to be asked about the runtime. These questions reveal two missing layers in QuarkuShop:

- **The Security Layer**: All the authentication and authorization parts.

- **The Monitoring Layer**: All the metrics, I.e., the measurement and tracking components.

187

© Nebrass Lamouchi 2021
N. Lamouchi, *Pro Java Microservices with Quarkus and Kubernetes*,
https://doi.org/10.1007/978-1-4842-7170-4_6

Implementing the Security Layer

Security! One of the most painful topics for developers, 😃 but it's probably the most critical subject in any enterprise application. Security has been always a very challenging subject in IT: technology and frameworks keep evolving and hackers are evolving more and more. 🙁

For this QuarkuShop, we will use the dedicated Quarkus components and the recommended practices and design choices. This chapter discusses how to implement a typical authentication and authorization engine.

 I reference the authentication and authorization process as *auth²*.

Analyzing Security Requirements and Needs

Before writing any code, we start by creating the design, using UML diagrams for example. The same is true for the security layer; we need to create the design before implementing the code. But which design? The code is there. What will we be designing?

The full QuarkuShop features have been implemented, but there is a lot to be designed.

I like to compare building software to building houses. What we have done up to now is:

- Built the house, which is the same as writing the source code.

- Validated the conformity of the building with the plans, which is the same as writing tests.

- Connected the house to the electricity, water, and sewerage networks, which is the same as configuring access to databases, SonarCloud, etc.

- Got the furniture and decorated the house, which is the same as creating the CI/CD pipelines.

The house is now ready and the owners want to have a security system. We start by checking the windows and doors to locate possible access points, which is where we place the locks. Only key holders can enter, depending on the person, and the owner will allocate the keys. For example, only the driver will have the car garage key. The gardener will have two keys: one to the external door and one to the garden shed, where the tools are stored. The family members living in the house will have all the keys without exceptions.

We will have also cameras and sensors to monitor and audit access to the house. When we suspect illegal access to the house, we can check the cameras and see what happened.

This home security system deployment process is somehow the same as adding the Security layer of an application. We follow the same basic steps:

1. We analyze and locate all the access points to our application. This process is called *attack surface analysis.*

   Attack surface analysis helps you:

   - Identify which functions and parts of the system you need to review/test for security vulnerabilities.

   - Identify high-risk areas of code that require defense-in-depth protection; what parts of the system that you need to defend.

   - Identify when you have changed the attack surface and need to do some kind of threat assessment.

   —OWASP Cheat Sheet Series
   https://cheatsheetseries.owasp.org/cheatsheets/
   Attack_Surface_Analysis_Cheat_Sheet.html

2. We will put locks on these access points. These locks are part of the *authentication* process.

   Authentication is the process of verifying that an individual, entity, or website is whom it claims to be. Authentication in the context of web applications is commonly performed by submitting a username or ID and one or more items of private information that only a given user should know.

   —OWASP Cheat Sheet Series
   https://cheatsheetseries.owasp.org/cheatsheets/
   Authentication_Cheat_Sheet.html

3. We will define an access control mechanism to be sure that only the allowed person can access a given "door". This process is called *authorization.*

Authorization is the process where requests to access a particular resource should be granted or denied. It should be noted that authorization is not equivalent to authentication - as these terms and their definitions are frequently confused. Authentication is providing and validating identity. The authorization includes the execution rules that determine which functionality and data the user (or Principal) may access, ensuring the proper allocation of access rights after authentication is successful.

—OWASP Cheat Sheet Series
https://cheatsheetseries.owasp.org/cheatsheets/
Access_Control_Cheat_Sheet.html

QuarkuShop is a Java Enterprise application that exposes REST APIs, which is the only communication channel with the application users.

The users of QuarkuShop can be divided into three categories:

- **Visitor or Anonymous**: An unauthenticated customer

- **User**: An authenticated customer

- **Admin**: The application superuser

The next step is to define which user category is allowed to access each REST API service. This can be done using the *authorization matrix.*

Defining Authorization Matrices for REST APIs

Authorization Matrix for the Cart REST API

Operation	Anonymous	User	Admin
Get All Carts	⊗	⊘	⊘
Get Active Carts	⊗	⊘	⊘
Get Carts by Customer ID	⊗	⊘	⊘
Create a New Cart for a Given Customer	⊗	⊘	⊘
Get a Cart by ID	⊗	⊘	⊘
Delete a Cart by ID	⊗	⊘	⊘

Authorization Matrix for the Category REST API

Operation	Anonymous	User	Admin
List All Categories	✓	✓	✓
Create New Category	✗	✗	✓
Get Category by ID	✓	✓	✓
Delete Category by ID	✗	✗	✓
Get Products by Category ID	✓	✓	✓

Authorization Matrix for the Customer REST API

Operation	Anonymous	User	Admin
Get All Customers	✗	✗	✓
Create a New Customer	✗	✗	✓
Get Active Customers	✗	✗	✓
Get Inactive Customers	✗	✗	✓
Get Customer by ID	✗	✗	✓
Delete Customer by ID	✗	✗	✓

Authorization Matrix for the Order REST API

Operation	Anonymous	User	Admin
Get All Orders	✗	✗	✓
Create a New Order	✗	✓	✓
Get Orders by Customer ID	✗	✓	✓
Check if There Is an Order for a Given ID	✗	✓	✓
Get Order by ID	✗	✓	✓
Delete Order by ID	✗	✓	✓

Authorization Matrix for the Order-Item REST API

Operation	Anonymous	User	Admin
Create a New Order-Item	⊗	⊘	⊘
Get Order-Items by Order ID	⊗	⊘	⊘
Get Order-Item by ID	⊗	⊘	⊘
Delete Order-Item by ID	⊗	⊘	⊘

Authorization Matrix for the Payment REST API

Operation	Anonymous	User	Admin
Get All Payments	⊗	⊗	⊘
Create a New Payment	⊗	⊘	⊘
Get Payments for Amounts Inferior or Equal a Limit	⊗	⊘	⊘
Get a Payment by ID	⊗	⊘	⊘
Delete a Payment by ID	⊗	⊗	⊘

Authorization Matrix for the Product REST API

Operation	Anonymous	User	Admin
Get All Products	⊘	⊘	⊘
Create a New Product	⊗	⊗	⊘
Get Products by Category ID	⊘	⊘	⊘
Count All Products	⊘	⊘	⊘
Count Products by Category ID	⊘	⊘	⊘
Get a Product by ID	⊘	⊘	⊘
Delete a Product by ID	⊗	⊗	⊘

Authorization Matrix for the Review REST API

Operation	Anonymous	User	Admin
Get Reviews by Product ID	⊘	⊘	⊘
Create a New Review by Product ID	⊗	⊘	⊘
Get a Review by ID	⊘	⊘	⊘
Delete a Review by ID	⊗	⊗	⊘

Implementing the Security Layer

We will use dedicated Identity storage to handle the QuarkuShop users' credentials. We use Keycloak for this purpose.

WHAT IS KEYCLOAK?

Keycloak is an open-source identity and access management (IAM) solution aimed at modern applications and services. It makes it easy to secure applications and services with little to no code.

Users authenticate with Keycloak rather than with individual applications. This means that your applications don't have to deal with login forms, authenticating users, and storing users. Once logged-in to Keycloak, users don't have to log in again to access a different application. This also applied to logout.

Keycloak provides single-sign out, which means users only have to log out once to be logged out of all applications that use Keycloak.

Keycloak is based on standard protocols and provides support for OpenID Connect, OAuth 2.0, and SAML.

If role-based authorization doesn't cover your needs, Keycloak provides fine-grained authorization services as well. This allows you to manage permissions for all your services from the Keycloak admin console and gives you the power to define exactly the policies you need.

We will implement this security policy in four steps:

1. Preparing and configuring Keycloak.

2. Implementing the auth^2 Java components in QuarkuShop.

3. Updating the integration tests to support auth^2.

4. Adding Keycloak to our Production environment.

Preparing and Configuring Keycloak

The first step in Security implementation is to have a Keycloak instance. This section discusses creating and configuring Keycloak step-by-step.

ℹ   In many tutorials, there are prepared configurations that can be imported to Keycloak to get started easily. You will not be doing this here. You will be going step by step to perform all the needed configuration. This is the best way to learn: learning by doing.

Start by creating the Keycloak instance in Docker container:

```
docker run -d --name docker-keycloak \
        -e KEYCLOAK_USER=admin \          ①
        -e KEYCLOAK_PASSWORD=admin \      ①
        -e DB_VENDOR=h2 \                 ②
        -p 9080:8080 \                    ③
        -p 8443:8443 \                    ③
        -p 9990:9990 \                    ③
        jboss/keycloak:11.0.0             ④
```

① By default, there is no `admin` user created, so you won't be able
to log in to the `admin` console. To create an `admin` account,
you need to use environment variables to pass in an initial
username and password.

② Use `H2` as the Keycloak database.

③ List the exposed ports.

④ This is based on Keycloak 11.0.0.

Open `http://localhost:9080` to access the welcome page:

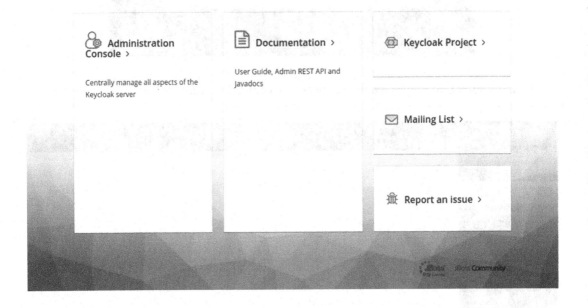

195

Next, click Administration Console to authenticate to the console. Use the `admin` credentials for the username and password:

Next, you need to create a new *realm*. Start by clicking Add Realm:

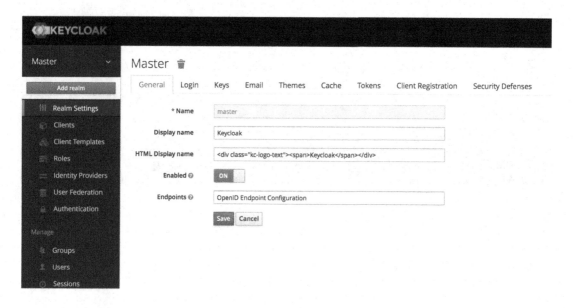

WHAT IS A KEYCLOAK REALM?

A *realm* is the core concept in Keycloak. A realm manages a set of users, credentials, roles, and groups. A user belongs to and logs in to a realm. Realms are isolated from one another and can only manage and authenticate the users that they control.

When you boot up Keycloak for the first time, it creates a predefined realm for you. This initial realm is the `master` realm. It is the highest level in the hierarchy of realms. Admin accounts in this realm have permissions to view and manage any other realm created on the server instance. When you define your initial `admin` account, you create an account in the `master` realm. Your initial login to the admin console will also be via the `master` realm.

You will land next on the first step of creating a new realm. Call the realm `quarkushop-realm` then click Create:

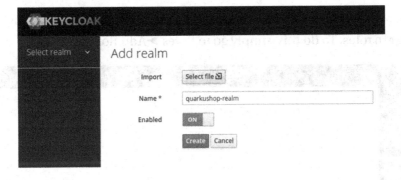

Next, you will get the `quarkushop-realm` configuration page:

In the `quarkushop-realm`, you need to define the roles that you will be using: the `user` and `admin` roles. To do this, simply go to Roles ➤Add Role:

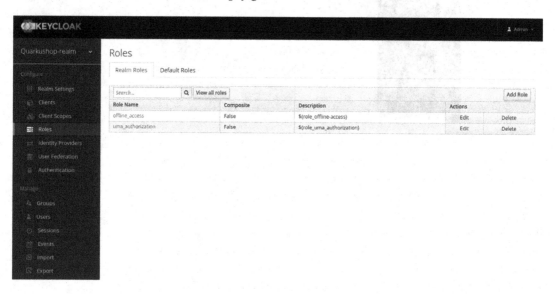

Now you can create the admin role:

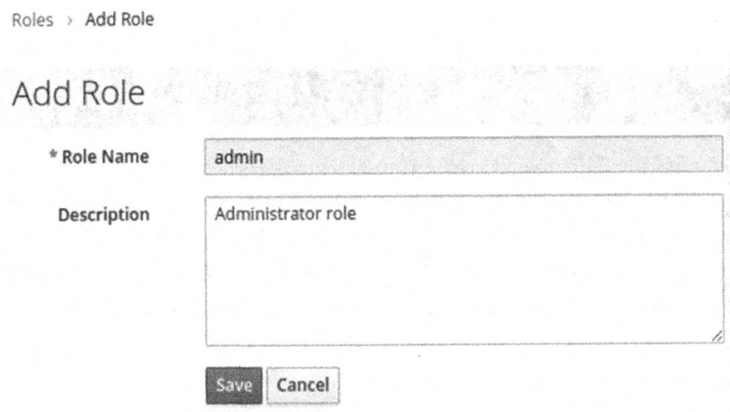

Roles > Add Role

Add Role

* Role Name   admin

Description   Administrator role

Save Cancel

Create the user role as well:

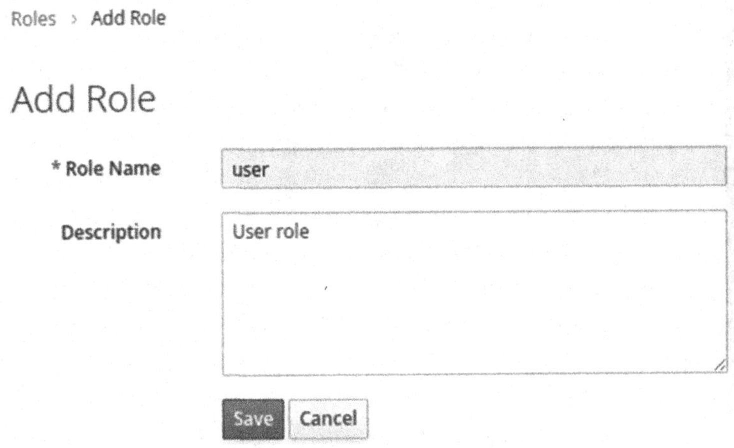

Roles > Add Role

Add Role

* Role Name   user

Description   User role

Save Cancel

Now that you have created the roles, you need to create the users. Just go to the Users menu:

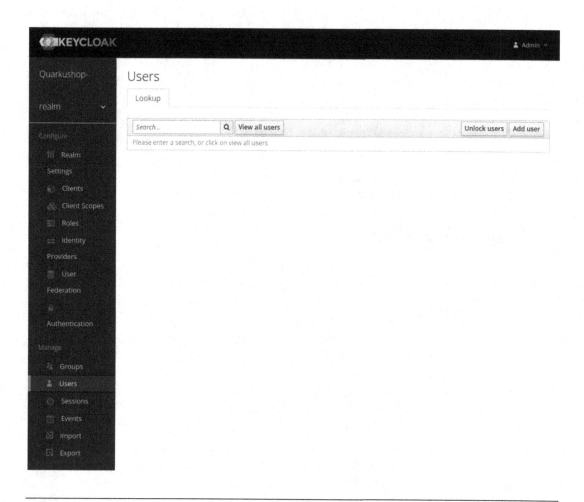

💡   Sometimes on this screen, the list of users isn't loaded when you open the page. If this happens, just click View All Users to load the list.

Click Add User to create the users (for this example, Nebrass, Jason, and Marie):

Users › Add user

Add user

ID	
Created At	
Username *	nebrass
Email	nebrass@quarkushop.store
First Name	Nebrass
Last Name	Lamouchi
User Enabled ❔	**ON**
Email Verified ❔	**ON**
Required User Actions ❔	Select an action...

Save   Cancel

Then after clicking Save, click the Credentials tab, where you will define the user passwords.

⚠   Don't forget to set the `Temporary` to `OFF` to prevent Keycloak from asking you to update the password on the first login. Then, click Set Password:

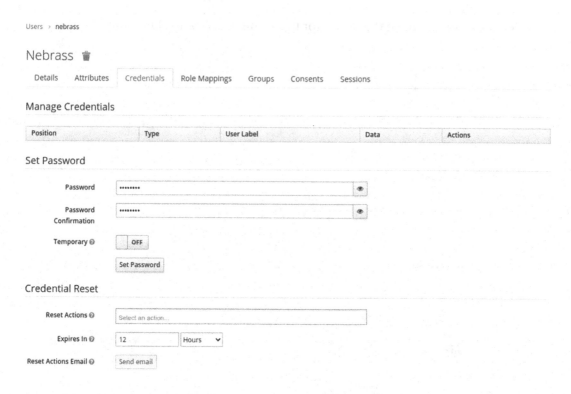

Next, go to the Role Mappings tab and add all the roles to Nebrass. ☻ Yes! I'll be the admin of this app. 😬

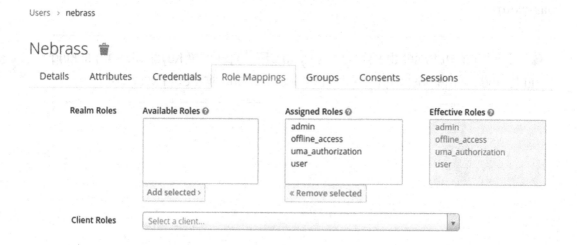

Now create the Jason user and define a password:

Users > Add user

Add user

ID	
Created At	
Username *	jason
Email	jason@quarkushop.store
First Name	Jason
Last Name	Bourne
User Enabled @	ON
Email Verified @	ON
Required User Actions @	Select an action...

Save Cancel

Add the user role to Jason:

Users > jason

Jason 🗑

Details	Attributes	Credentials	Role Mappings	Groups	Consents	Sessions

Realm Roles

Available Roles @	Assigned Roles @	Effective Roles @
admin	offline_access uma_authorization user	offline_access uma_authorization user
Add selected >	« Remove selected	

Client Roles   Select a client...

Next, create the Marie user and define a password:

Users > Add user

Add user

ID	
Created At	
Username *	marie
Email	marie@quarkushop.store
First Name	Marie
Last Name	Hugo
User Enabled @	ON
Email Verified @	ON
Required User Actions @	Select an action...

Save Cancel

Add the user role to Marie:

Users > marie

Marie 🗑

Details   Attributes   Credentials   Role Mappings   Groups   Consents   Sessions

Realm Roles

Available Roles @

admin

Add selected >

Assigned Roles @

offline_access
uma_authorization
user

« Remove selected

Effective Roles @

offline_access
uma_authorization
user

Client Roles   Select a client...

You are finished configuring roles and users! Now, click Clients to list the realm clients.

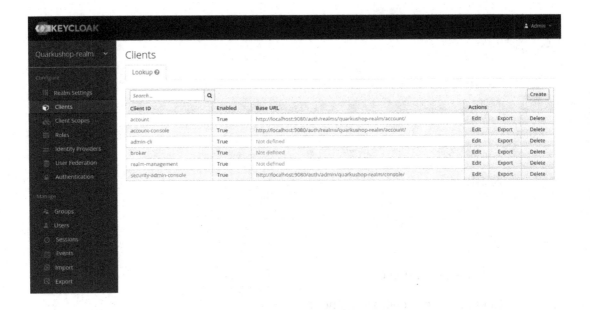

WHAT IS A REALM CLIENT?

Clients are entities that can request Keycloak to authenticate a user. Most often, clients are applications and services that want to use Keycloak to secure themselves and provide a single sign-on solution. Clients can also be entities that just want to request identity information or an access token so that they can securely invoke other services on the network that are secured by Keycloak.

Click Create to add a new client with the following settings:

Clients > **Add Client**

Add Client

Import	Select file ⤓
Client ID * ❷	quarkushop
Client Protocol ❷	openid-connect ▾
Root URL ❷	http://localhost:8080
	Save Cancel

- Client ID: quarkushop

- Client protocol: openid-connect

- Root URL: http://localhost:8080/

Click Save to get the client configuration screen:

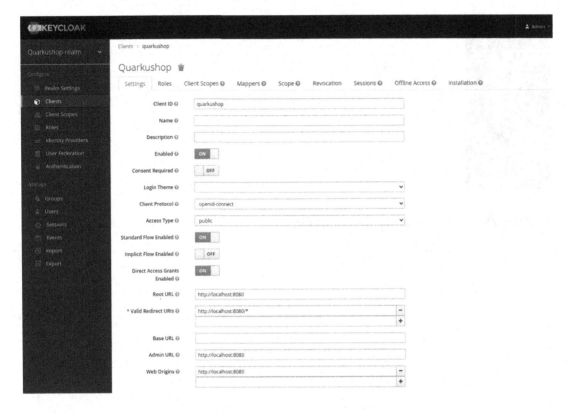

It's mandatory to define a protocol mapper for your client.

WHAT IS A PROTOCOL MAPPER?

Protocol mappers perform transformations on tokens and documents. They can do things like map user data to protocol claims and transform any requests going between the client and auth server.

Click the Mappers tab to configure a mapper:

Then click Create to add a new mapper:

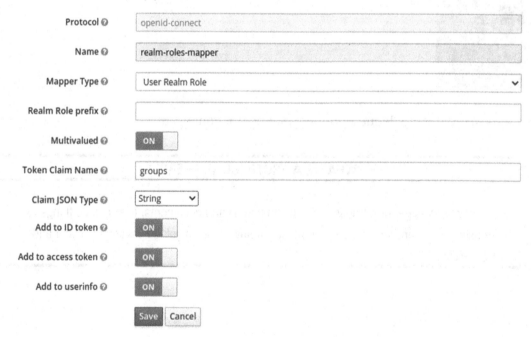

> ℹ️ *Why Do We Define* Token Claim Name *as Groups?*

We will use the protocol mapper to map the User Realm role (which can be user or admin) to a property called groups, which we will add as a plain string to the ID token, the access token, and the userinfo.

The choice of groups is based on the MpJwtValidator Java class from the Quarkus SmallRye JWT library (which is the Quarkus implementation for managing the JWT); where we define the SecurityIdentity roles using jwtPrincipal.getGroups():

```
JsonWebToken jwtPrincipal = parser.parse(request.getToken().getToken());
uniEmitter.complete(
        QuarkusSecurityIdentity.builder().setPrincipal(jwtPrincipal)
            .addRoles(jwtPrincipal.getGroups())
            .addAttribute(SecurityIdentity.USER_ATTRIBUTE, jwtPrincipal)
            .build()
);
```

This is why we defined our mapper to affect the User roles to the Groups property embedded in the JWT token. 😉

You can now test if the Keycloak instance is running as expected. Simply request an access_token using the cURL command:

```
curl -X POST http://localhost:9080/auth/realms/quarkushop-realm/protocol/
openid-connect/token \
        -H 'content-type: application/x-www-form-urlencoded' \
        -d 'client_id=quarkushop' \
        -d 'username=nebrass' \
        -d 'password=password' \
        -d 'grant_type=password' | jq '.'
```

ℹ️   The URL `http://localhost:9080/auth/realms/quarkushop-realm/`
`protocol/openid-connect/token` is composed of:

http://localhost:9080/auth/realms/quarkushop-realm/protocol/openid-connect/token

| Keycloak URL | Keycloak Realm API | Keycloak Realm name | OpenID Connect URI |

We want to access to the token's endpoint

💡   The `jq` is a lightweight and flexible command-line JSON processor that I'm
using to format the JSON output.

You will get a JSON response like this:

```
{
  "access_token": "eyJhbGciOiJSUzI1NiIsInR5cCIgOiAiSldUIiwia2lkIiA6ICJKcmlx
WGQzYVBNOS13djhXUmVJekZkRnRJa3Z1WG5uNDd4aOJmT195R19zInO.eyJleHAiOjE1OTTcOOT
EwNTIsImlhdCI6MTU5NzQ5MDc1MiwianRpIjoiZmIxZmQxOWMtNWJlMCOoYTgwLWExOTUtOTA
xZjFkOTI3NDI5IiwiaXNzIjoiaHR0cDovL2xvY2FsaG9zdDo5MDgwL2F1dGgvcmVhbG1zL3F1
YXJrdXNob3AtcmVhbG0iLCJhdWQiOiJhY2NvdW50Iiwic3ViIjoiMzU1ODc3YWQtMjY3Ny00O
DJiLWE5NWYtYTI4ZjdmZGI1OTk5IiwidHlwIjoiQmVhcmVyIiwiYXpwIjoicXVhcmt1c2hvcCI
sInNlc3Npb25fc3RhdGUiOiJjM2E4ZmU3Mi02MzRmLTRiNmUtYTZkMSO3MTkyOGI2YTBlN2YiL
CJhY3IiOiIxIiwiYWxsb3dlZC1vcmlnaW5zIjpbImh0dHA6Ly9sb2NhbGhvc3Q6ODA4MCJdLCJ
yZWFsbV9hY2Nlc3MiOnsicm9sZXMiOlsib2ZmbGluZV9hY2Nlc3MiLCJhZG1pbiIsInVtYV9hdX
Rob3JpemF0aW9uIiwidXNlciJdfSwicmVzb3VyY2VfYWNjZXNzIjp7ImFjY291bnQiOnsicm9sZ
XMiOlsibWFuYWdlLWFjY291bnQiLCJtYW5hZ2UtYWNjb3VudC1saW5rcyIsInZpZXctcHJvZmls
ZSJdfXOsInNjb3BlIjoiZW1haWwgcHJvZmlsZSIsImVtYWlsX3ZlcmlmaWVkIjpOcnVlLCJuYW1
lIjoiTmVicmFzcyBMYW1vdWNoaSIsImdyb3Vwcyl6WyJvZmZsaW5lX2FjY2VzcyIsImFkbWluIi
widWthX2F1dGhvcml6YXRpb24iLCJ1c2VyIl0sInByZWZlcnJlZF91c2VybmFtZSI6Im5lYnJhc
3MiLCJnaXZlbl9uYW1lIjoiTmVicmFzcyIsImZhbWlseV9uYW1lIjoiTGFtb3VjaGkiLCJlbWFp
bCI6Im5lYnJhc3NAcXVhcmt1c2hvcC5zdG9yZSJ9.HZmicWhE9V8g74of9KGcZOVGvwC_
oo2zs4-ElBBuV6XSWDUoiFLJVkSUzOV4WFzwvsM7V7_aZRzihZqq6QTtezweyhZIauo3pjmmtbM
nq16WUFV-4oJWzk3P_6T5y74sh93aPuQtnw5hSQ4L68RjwQ6HIcaHJFkqrh6fX7uyOZiHuPnRzh
v38uQrD9YMC_z3tApWKTS2TA9igizZrlJCDfTdfiThUDuXEgOmw-pffYx1BASfL1400cOapGPqi
```

rNkSgSrCpuFvikXlRdeu3YnI1JQ6S7Jn-qQI-bdCD5MO_ynaUiJn_p6sZqI6ioSmLGyA__
S5J7nj_BO--fdIlolUA",
  "expires_in": 300,
  "refresh_expires_in": 1800,
  "refresh_token": "...",
  "token_type": "bearer",
  "not-before-policy": 0,
  "session_state": "c3a8fe72-634f-4b6e-a6d1-71928b6a0e7f",
  "scope": "email profile"
}

ℹ   For prettier output, I omitted the value of `refresh_token`, as it's very long and useless.

Copy the `access_token` value. Then go to `jwt.io` and paste the JWT `access_token` there to decode it:

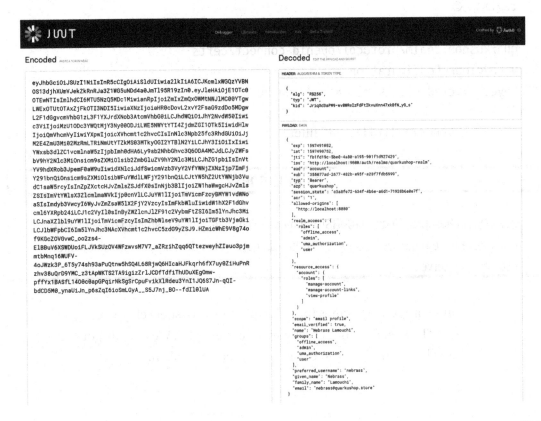

Note that there is a JSON attribute called groups that holds the Roles array that we assigned to Nebrass in Keycloak.

Good! ☺ Keycloak is running and working like expected. You'll now begin implementing security on the Java side.

Implementing the auth^2 Java Components in QuarkuShop

Java Configuration Side

The first step is to add the Quarkus SmallRye JWT dependency to QuarkuShop:

```
./mvnw quarkus:add-extension -Dextensions="io.quarkus:quarkus-smallrye-jwt"
```

Next, add the Security configuration to the application.properties:

```
1  ### Security
2  quarkus.http.cors=true   ①
3  # MP-JWT Config
4  mp.jwt.verify.issuer=http://localhost:9080/auth/realms/quarkushop-
   realm   ②
5  mp.jwt.verify.publickey.location=http://localhost:9080/auth/realms/
   quarkushop-realm/protocol/openid-connect/certs   ③
6  # Keycloak Configuration
7  keycloak.credentials.client-id=quarkushop   ④
```

① Enables the HTTP CORS filter.

WHAT IS CORS?

Cross-Origin Resource Sharing (CORS) is a mechanism that allows restricted resources on a web page to be requested from another domain outside the domain from which the first resource was served.

---

② Config property specifies the value of the iss (issuer) claim of the JWT token that the server will accept as valid. We already got this value in the iss field of the decrypted JWT token.

③ Config property allows for an external or internal location of the public key to be specified. The value may be a relative path or an URL. When using Keycloak as the identity manager, the value will be the `mp.jwt.verify.issuer` plus `/protocol/openid-connect/certs`.

④ A custom property with a key called `keycloak.credentials. client-id`, which holds the value `quarkushop`, which is the Realm client ID.

Java Source Code Side

In the Java code, you need to protect the REST APIs based on the authorization matrix that we created for each service.

Let's begin with the Carts REST API, where all operations are allowed for users and admins. Only the authenticated subjects are allowed on the Carts REST API. To satisfy this requirement, we have an `@Authenticated` annotation from the `io.quarkus. security` package, which will grant access only to authenticated subjects.

❗ To differentiate between an *application user* and the *role user*, I will refer to an application user as a *subject*. The term subject came in the old good Java Authentication and Authorization Service (JAAS) to represent the caller that is making a request to access a resource. A subject may be any *entity*, including as a *person* or *service*.

As all the operations in the `CartResource` require an authenticated subject, you have to annotate the `CartResource` class with `@Authenticated` so it will be applied to all the operations. See Listing 6-1.

Listing 6-1. com.targa.labs.quarkushop.web.CartResource

```
@Authenticated
@Path("/carts")
@Tags(value = @Tag(name = "cart", description = "All the cart methods"))
public class CartResource {
    ...
}
```

The next REST API is the Category API, where only the admin can create and delete categories. All the other operations are allowed by everyone (the admin, user, and anonymous). To grant access to a specific role only, use the @RolesAllowed annotation from the javax.annotation.security package.

ℹ️   *JavaDoc of javax.annotation.security.RolesAllowed*

@RolesAllowed: Specifies the list of security roles permitted to access the method(s) in an application.

The value of the @RolesAllowed annotation is a list of security role names. This annotation can be specified on a class or on methods:

- Specifying it at a class level means that it applies to all the operations in the class.

- Specifying it on a method means that it applies to that method only.

- If applied to the class and operations levels, the method value overrides the class value when the two conflict.

Based on the JavaDoc, we will pass the desired role as the value of the annotation. Apply the @RolesAllowed("admin") annotation to the operations where you create and delete categories:

```
@Path("/categories")
@Tags(value = @Tag(name = "category", description = "All the category
methods"))
public class CategoryResource {
    ...

    @RolesAllowed("admin")
    @POST
        public CategoryDto create(CategoryDto categoryDto) {
        return this.categoryService.create(categoryDto);
    }
```

```
@RolesAllowed("admin")
@DELETE
@Path("/{id}")
public void delete(@PathParam("id") Long id) {
    this.categoryService.delete(id);
}
}
```

For the Customer REST API, only the admin is allowed to access all the services. Annotating the `CustomerResource` class with `@RolesAllowed("admin")` will apply this policy.

Next is the Order REST API, where the authenticated subjects can access all the operations, except for the `findAll()` method, which is allowed only for `admin`. So we combine the two `@Authenticated` annotations in the class level and `@RolesAllowed` on the method requiring a specific role:

```
@Authenticated
@Path("/orders")
@Tag(name = "order", description = "All the order methods")
public class OrderResource {

    ...

    @RolesAllowed("admin")
    @GET
    public List<OrderDto> findAll() {
        return this.orderService.findAll();
    }
    ...
}
```

> ❶ While we are using `@RolesAllowed` in the local method, we are overriding the policy applied by the class level `@Authenticated`.

After `OrderResource`, we will deal with the OrderItem REST API, where only authenticated subjects are allowed to access all the services. Annotating the `OrderItemResource` class with `@Authenticated` will apply this policy.

The PaymentResource grants access only to authenticated subjects, except that deleting and listing all payments are granted only to the admin:

```
@Authenticated
@Path("/payments")
@Tag(name = "payment", description = "All the payment methods")
public class PaymentResource {

    ...

    @RolesAllowed("admin")
    @GET
    public List<PaymentDto> findAll() {
        return this.paymentService.findAll();
    }

    @RolesAllowed("admin")
    @DELETE
    @Path("/{id}")
    public void delete(@PathParam("id") Long id) {
        this.paymentService.delete(id);
    }
    ...
}
```

For the Product REST API, all operations are allowed by everyone, except for creating and deleting products, which are allowed only by the admin:

```
@Path("/products")
@Tag(name = "product", description = "All the product methods")
public class ProductResource {

    ...

    @RolesAllowed("admin")
    @POST
        public ProductDto create(ProductDto productDto) {
        return this.productService.create(productDto);
    }
```

```
    @RolesAllowed("admin")
    @DELETE
    @Path("/{id}")
    public void delete(@PathParam("id") Long id) {
        this.productService.delete(id);
    }
    ...
}
```

Finally, the last REST API is ReviewResource:

```
@Path("/reviews")
@Tag(name = "review", description = "All the review methods")
public class ReviewResource {

    ...

    @Authenticated
    @POST
    @Path("/product/{id}")
        public ReviewDto create(ReviewDto reviewDto, @PathParam("id") Long id) {
        return this.reviewService.create(reviewDto, id);
    }

    @RolesAllowed("admin")
    @DELETE
    @Path("/{id}")
    public void delete(@PathParam("id") Long id) {
        this.reviewService.delete(id);
    }
}
```

Great! You have applied the first-level authorization layer! 😊

Don't be too confident, though. 😡 This implementation leaks more levels of authorization. For example, users are authorized to delete Orders or OrderItems, but we can't verify that the authenticated subject is only deleting his own Orders or OrderItems and not those of other users. We know how to define access rules based on roles, but how can we gather more information about the authenticated subject?

For this purpose, we will create a new REST API called UserResource. When invoked, UserResource will return the current authenticated subject information as a response.

UserResource will look like this:

```
@Path("/user")
@Authenticated
@Tag(name = " user", description = "All the user methods")
public class UserResource {

    @Inject
    JsonWebToken jwt;                                              ①

    @GET
    @Path("/current/info")
    public JsonWebToken getCurrentUserInfo() {                     ②
        return jwt;
    }

    @GET
    @Path("/current/info/claims")
    public Map<String, Object> getCurrentUserInfoClaims() {       ③
        return jwt.getClaimNames()
                .stream()
                .map(name -> Map.entry(name, jwt.getClaim(name)))
                .collect(Collectors.toMap(
                        entry -> entry.getKey(),
                        entry -> entry.getValue())
                );
    }
}
```

① Inject a JsonWebToken, which is an implementation of the specification that defines the use of JWT as a bearer token. This injection will use an instance of the JWT token in the incoming request.

② The JsonWebToken will return the injected JWT token.

③ The getCurrentUserInfoClaims() method will return the list
of the available claims and their respective values embedded in
the JWT token. The claims will be extracted from the JWT token
instance injected in the UserResource.

Let's test this new REST API. Start by getting a new access_token:

```
export access_token=$(curl -X POST http://localhost:9080/auth/realms/
quarkushop-realm/protocol/openid-connect/token \
    -H 'content-type: application/x-www-form-urlencoded' \
    -d 'client_id=quarkushop' \
    -d 'username=nebrass' \
    -d 'password=password' \
    -d 'grant_type=password' | jq --raw-output '.access_token')
```

Then, invoke the /user/current/info REST API:

```
curl -X GET -H "Authorization: Bearer $access_token"
http://localhost:8080/api/user/current/info | jq '.'
```

You will get as a response the JWT token:

```
{
  "audience": [
    "account"
  ],
  "claimNames": [
    "sub", "resource_access", "email_verified", "allowed-origins", "raw_
    token", "iss",
    "groups", "typ", "preferred_username", "given_name", "aud", "acr",
    "realm_access",
    "azp", "scope", "name", "exp", "session_state", "iat", "family_name",
    "jti", "email"
  ],
  "expirationTime": 1597530481,
  "groups": ["offline_access", "admin", "uma_authorization", "user"],
  "issuedAtTime": 1597530181,
```

```
  "issuer": "http://localhost:9080/auth/realms/quarkushop-realm",
  "name": "nebrass",
  "rawToken": "eyJhbGci...L5A",
  "subject": "355877ad-2677-482b-a95f-a28f7fdb5999",
  "tokenID": "7416ee6e-e74c-45ae-bf85-8889744eaacf"
}
```

Good, we have the available claims. Let's get their respective values:

```
{
  "sub": "355877ad-2677-482b-a95f-a28f7fdb5999",
  "resource_access": {
    "account": {
      "roles": ["manage-account", "manage-account-links", "view-profile"]
    }
  },
  "email_verified": true,
  "allowed-origins": ["http://localhost:8080"],
  "raw_token": "eyJhbGci...L5A",
  "iss": "http://localhost:9080/auth/realms/quarkushop-realm",
  "groups": ["offline_access", "admin", "uma_authorization", "user"],
  "typ": "Bearer",
  "preferred_username": "nebrass",
  "given_name": "Nebrass",
  "aud": ["account"],
  "acr": "1",
  "realm_access": {
    "roles": ["offline_access", "admin", "uma_authorization", "user"]
  },
  "azp": "quarkushop",
  "scope": "email profile",
  "name": "Nebrass Lamouchi",
  "exp": 1597530481,
  "session_state": "68069099-f534-434f-8d08-d8d75b8ff1c6",
  "iat": 1597530181,
  "family_name": "Lamouchi",
```

```
    "jti": "7416ee6e-e74c-45ae-bf85-8889744eaacf",
    "email": "nebrass@quarkushop.store"
}
```

Wonderful! 😊 Now you know how to access the security details that you can use to identify the authenticated subjects exactly. By the way, you can have the same information about the JWT token. You can get the same JWT token an alternative way:

```
@GET()
@Path("/current/info-alternative")
public Principal getCurrentUserInfoAlternative(@Context SecurityContext
ctx) {
    return ctx.getUserPrincipal();
}
```

The @Context SecurityContext ctx passed as the method parameter is used to inject the SecurityContext in the current context.

💡   SecurityContext is an injectable interface that provides access to security-related information like the Principal.

ℹ️   The Principal interface represents the abstract notion of a principal, which can be used to represent any entity, such as an individual, a corporation, or a login ID. In this case, the principal is the JWT token. 😬

🔥   I will not dig into the full implementation of the authorization layer. I will stop here; otherwise, I would need to spend two more chapters just on this content.

The last step of the security part is to add a REST API that returns an access_token for a given username and password. This can be useful, especially with the Swagger UI. Speaking of Swagger UI, we need to make it aware of our Security layer.

We will start by creating the TokenService, which will be the REST client that makes the request of the access_token from Keycloak.

As we are using Java 11, we can enjoy one of its great new features: the brand new HTTP client.

As you did before using the cURL command, you need to use the Java 11 HTTP client to request an access_token:

```java
@RequestScoped                                          ①
public class TokenService {

    @ConfigProperty(name = "mp.jwt.verify.issuer", defaultValue = "undefined")
    Provider<String> jwtIssuerUrlProvider;   ②

    @ConfigProperty(name = "keycloak.credentials.client-id", defaultValue =
    "undefined")
    Provider<String> clientIdProvider;        ③

    public String getAccessToken(String userName, String password)
                    throws IOException, InterruptedException {

        String keycloakTokenEndpoint =
                    jwtIssuerUrlProvider.get() + "/protocol/openid-connect/
                    token";

        String requestBody = "username=" + userName + "&password=" + password +
                    "&grant_type=password&client_id=" + clientIdProvider.get();

        if (clientSecret != null) {
            requestBody += "&client_secret=" + clientSecret;
        }

        HttpClient client = HttpClient.newBuilder().build();

        HttpRequest request = HttpRequest.newBuilder()
                .POST(BodyPublishers.ofString(requestBody))
                .uri(URI.create(keycloakTokenEndpoint))
                .header("Content-Type", "application/x-www-form-urlencoded")
                .build();

        HttpResponse<String> response = client.send(request, HttpResponse.
        BodyHandlers.ofString());

        String accessToken = "";

        if (response.statusCode() == 200) {
```

```
        ObjectMapper mapper = new ObjectMapper();
        try {
            accessToken = mapper.readTree(response.body()).get("access_
            token").textValue();
        } catch (IOException e) {
            e.printStackTrace();
        }
    } else {
        throw new UnauthorizedException();
    }

    return accessToken;
    }
}
```

① The annotation creates an instance of TokenService for every
  HTTP request.

② Gets the mp.jwt.verify.issuer property value to build the
  Keycloak token's endpoint URL.

③ Gets the keycloak.credentials.client-id property value,
  which is needed to request the access_token.

💡   We are getting the property value as Provider<String> and not String to
avoid failing the native image build.

Next, add the getAccessToken() method:

```
@Path("/user")
@Authenticated
@Tag(name = " user", description = "All the user methods")
public class UserResource {

    @Inject JsonWebToken jwt;

    @POST
    @PermitAll
```

223

```
@Path("/access-token")
@Produces(MediaType.TEXT_PLAIN)
public String getAccessToken(@QueryParam("username") String username,
                             @QueryParam("password") String password)
                throws IOException, InterruptedException {
    return tokenService.getAccessToken(username, password);
}
...
}
```

Excellent! 😄 You can test the new method from the Swagger UI:

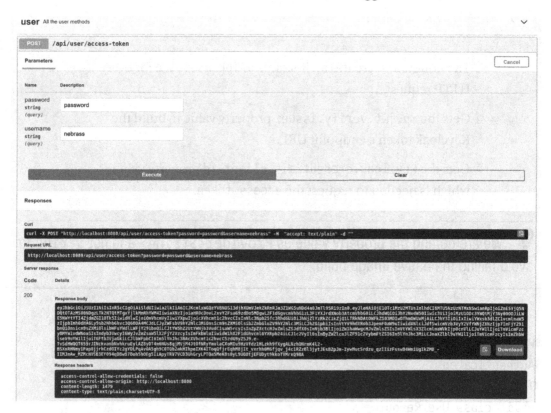

Yippee! 😄 You now need to find a way to make Swagger UI apply the access_token to request all the REST APIs.

I thought this would be a long trip, but it was a very easy task. Just 10 lines of code are enough to make the party: 😄

```java
@SecurityScheme(
        securitySchemeName = "jwt",                   ①
        description = "JWT authentication with bearer token",
        type = SecuritySchemeType.HTTP,               ①
        in = SecuritySchemeIn.HEADER,                 ①
        scheme = "bearer",                            ①
        bearerFormat = "Bearer [token]")             ①
@OpenAPIDefinition(
        info = @Info(                                 ②
                title = "QuarkuShop API",
                description = "Sample application for the book 'Playing
                with Java Microservices with Quarkus and Kubernetes'",
                contact = @Contact(name = "Nebrass Lamouchi", email =
                "lnibrass@gmail.com", url = "https://blog.nebrass.fr"),
                version = "1.0.0-SNAPSHOT"
        ),
        security = @SecurityRequirement(name = "JWT") ③
)
public class OpenApiConfig extends Application {
}
```

① @SecurityScheme defines a security scheme that can be used by the OpenAPI operations.

② Add a description for the OpenAPI definition.

③ Link the created security schema jwt to the OpenAPI definition.

Check the Swagger UI again:

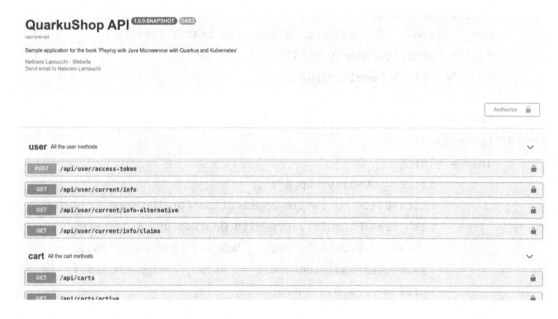

Note that there is the lock icon 🔒.

Use the getAccessToken() operation to create an access_token and then click Authorize 🔓 to pass the generated access_token to the SecurityScheme. Finally, click Authorize:

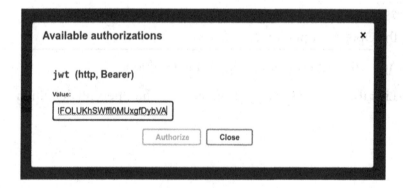

Now, when you click any operation, Swagger UI will include the access_token as a bearer to every request.

Excellent! You now have the Keycloak and the Security Java components. Next, you need to refactor the tests to be aware of the Security layer.

Update the Integration Tests to Support auth[2]

For the tests, you need to dynamically provision the Keycloak instance, as you did for the database using the `Testcontainers` library.

We will use the same library to provision Keycloak. We will not use a plain Docker container as we did with PostgreSQL, because there, Flyway populated the database for us. For Keycloak, we don't have a built-in mechanism that will create the Keycloak realms for us. The only possible solution is to use a Docker Compose file that will import a sample Keycloak realms file. Fortunately, `Testcontainers` has great support to provision Docker Compose files.

To provision the containers from a Docker Compose file using `TestContainers`, use this:

```
public static DockerComposeContainer KEYCLOAK = new DockerComposeContainer(
    new File("src/main/docker/keycloak-test.yml"))
        .withExposedService("keycloak_1", 9080,
            Wait.forListeningPort().withStartupTimeout(Duration.
            ofSeconds(30)));
```

We will use a sample Keycloak realm that contains the following:

- Two users:

    - Admin (username `admin`, password `test`, role `admin`)

    - Test (username `user`, password `test`, role `user`)

- The Keycloak client has a `client-id=quarkus-client:` and
  `` `secret=mysecret. ``

The `QuarkusTestResourceLifecycleManager` will communicate with the provisioned Keycloak instance using the `TokenService` that we created, and it will use the sample Realm credentials to get `access_tokens` that we will use in the integration tests.

We will get two `access_tokens`: one for the `admin` role and one for the `user` role. We will store them, along with `mp.jwt.verify.publickey.location` and `mp.jwt.verify.issuer`, as system properties in the current test scope.

The custom QuarkusTestResourceLifecycleManager will look like this:

```
public class KeycloakRealmResource implements
QuarkusTestResourceLifecycleManager {

    @ClassRule
    public static DockerComposeContainer KEYCLOAK = new
    DockerComposeContainer(
        new File("src/main/docker/keycloak-test.yml"))
        .withExposedService("keycloak_1",
                9080,
                Wait.forListeningPort().withStartupTimeout(Duration.
                ofSeconds(30)));

    @Override
    public Map<String, String> start() {
        KEYCLOAK.start();

        String jwtIssuerUrl = String.format(
                "http://%s:%s/auth/realms/quarkus-realm",
                KEYCLOAK.getServiceHost("keycloak_1", 9080),
                KEYCLOAK.getServicePort("keycloak_1", 9080)
        );

        TokenService tokenService = new TokenService();
        Map<String, String> config = new HashMap<>();
        try {
            String adminAccessToken = tokenService.
            getAccessToken(jwtIssuerUrl,
                "admin", "test", "quarkus-client", "mysecret"
            );

            String testAccessToken = tokenService.
            getAccessToken(jwtIssuerUrl,
                "test", "test", "quarkus-client", "mysecret"
            );

            config.put("quarkus-admin-access-token", adminAccessToken);
            config.put("quarkus-test-access-token", testAccessToken);
```

```
        } catch (IOException | InterruptedException e) {
                e.printStackTrace();
        }

        config.put("mp.jwt.verify.publickey.location", jwtIssuerUrl + "/
        protocol/openidconnect/certs");
        config.put("mp.jwt.verify.issuer", jwtIssuerUrl);

        return config;
    }

    @Override
    public void stop() {
            KEYCLOAK.stop();
    }
}
```

We will use it with the @QuarkusTestResource(KeycloakRealmResource.class)
annotation.

In the @BeforeAll method, we get the access_tokens from the systems properties to
make them ready to be used in tests. A typical test skull will look like this:

```
@QuarkusTest
@QuarkusTestResource(TestContainerResource.class)
@QuarkusTestResource(KeycloakRealmResource.class)
class CategoryResourceTest {

    static String ADMIN_BEARER_TOKEN;
    static String USER_BEARER_TOKEN;

    @BeforeAll
    static void init() {
      ADMIN_BEARER_TOKEN = System.getProperty("quarkus-admin-access-token");
      USER_BEARER_TOKEN = System.getProperty("quarkus-test-access-token");
    }

    ...
}
```

To use these tokens in a test:

```
@Test
void testFindAllWithAdminRole() {
   given().when()
          .header(HttpHeaders.AUTHORIZATION, "Bearer " + ADMIN_BEARER_TOKEN)
          .get("/carts")
          .then()
          .statusCode(OK.getStatusCode())
          .body("size()", greaterThan(0));
}
```

You need to test and verify the authorization rules in tests, for example, to verify that a given profile is not Unauthorized:

```
@Test
void testFindAll() {
    get("/carts").then()
          .statusCode(UNAUTHORIZED.getStatusCode());
}
```

To verify that, for a given request, the subject is not allowed on a REST API, use this:

```
@Test
void testDeleteWithUserRole() {
   given().when()
          .header(HttpHeaders.AUTHORIZATION, "Bearer " + USER_BEARER_TOKEN)
          .delete("/products/1")
          .then()
          .statusCode(FORBIDDEN.getStatusCode());
}
```

Good! I implemented all the tests; you can find them in my ⭘ GitHub repository. 😎

Adding Keycloak to the Production Environment

The last step is to add the production Keycloak entries to Docker Compose in the Production VM. We also need to add the Production realms.

You can export the realm from the local Keycloak instance in very few steps.

To export the realm from the local Keycloak container (called docker-keycloak), use this:

```
$docker exec -it docker-keycloak bash

bash-4.4$ cd /opt/jboss/keycloak/bin/

bash-4.4$ mkdir backup

bash-4.4$ ./standalone.sh -Djboss.socket.binding.port-offset=1000 \
    -Dkeycloak.migration.realmName=quarkushop-realm \
    -Dkeycloak.migration.action=export \
    -Dkeycloak.migration.provider=dir \
    -Dkeycloak.migration.dir=./backup/
```

To copy the stored realm from the docker-keycloak container to a local directory, use this:

```
$ mkdir ~/keycloak-realms

$ docker cp docker-keycloak:/opt/jboss/keycloak/bin/backup ~/keycloak-realms
```

You will get two Keycloak realm files—quarkushop-realm-realm.json and quarkushop-realm-users-0.json—in ~/keycloak-realms.

You need to edit the quarkushop-realm-realm.json file and change sslRequired from external to none:

```
{
    ...
    "sslRequired": "none",
    ...
}
```

ℹ   The "sslRequired": "none" property disables the required SSL certificate for any request.

Then, copy the two files—quarkushop-realm-realm.json and quarkushop-realm-users-0.json—to the /opt/realms directory in the Azure VM instance, which is the Production environment.

Here we are in the Azure VM instance. 😄 We will finish the last step: adding the Keycloak service to the /opt/docker-compose.yml file:

```
 1 version: '3'
 2 services:
 3   quarkushop:
 4     image: nebrass/quarkushop-monolithic-application:latest
 5     environment:
 6       - QUARKUS_DATASOURCE_JDBC_URL=jdbc:postgresql://postgresql-
         db:5432/demo
 7       -
  MP_JWT_VERIFY_PUBLICKEY_LOCATION=http://51.103.50.23:9080/auth/realms/
  quarkushoprealm/protocol/openid-connect/certs   ①
 8       - MP_JWT_VERIFY_ISSUER=http://51.103.50.23:9080/auth/realms/
         quarkushop-realm ①
 9     ports:
10       - 8080:8080
11   postgresql-db:
12     image: postgres:13
13     volumes:
14       - /opt/postgres-volume:/var/lib/postgresql/data
15     environment:
16       - POSTGRES_USER=developer
17       - POSTGRES_PASSWORD=p4SSWord
18       - POSTGRES_DB=demo
19       - POSTGRES_HOST_AUTH_METHOD=trust
20     ports:
21       - 5432:5432
22   keycloak:                                    ②
23     image: jboss/keycloak:latest
24     command:
25       [
```

```
26        '-b','0.0.0.0',
27
28        '-Dkeycloak.migration.action=import',
29        '-Dkeycloak.migration.provider=dir',
30        '-Dkeycloak.migration.dir=/opt/jboss/keycloak/realms',
31        '-Dkeycloak.migration.strategy=OVERWRITE_EXISTING',
32        '-Djboss.socket.binding.port-offset=1000',
33        '-Dkeycloak.profile.feature.upload_scripts=enabled',
34     ]
35
36
37  volumes:
38    - ./realms:/opt/jboss/keycloak/realms
39  environment:
40    - KEYCLOAK_USER=admin        ③
41    - KEYCLOAK_PASSWORD=admin     ③
42    - DB_VENDOR=POSTGRES          ④
43    - DB_ADDR=postgresql-db       ⑤
44    - DB_DATABASE=demo            ⑥
45    - DB_USER=developer           ⑥
46    - DB_SCHEMA=public            ⑥
47    - DB_PASSWORD=p4SSWOrd        ⑥
48  ports:
49    - 9080:9080
50  depends_on:                     ⑦
51    - postgresql-db               ⑦
```

① Overrides the `MP_JWT_VERIFY_PUBLICKEY_LOCATION` and `MP_JWT_VERIFY_ISSUER` properties to ensure that the application points to the Azure VM instance instead of the `localhost`.

② Adds the Keycloak Docker service.

③ Defines the Keycloak cluster's username and password.

④ Defines the Keycloak Database vendor as PostgreSQL, as we have a PostgreSQL DB instance in our services.

⑤ Defines the DB host as the `postgresql-db`, which will be resolved dynamically by Docker with the service IP.

⑥ Defines the Keycloak database credentials as the same as the PostgreSQL credentials.

⑦ Expresses the dependency between the Keycloak and PostgreSQL services.

⚠ As you can see, all the credentials are listed as plain text in the `docker-compose.yml` file.

You can protect these credentials using Docker Secrets. Each password will be stored in a Docker secret.

```
docker service create --name POSTGRES_USER --secret developer
docker service create --name POSTGRES_PASSWORD --secret p4SSWOrd
docker service create --name POSTGRES_DB --secret demo
docker service create --name KEYCLOAK_USER --secret admin
docker service create --name KEYCLOAK_PASSWORD --secret admin
```

⚠ Unfortunately, this feature is available only for Docker Swarm clusters.

To protect the credentials, store them in an `~/.env` file on the Azure VM instance:

```
POSTGRES_USER=developer
POSTGRES_PASSWORD=p4SSWOrd
POSTGRES_DB=demo
KEYCLOAK_USER=admin
KEYCLOAK_PASSWORD=admin
```

Then, change `docker-compose.yml` to use the `~/.env` elements:

```
version: '3'
services:
  quarkushop:
    image: nebrass/quarkushop-monolithic-application:latest
    environment:
```

```
        - QUARKUS_DATASOURCE_JDBC_URL=jdbc:postgresql://postgresql-
          db:5432/${POSTGRES_DB}
        - MP_JWT_VERIFY_PUBLICKEY_LOCATION=http://51.103.50.23:9080/auth/
          realms/quarkushop-realm/protocol/openid-connect/certs
        - MP_JWT_VERIFY_ISSUER=http://51.103.50.23:9080/auth/realms/
          quarkushop-realm
      ports:
        - 8080:8080
  postgresql-db:
    image: postgres:13
    volumes:
        - /opt/postgres-volume:/var/lib/postgresql/data
    environment:
        - POSTGRES_USER=${POSTGRES_USER}
        - POSTGRES_PASSWORD=${POSTGRES_PASSWORD}
        - POSTGRES_DB=${POSTGRES_DB}
        - POSTGRES_HOST_AUTH_METHOD=trust
    ports:
        - 5432:5432
  keycloak:
    image: jboss/keycloak:latest
    command:
      [
        '-b',
        '0.0.0.0',
        '-Dkeycloak.migration.action=import',
        '-Dkeycloak.migration.provider=dir',
        '-Dkeycloak.migration.dir=/opt/jboss/keycloak/realms',
        '-Dkeycloak.migration.strategy=OVERWRITE_EXISTING',
        '-Djboss.socket.binding.port-offset=1000',
        '-Dkeycloak.profile.feature.upload_scripts=enabled',
      ]
    volumes:
        - ./realms:/opt/jboss/keycloak/realms
```

```
environment:
    - KEYCLOAK_USER=${KEYCLOAK_USER}
    - KEYCLOAK_PASSWORD=${KEYCLOAK_PASSWORD}
    - DB_VENDOR=POSTGRES
    - DB_ADDR=postgresql-db
    - DB_DATABASE=${POSTGRES_DB}
    - DB_USER=${POSTGRES_USER}
    - DB_SCHEMA=public
    - DB_PASSWORD=${POSTGRES_PASSWORD}
ports:
    - 9080:9080
depends_on:
    - postgresql-db
```

Good! The Docker Compose services are ready to go! 😁

We need just to add an exception to the Azure VM instance networking rules for the Keycloak port. In the Azure VM instance, go to the Networking section and add an exception for port 9080:

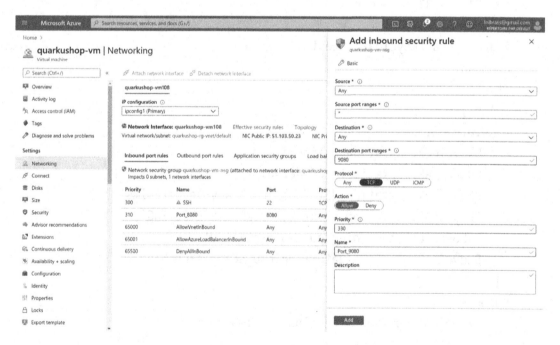

Excellent! 🙉 The production environment has all the needed elements to deploy a new version of the QuarkuShop container without risking the PostgreSQL DB or the Keycloak cluster.

Go to the production Swagger UI and enjoy QuarkuShop: the greatest online store! 😄

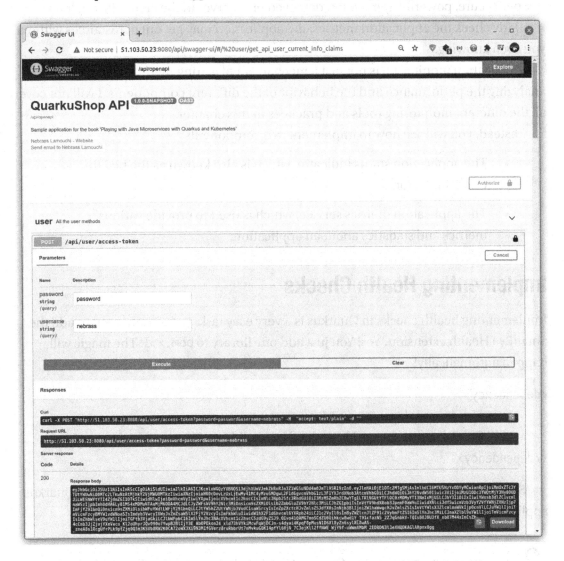

Good! 😃 It's time to move to the next anti-disaster layer: *monitoring* 👁.

Implementing the Monitoring Layer

Security is not the only critical extra layer in an application. Metrics monitoring is also a very important layer that can prevent disasters. Imagine a situation where you have a super-secure, powerful application deployed on a server in the cloud. If you don't regularly check the application metrics, the application may get out of resources without you even knowing.

Application monitoring is not just a mechanism of getting metrics; it includes analyzing the performance and the behavior of the different components. I will not cover all the different monitoring tools and practices in this chapter.

Instead, you will see how to implement two components:

- The application status indicator, which is also known as the health check indicator.

- The application metrics service, which is used to provide various metrics and statistics about an application.

Implementing Health Checks

Implementing health checks in Quarkus is a very easy task: you simply need to add the SmallRye Health extension. Yes! You just add one library to `pom.xml`! The magic will happen automatically!

```
<dependency>
    <groupId>io.quarkus</groupId>
    <artifactId>quarkus-smallrye-health</artifactId>
</dependency>
```

SmallRye Health will automatically add the health check endpoints to your Quarkus application.

💡 For those who are used to Spring Boot, SmallRye Health is the equivalent of Actuator.

The new *health check* endpoints are:

- /health/live: The application is up and running.

- /health/ready: The application is ready to serve requests.

- /health: Accumulating all health check procedures in the application.

Run the application and do a cURL GET on http://localhost:8080/api/health:

```
curl -X GET http://localhost:8080/api/health | jq '.'
```
You will get a JSON response:

```
{
  "status": "UP",
  "checks": [
    {
      "name": "Database connections health check",
      "status": "UP"
    }
  ]
}
```

This JSON response confirms that the application is correctly running, and there is one check that was made confirming that the database is UP.

All the health REST endpoints return a simple JSON object with two fields:

- status: The overall result of all the health check procedures

- checks: An array of individual checks

Out of the box, Quarkus includes a database check. Let's create a health check for the Keycloak instance:

```
@Liveness
@ApplicationScoped
public class KeycloakConnectionHealthCheck implements HealthCheck {

    @ConfigProperty(name = "mp.jwt.verify.publickey.location", defaultValue =
    "false")
    private Provider<String> keycloakUrl;                                    ①
```

```java
    @Override
    public HealthCheckResponse call() {

        HealthCheckResponseBuilder responseBuilder =
                HealthCheckResponse.named("Keycloak
                connection health check");                      ③

        try {
            keycloakConnectionVerification();                   ④
            responseBuilder.up();                               ⑤
        } catch (IllegalStateException e) {
            // cannot access keycloak
            responseBuilder.down().withData("error",
            e.getMessage());                                    ⑤
        }

        return responseBuilder.build();                         ⑥
    }

    private void keycloakConnectionVerification() {
        HttpClient httpClient = HttpClient.newBuilder()         ②
                .connectTimeout(Duration.ofMillis(3000))
                .build();

        HttpRequest request = HttpRequest.newBuilder()
                .GET()
                .uri(URI.create(keycloakUrl.get()))
                .build();

        HttpResponse<String> response = null;

        try {
            response = httpClient.send(request,
            HttpResponse.BodyHandlers.ofString());
        } catch (IOException e) {
            e.printStackTrace();
        } catch (InterruptedException e) {
            e.printStackTrace();
```

```
            Thread.currentThread().interrupt();
        }

        if (response == null || response.statusCode() != 200) {
            throw new IllegalStateException("Cannot contact Keycloak");
        }
    }
}
```

① You get the mp.jwt.verify.publickey.location property,
  which you will use as the Keycloak URL.

② You instantiate the Java 11 HTTPClient with 3000 milliseconds
  of timeout.

③ You define the name of the health check as Keycloak
  connection health check.

④ You verify that the Keycloak URL is reachable and the response
  status code is HTTP 200.

⑤ If the keycloakConnectionVerification() throws an
  exception, the health check status will be down.

⑥ You build the health check response and send it back to the
  caller.

Let's cURL again the /health endpoint:

```
curl -X GET http://localhost:8080/api/health | jq '.'
```

The new JSON response will be: 😬

```
{
   "status": "UP",
   "checks": [
     {
       "name": "Keycloak connection health check",
       "status": "UP"
     },
     {
       "name": "Database connections health check",
```

```
      "status": "UP"
    }
  ]
}
```

Good! 😆 It's as simple as that!

There is more! SmallRye Health provides a very useful Health UI at `http://localhost:8080/api/health-ui/`:

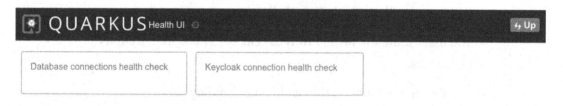

There is even a pooling service that can be configured to refresh the page in intervals you set:

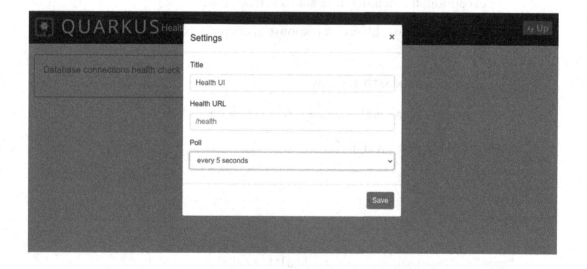

This Health UI is very useful, but unfortunately it's not activated by default in the prod profile. To enable it for every profile/environment, use this property:

```
### Health Check
quarkus.smallrye-health.ui.always-include=true
```

Excellent. ☺ It's time to move to the next step, in order to implement the *metrics service*.

Implementing the Metrics Service

Metrics are important and critical monitoring data. Quarkus has many dedicated libraries for metrics exposure, along with a very rich toolset to build custom application metrics. No surprise, the first library is also from the SmallRye family. It's called `quarkus-smallrye-metrics` and is used to expose metrics based on the MicroProfile specifications.

Starting with Quarkus v1.9, it's not recommended to use SmallRye metrics. Quarkus officially adopted Micrometer as the new standard for its metrics. This adoption is based on cloud market trends and needs.

ⓘ   To learn more about the transition from MicroProfile metrics to Micrometer metrics, see `https://quarkus.io/blog/micrometer-metrics/`.

The first step in implementing the metrics service is to add the `quarkus-micrometer` Maven dependency:

```
<dependency>
    <groupId>io.quarkus</groupId>
    <artifactId>quarkus-micrometer</artifactId>
</dependency>
```

This dependency will provide access to the Micrometer core metric types:

- **Counter**: Counters are used to measure values that only increase. For example, to measure how many times a REST API was called.

- **Gauge**: An indicator that shows a current value, like the number of created objects or threads.

- **Timer**: Used to measure short-duration latencies and their frequencies.

- **Distribution Summary**: Used to track the distribution of events. It is similar to a timer structurally, but records values that do not represent units of time. For example, a distribution summary could be used to measure the payload sizes of requests hitting a server.

All these objects need to be stored somewhere, which is the purpose of the *meter registry*. As Micrometer supports many monitoring systems (Prometheus, Azure Monitor, Stackdriver, Datadog, Cloudwatch, etc.), we will find a dedicated implementation for `MeterRegistry`. For this example, we use Prometheus as the monitoring system. In that case, you need to add its Maven dependency:

```
<dependency>
    <groupId>io.micrometer</groupId>
    <artifactId>micrometer-registry-prometheus</artifactId>
</dependency>
```

Now, restart the application and check the `http://localhost:8080/metrics` URL generated by Quarkus Micrometer:

```
# HELP jvm_threads_live_threads The current number of live threads
including both daemon and non-daemon threads
# TYPE jvm_threads_live_threads gauge
jvm_threads_live_threads 64.0
# HELP jvm_memory_max_bytes The maximum amount of memory in bytes that can
be used for memory management
# TYPE jvm_memory_max_bytes gauge
jvm_memory_max_bytes{area="nonheap",id="CodeHeap 'profiled nmethods'",}
1.63971072E8
jvm_memory_max_bytes{area="heap",id="G1 Survivor Space",} -1.0
jvm_memory_max_bytes{area="heap",id="G1 Old Gen",} 8.589934592E9
jvm_memory_max_bytes{area="nonheap",id="Metaspace",} -1.0
jvm_memory_max_bytes{area="nonheap",id="CodeHeap 'non-nmethods'",} 7598080.0
jvm_memory_max_bytes{area="heap",id="G1 Eden Space",} -1.0
jvm_memory_max_bytes{area="nonheap",id="Compressed Class Space",}
1.073741824E9
```

```
jvm_memory_max_bytes{area="nonheap",id="CodeHeap 'non-profiled nmethods'",}
1.63975168E8
...
```

These metrics are generated by Micrometer and are compatible with Prometheus. You can try to import them in a standalone Prometheus instance.

First, download Prometheus from `https://prometheus.io/download/`:

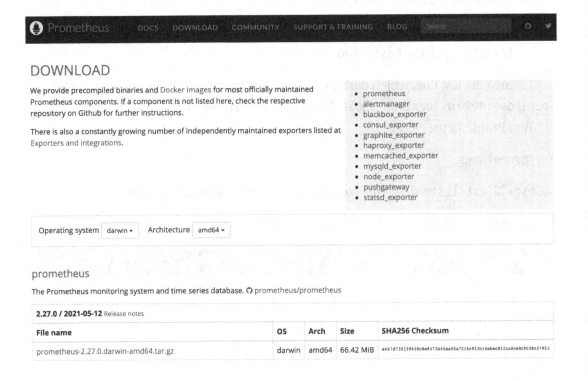

Choose a suitable edition for your machine/OS and download it. It's `darwin-amd64` in my case.

After decompressing the archive, edit the `prometheus-2.27.0.darwin-amd64/` `prometheus.yml` file as follows:

```
# my global config
global:
  scrape_interval:     15s # Set the scrape interval to every 15 seconds.
                           Default is every 1 minute.
  evaluation_interval: 15s # Evaluate rules every 15 seconds. The default
                           is every 1 minute.
```

```
...
scrape_configs:
  # The job name is added as a label `job=<job_name>` to any timeseries
scraped from this config.
  - job_name: 'prometheus'

    # metrics_path defaults to '/metrics'
    # scheme defaults to 'http'.

    static_configs:
    - targets: ['localhost:9090']
```

Change the last line, which defines the targeted /metrics API host location, from
localhost:9090 to localhost:8080. This is the *application URL*.

Run Prometheus:

```
$ ./prometheus
```

```
...msg="Start listening for connections" address=0.0.0.0:9090
```

You can access it from http://localhost:9090/:

In the Expression input, enter `system_cpu_usage` and click Execute. Then click the Graph tab:

Now, you can create your own custom application metrics provider for TokenService:

```
@Slf4j
@RequestScoped
public class TokenService {
    private static final String TOKENS_REQUESTS_TIMER =
    "tokensRequestsTimer";    ①
    private static final String TOKENS_REQUESTS_COUNTER =
    "tokensRequestsCounter";    ②
```

```
@Inject MeterRegistry registry;
...
@PostConstruct
public void init() {
    registry.timer(TOKENS_REQUESTS_TIMER, Tags.empty());         ①
    registry.counter(TOKENS_REQUESTS_COUNTER, Tags.empty());     ②
}

public String getAccessToken(String userName, String password) {
    var timer = registry.timer(TOKENS_REQUESTS_TIMER);           ①
    return timer.record(() -> { var accessToken = "";
        try {
            accessToken = getAccessToken(jwtIssuerUrlProvider.get(),
                            userName, password, clientIdProvider.get(),
                            null);
            registry.counter(TOKENS_REQUESTS_COUNTER).increment();   ②
        } catch (IOException e) { log.error(e.getMessage());
        } catch (InterruptedException e) {
            Thread.currentThread().interrupt();
            log.error("Cannot get the access_token");
        }
        return accessToken;
    });
}
...
}
```

① Create a timer called tokensRequestsTimer for the duration of
executing the getAccessToken() method.

② Create a counter called tokensRequestsCounter, which will
increment each time the getAccessToken() method is invoked.

Go to the Swagger UI and request an `access_token` many times to generate some metrics. Then go back to the Prometheus UI to check the new metrics:

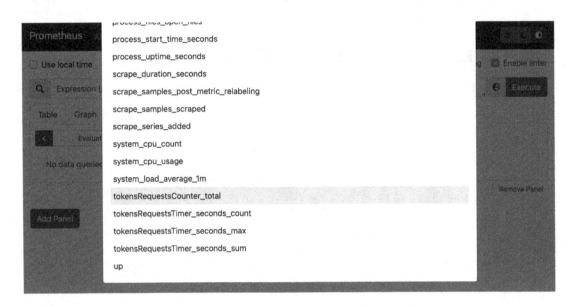

Take a look at the value reached by the `tokensRequestsCounter`, based on the previous screenshot. Its Prometheus expression is:

You can check the Max value for the `tokensRequests` timer, which matches the `tokensRequestsTimer_seconds_max` expression in Prometheus:

Great! 😄 You have now the basic health check and monitoring components that ensure your application is healthy and has all the required resources.

Conclusion

I consider security and monitoring to be anti-disaster layers, but even with the application of these components, the application still faces many risks. One of them is high availability.

CHAPTER 7

Microservices Architecture Pattern

Introduction

So far, we have developed QuarkuShop as a single-block application. All the components are packaged in a single package. This single block is called a *monolith*.

Based on the Oxford English Dictionary, a monolith is "a single, very large organization that is very slow to change". In the software architecture world, a monolith or monolithic application, is a single-block application where all the components are combined into a single package.

In the QuarkuShop project, if developers want to update the definition of a `Product` entity, for example, they will access the same codebase as another developer who is working on the `PaymentService`. After these updates, they must rebuild and redeploy the updated version of the application.

During runtime, QuarkuShop is deployed as one package, the Native JAR that we packaged in a Docker container using the CI/CD pipelines. All the Java code and the HTML/CSS resources (we have a web page in `src/main/resources/META-INF/resources`) will be running in the same block, even if we embedded some React or Angular code in the JAR.

QuarkuShop handles the HTTP requests, executes some domain-specific logic, retrieves and updates data from the database, and handles payloads to be sent to the REST client.

Because of all these points, QuarkuShop is a monolith. 😈

Is this a good or bad thing? ☺

© Nebrass Lamouchi 2021
N. Lamouchi, *Pro Java Microservices with Quarkus and Kubernetes*,
https://doi.org/10.1007/978-1-4842-7170-4_7

During training and discussion sessions, when I say that an application is a monolith, many people assume that this is a bad thing. This chapter describes the pros/cons of this architecture, and I will let you decide if it's good or bad, or good+bad (a little of both). 😁

The primary benefit of a monolithic application is its *simplicity*. It is easy to develop, deploy, and scale only one block.

Since the entire application's codebase is in one place, only one slot has to be configured for building and deploying the application.

Monoliths are very easy to work on, especially in the beginning, and it's the default choice when starting a new project. While the complexity will grow over time, agile management of the codebase will help to maintain productivity over the lifetime of a monolithic application. Keeping an eye on how the code is written and how the architecture is evolving will protect the project from becoming a big plate of spaghetti.

⚠ Although I'm telling you that agility will guarantee that the project will remain clean and easy to work on, there is no reciprocal. Monolithic application components are very tightly coupled and can become very complex as a product evolves. Thus, it can be extremely difficult for developers to manage them over time.

"The way to build a complex system that works is to build it from very simple systems that work."

—Kevin Kelly

In real-world projects, medium or huge, it's very common for a developer to work only on a specific part of the application. It's also common for each developer to understand only part of a monolith, meaning very few developers can explain the entirety of the application. Since monoliths must be developed and deployed as one unit, it can be difficult to break development efforts into independent teams. Each code change must be carefully coordinated, which slows down development.

This situation can be difficult for new developers, who don't want to deal with a massive codebase that has evolved over the years. As a result, more time is spent finding the correct line of code and making sure it doesn't have side effects. In the same vein, less time is spent writing new features that will improve the application.

Adopting new technology in a monolith can mean rewriting the whole application, which is costly and time-intensive drudgery.

Monoliths are popular because they are simpler to begin building than their alternative, *microservices*.

Microservices Architecture

While a monolith is a single, large unit, a microservice architecture uses small, modular units of code that can be deployed independently of the rest of a product's components.

"Simple can be harder than complex. You have to work hard to get your thinking clean to make it simple."

—Steve Jobs

Benefits of a Microservices Architecture

A microservices architecture allows a big application to be broken into small, loosely coupled services. This approach brings with it a lot of benefits:

- Our QuarkuShop application was developed using a monolithic architecture, and over time it has grown with a lot of new features. The codebase is huge and new people are joining our team. It is very difficult for them to get started with the given application, as there is no clear separation between the various components of the application. The microservices approach allows us to see our application as small, loosely coupled components, so anyone can get started with the existing application in a short period. It won't be too difficult to add a new fix to the codebase.

- Imagine that today is Black Friday, which is the busiest shopping day of the year, so we get a huge amount of traffic to our site. Our product catalog is highly requested, which causes the whole application to go down. If this happens in a microservices architecture, we won't face such failures, as it runs multiple services independently. If one service goes down, it doesn't affect any other services.

- We are developers who spent a lot of time understanding our application codebase. We are excited about adding new features, such as a product search engine. We would have to redeploy the whole application to show these features to end users. We would be working on many such features, just think about the time it would take every time in deployment. So if the application is huge, it takes a lot of effort and time, which definitely will cause loss of productivity. Nobody likes to wait to see the result of code changes. In a microservices architecture, we try to make the codebase as small as possible in each service, so it doesn't take so much time in terms of building, deployments, etc.

- Today we are getting a huge amount of traffic. Nothing is broken and the servers are up. Let's say we need to scale some components of our application, the product catalog for example. We can't scale individual components in a monolithic architecture. But, in a microservices architecture, we can scale any component separately by adding more nodes dynamically.

- Tomorrow, we want to move to a new framework or technology stack. It is hard to upgrade a monolith, as it has become very big and complex over time. It is not that difficult to update a microservices architecture, as the components are small and flexible.

That's how microservices architecture makes our life easy. There are various strategies available that help us divide the application into small services, such as by domain-driven design, by business capability, etc.

What Really Is a Microservice?

A *microservice* typically implements a set of distinct features or functionality, such as order management, customer management, etc. Each microservice is a mini-application that has its own business logic along with its boundaries, such as REST web services. Some microservices expose an API that's consumed by other microservices or by the application's clients. Other microservices might implement a web UI. We can also have communication using messaging queues.

Each functional area of the application is now implemented by its own microservice. Moreover, the web application is split into a set of smaller web applications.

Each backend service generally exposes a REST API and most services consume APIs provided by other services. The UI services invoke other services to render web pages. Services might also use asynchronous message-based communication.

Some REST APIs are also exposed to client apps that don't have direct access to the backend services. Instead, communication is mediated by an intermediary known as an *API Gateway.* The API Gateway is responsible for tasks such as load balancing, caching, access control, API metering, and monitoring.

The Microservices Architecture pattern significantly impacts the relationship between the application and the database. Rather than sharing a single database schema with other services, each service has its database schema. On the one hand, this approach is at odds with the idea of an enterprise-wide data model. Also, it often results in duplication of some data. However, having one database schema per service is essential if you want to benefit from microservices, because it ensures loose coupling.

Each service has a database. Moreover, a service can use a type of database that is best suited to its needs, the so-called *polyglot persistence architecture.*

On the surface, the Microservices Architecture pattern is similar to SOA. With both approaches, the architecture consists of a set of services. However, one way to think about the Microservices Architecture pattern is that it's SOA without the commercialization and perceived baggage of Web Service Specifications (WS) and an Enterprise Service Bus (ESB). Microservice-based applications favor simpler, lightweight protocols such as REST, rather than heavy protocols. They also very much avoid using ESBs and instead implement ESB-like functionality in the microservices themselves.

Conclusion: Making the Switch

So, is it possible to switch from a monolithic to a microservices architecture without starting from scratch? Is it worth it? ☺ Big names like Netflix, Amazon, and Twitter have all shifted from monolithic to microservices architectures and have no intention of going back.

Changing architectures can be done in stages. You extract microservices one-by-one out of your monolithic application until you are done. ☺ A good architecture choice can transform your applications and organization for the better. If you're thinking about switching over, you will get a great migration guide in the following chapters.

CHAPTER 8

Splitting the Monolith: Bombarding the Domain

Introduction

We have defined what a microservice architecture is and discussed the problems it solves. We also learned about the many benefits of adopting a microservices architecture. But how can you migrate your monolithic application to a microservices architecture? How can you apply this pattern? How can you split your monolith without rewriting the whole application?

This chapter answers those questions. We will use domain-driven design as an approach to split the QuarkuShop monolith. Domain-driven design (DDD) is a software development method that simplifies software modeling and design.

What Is Domain-Driven Design?

The domain-driven design has many advantages:

- Focuses on the core business domain and business logic.

- The best way to ensure that the design is based on a model of the domain.

- A tight collaboration between technical and business teams.

To understand domain-driven design, you need to understand its many concepts.

259

© Nebrass Lamouchi 2021
N. Lamouchi, *Pro Java Microservices with Quarkus and Kubernetes*,
https://doi.org/10.1007/978-1-4842-7170-4_8

Context

Context is the specific environment in which an action or a term comes under a specific meaning. That meaning can change in a different environment.

Domain

A domain is a group of knowledge and specifications targeted by the software development.

Model

A model is an abstract representation of the actors and components from the domain.

Ubiquitous Language

People in different roles in the company have different knowledge of the business problem that they are facing. For example, if you are developing a trading platform, you will typically have a team composed of a project manager, developers, DevOps, testers, and business analysts. Usually, the business analysts are the people who have the business knowledge, trading in this case, and their role is to translate the business specifications and requirements for the other team members who are not necessarily proficient in economics and financials.

This jargon will guarantee that all the team members have the same understanding of the business context.

The language/jargon used in the presentations, meetings, user stories, and tickets is called the *ubiquitous language.*

Strategic Design

Strategic design is one of the most important paradigms in the domain-driven design world. It helps to split the domain, which is always complex, into smaller parts. This split can be dangerous and can change crucial concepts in the business logic. Here comes the strategic design's power: it brings many methodologies and principles that guarantee the main domain's full integrity.

You will discover the main components of the strategic design in the next sections.

Bounded Context

A *bounded context* is a logical collection of components that belong to the same business subdomain. Each subdomain is handled by a dedicated team, which will optimize new developments and bug fixes. It's easier to work on small parts than on big blocks.

A *bounded context* has a defined scope that will cover all related models. Each element needs to be attributed to only one specific bounded context. Semantically, an element can belong to two or more bounded contexts, but a decision needs to be made to attribute it to the main bounded context.

Let's examine the table reservation example that we've been using. When you started designing the system, you would have seen that the guest would visit the application and request a table reservation at a selected restaurant, date, and time. The backend system informs the restaurant about the booking information. Similarly, the restaurant keeps their system updated with table bookings, given that the restaurant can also book tables. So, when you look at the system's finer points, you see three domain models:

- The Product domain model

- The Order domain model

- The Customer domain model

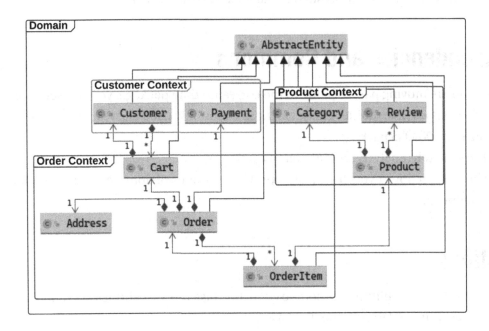

They have their own bounded context, and you need to make sure that the interface between them works fine.

Bombarding QuarkuShop

Here, you will learn how to split the QuarkuShop application into many steps.

Codebase

The first step is to create a package for each bounded context. Then, you will move each class to its related bounded context package. With NetBeans (and other IDEs), you can move and refactor code easily with a few clicks. While moving code, you might find some new bounded context that you missed.

At this point, the only way to guarantee that the refactoring did not break your application is through testing!

This task is a direct application of the design created in the previous steps. This task looks easy in this example. But when dealing with huge applications, it will be hard and will take several weeks or even months. To optimize the restructuring operations, you can use structure analysis tools such as Stan4j and Structure101.

Dependencies and Commons

While you are moving parts of code to the corresponding package, you will see some common classes (like utilities classes). These commonly used classes must be moved to a dedicated COMMONS package.

The structure analysis tools are handy at this point.

The next section covers the most important elements of domain splitting: entities and relationships.

Entities

At this level, you're splitting the source code. Because the Java entities are mapped to SQL tables, you need to split the database as well.

For the database access code, you have one repository for each entity. The relationships between entities reveal the foreign key relationships between tables, which represent the database-level constraints.

In QuarkuShop, a given entity will belong to one specific bounded context. But moving the entities into separate packages is not the last step. You need to break the JPA mapping relationships by breaking the relationships between the tables that belong to different bounded contexts. You will see by example how this can be done while respecting the application's business logic integrity.

Example: Breaking Foreign Key Relationships

The QuarkuShop application stores the product information in a dedicated table, which is mapped and managed by the ORM. The `OrderItem` object stores the reference of the ordered product with the ordered quantity in a dedicated table. The reference of the `Product` record in the `OrderItem` table consists of a foreign key constraint.

So how can you break this relationship?

The answer is easily. 😄

First of all, you need to change the `Product` reference in the `OrderItem` from `Product` to `Long`, which is the primary key type for the `Product` entity.

The original code is as follows:

```
@ManyToOne(fetch = FetchType.LAZY)
private Product product;
```

And after refactoring, it looks like this:

```
private Long product;
```

The `@ManyToOne` annotation is useless, as there is no JPA entity targeted. Now it's just a `Long` attribute.

This modification will limit the amount of "knowledge" that the `OrderItem` has about the product. So when you are reading the `OrderItem` records, you need to have a component in the `Order` service that reads the data for a given product ID from the `Product` service. This communication between services will be done using REST, as it's a synchronous communication.

This exchange is represented in this schema:

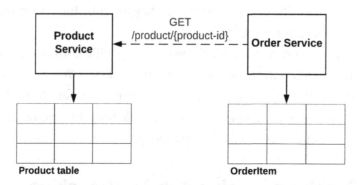

You have two database calls instead of one, as these two microservices are separated, whereas you have only one call in the monolith. Maybe you are wondering about performance issues? The extra call will take some extra time, but it's not significant. If you test performance before splitting, you should have visibility while making changes.

Because the foreign key relationship is deleted from the code, there will not be a constraint in the SQL database. I know that many database administrators will not be happy about the data integrity. Don't be sad, guys! You can always develop a verification batch that ensures that data is well-built and not corrupted without constraints. You also need to consider this point when deleting a `Product`. You need to come up with a strategy about the stored `Product` IDs in the `OrderItem` records.

Each of the microservices will be free to store its tables. It can use the same database/schema shared by all the microservices, or you can even create a dedicated database server instance for each microservice.

Conclusion

In this chapter, you learned how to split the QuarkuShop application based on the domain-driven design guidelines. Each microservice represents a bounded context. The task is huge, but doing it incrementally will reduce the effort needed to reach the goal.

The microservices are there. You simply need to settle them in the Production environment, where they will be consumed. In the next chapter, you'll discover the world of deployment.

CHAPTER 9

Applying DDD to the Code

You learned, in the previous chapter, how to use domain-driven design (DDD) to split your domain into bounded contexts.

In this chapter, you learn how to split your code using the cut lines defined in the previous chapter.

Applying Bounded Contexts to Java Packages

Our classes are already classified by component type, such as *repository*, *service*, etc.

We will move every component in a new package that includes the bounded context name. The name of each component has this format:

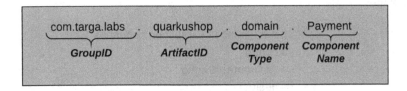

After refactoring, the naming format will be:

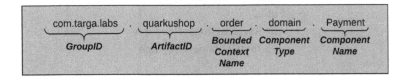

© Nebrass Lamouchi 2021
N. Lamouchi, *Pro Java Microservices with Quarkus and Kubernetes*,
https://doi.org/10.1007/978-1-4842-7170-4_9

After renaming all the components, you'll have a Project Tree that looks like this:

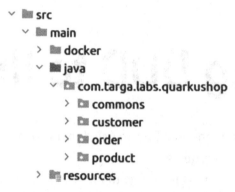

Wait! You might wonder what the `commons` and `configuration` packages contain. Let's discuss that now.

The Birth of the Commons Package

Recall that the common components have to be collected into a dedicated `commons` package, which will be shared by all the bounded contexts. Here's what I have in my `commons` package:

Note that these classes are composed of configuration and utility classes. Think of them like the Apache Commons library that you find in almost every Java project directly, or grabbed indirectly by one of the dependencies. This `commons` library is composed of four packages:

- `config`: Contains the `OpenApiConfig` used to configure the OpenAPI implementation and the Swagger UI.

- `health`: Contains the custom Keycloak health check.

- `security`: Contains the `TokenService` used to grab the JWT token.

- `utils`: Contains utility classes to provision Keycloak and PostgreSQL for tests.

ℹ️   Note that these utility classes are needed in all components, without having a specific flavor for a given microservice. But you can always get rid of the `commons` library.

I had a bad habit of sharing DTOs in the `commons` project. But, Georgios Andrianakis, our great technical reviewer, suggested that I stop doing this! I thought about it, and I agreed that it was a bad idea, even for proof-of-concepts projects.

⚠️   When we talked about microservices, we said that after the splitting, the microservices can talk to each other. So, imagine this case: `Order` wants to get a `Product` from the `Product` microservice using a given `Product ID`. The REST API in the `Product` will return a `ProductDTO` object populated by the data of a `Product` record, which will be serialized to JSON and will be returned to the requesting service, which is `Order`. At this level, each microservice has a definition of `Product`. Based on many elements like the project specifications, documentation, and even through the OpenAPI resources, different microservices can communicate easily. If the DTOs were shared in the `commons` library, we could lose one of the benefits of microservices: being free from tight coupling.

Locating the Bounded Contexts Relationships

This step aims to break dependencies between bounded contexts (BCs). To be able to break them, you need first to find these dependencies. There are many ways to find them. For example, by reviewing the class diagrams, the source code, etc. In the previous chapter, we talked about tools that can help you highlight the dependencies between blocks in your monolith.

I am mainly using STAN (STAN4J), a powerful structure analysis for Java. STAN supports a set of carefully selected metrics, suitable to cover the most important aspects of structural quality. Special focus has been set on visual dependency analysis, a key to structure analysis.

STAN is available in two variants:

- As a standalone application for Windows and macOS, which is targeted to architects and project managers who are typically not using the IDE.

- As an extension to the Eclipse Integrated Development Environment (IDE), which allows the developer to quickly explore the structure of any bunch of code.

We will be using the second choice. I got a fresh install of Eclipse IDE and installed the IDE extension as described in `http://stan4j.com/download/ide/`.

Our monolith is a Maven-based project, so it can easily be imported into Eclipse IDE. After importing, just follow these steps:

1. Right-click the project.

2. Choose Run As ➤ Maven Build.

3. Choose the Maven configuration, if you already have one.

4. In Goals, just enter `clean install -DskipTests` and choose Run.

5. You're done!

Next, create a structure analysis of the project:

1. Right-click the project.

2. Choose Run As ➤ Structure Analysis.

3. Yippee! ☻ The structure diagram is here!

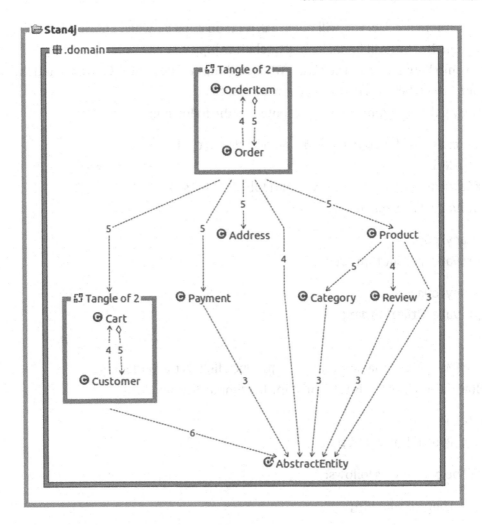

Breaking the BC Relationships

Now, you will break the relationships between the bounded contexts. You can start with the relationships between entities. Generally the relationships are more effective between tables in the database. Here, the entity classes are treated as relational tables (a JPA concept), so the relationships between entity classes are as follows:

- @ManyToOne relation

- @OneToMany relation

- @OneToOne relation

- @ManyToMany relation

269

To be more precise, you will not break relationships between entities that belong to the same BC, but will break inter-BC relationships. For example, consider the relationship between the `OrderItem`, which belongs to the `Order Context`, and the `Product`, which belongs to the `Product Context`.

In Java, this relationship is represented by the following:

```java
public class OrderItem extends AbstractEntity {
    @NotNull
    @Column(name = "quantity", nullable = false)
    private Long quantity;

    @ManyToOne
    private Product product;

    @ManyToOne
    private Order order;
}
```

The `@ManyToOne` that annotates the `product` field is the target here.

How do you break this relationship? It's simple, this block:

```java
@ManyToOne
private Product product;
```

Will be changed as follows:

```java
private Long productId;
```

So, you may wonder why we replace the `Product` type with the `Long` type? It's simple. `Long` is the type of the `Product`'s ID.

Great! You have to do the same thing to the `Product` class, if the relationship between `OrderItem` and `Product` is a bidirectional relationship.

When you try to build the project using `mvn clean install`, you will get compilation problems. This is obvious, because you edited `OrderItem`, so many components using this class have to be aware of these modifications. Here, it is the `OrderItemService` that is the trouble.

Let's look at the blocks in the OrderItemService class that have errors. Here's the first one:

```
public OrderItemDto create(OrderItemDto orderItemDto) {
    log.debug("Request to create OrderItem : {}", orderItemDto);

    var order = this.orderRepository
        .findById(orderItemDto.getOrderId())
        .orElseThrow(() -> new IllegalStateException("The Order does not
        exist!"));

    var product = this.productRepository
        .findById(orderItemDto.getProductId())
        .orElseThrow(() -> new IllegalStateException("The Product does
        not exist!"));

    return mapToDto(
        this.orderItemRepository.save(
            new OrderItem(
                    orderItemDto.getQuantity(),
                    product,
                    order
        )));
}
```

We are getting a Product instance from the ProductRepository, and we are passing it to the OrderItem constructor. There is no Product field in the OrderItem class anymore (you changed it to Product ID), so you need to pass the ID to the OrderItem constructor, instead of to the Product.

So, the Product object doesn't exist in the Order bounded context anymore. How can we deal with the Product and ProductRepository classes now?

Did you forget? We have in the scope of the Order bounded context, the commons module, which contains the ProductDTO and we can use for free!

For the ProductRepository, it's obvious. It will be replaced with a REST client that will gather the Product data from the Product microservice and populate the known ProductDTO object when needed. But here, we only need the Product ID to create the OrderItem instance. So, in this case, we don't need to get the Product record.

The second block is the method that maps the OrderItem to an OrderItemDto:

```java
public static OrderItemDto mapToDto(OrderItem orderItem) {
    return new OrderItemDto(
            orderItem.getId(),
            orderItem.getQuantity(),
            orderItem.getProductId(),
            orderItem.getOrder().getId()
    );
}
```

The reference of the Product has to be deleted from this method, as it was removed from the OrderItem class. We don't have a product as a member, but we do have the Product ID in the OrderItem class. So the orderItem.getProduct().getId() instruction has to be changed to orderItem.getProductId(). To get the product price to add/subtract from the order total price, we inject the ProductRepository in our OrderItemService.

The resulting OrderItemService will look like this:

```java
@Slf4j
@ApplicationScoped
@Transactional
public class OrderItemService {

    @Inject OrderItemRepository orderItemRepository;
    @Inject OrderRepository orderRepository;
    @Inject ProductRepository productRepository;

    public static OrderItemDto mapToDto(OrderItem orderItem) {
        return new OrderItemDto(orderItem.getId(),
                orderItem.getQuantity(), orderItem.getProductId(),
                orderItem.getOrder().getId());
    }

    public OrderItemDto findById(Long id) {
        log.debug("Request to get OrderItem : {}", id);
        return this.orderItemRepository.findById(id)
                    .map(OrderItemService::mapToDto).orElse(null);
    }
```

```java
public OrderItemDto create(OrderItemDto orderItemDto) {
    log.debug("Request to create OrderItem : {}", orderItemDto);
    var order = this.orderRepository
            .findById(orderItemDto.getOrderId()).orElseThrow(() ->
                new IllegalStateException("The Order does not exist!"));

    var orderItem = this.orderItemRepository.save(
            new OrderItem(orderItemDto.getQuantity(),
                    orderItemDto.getProductId(), order
            ));

    var product = this.productRepository.getOne(orderItem.getProductId());

    order.setPrice(order.getPrice().add(product.getPrice()));
    this.orderRepository.save(order);

    return mapToDto(orderItem);
}

public void delete(Long id) {
    log.debug("Request to delete OrderItem : {}", id);

    var orderItem = this.orderItemRepository.findById(id)
            .orElseThrow(() ->
                new IllegalStateException("The OrderItem does not
                exist!"));

    var order = orderItem.getOrder();
    var product = this.productRepository.getOne(orderItem.getProductId());

    order.setPrice(order.getPrice().subtract(product.getPrice()));

    this.orderItemRepository.deleteById(id);

    order.getOrderItems().remove(orderItem);
    this.orderRepository.save(order);
}

public List<OrderItemDto> findByOrderId(Long id) {
    log.debug("Request to get all OrderItems of OrderId {}", id);
    return this.orderItemRepository.findAllByOrderId(id)
```

```
        .stream()
        .map(OrderItemService::mapToDto)
        .collect(Collectors.toList());
  }
}
```

After this refactoring, you can use the great tool STAN to see how these modifications changed the structure of the project.

After some checks, the remaining modifications to do are:

- In the customer package:

    1. Cart: The private Order order; will change to private Long orderId;

    2. CartService: The Order reference will change to OrderDto

- In the order package:

    1. Order: The private Cart cart; will change to private Long cartId;

    2. OrderService: The Cart reference will change to CartDto

After these modifications, we still have an OrderService reference in the CartService. As mentioned, this OrderService will be replaced by a REST client that will make calls to the API exposed by the Order microservice. You can comment the lines, referencing the OrderService before analyzing the structure.

After this refactoring, here's how these modifications changed the structure of the project:

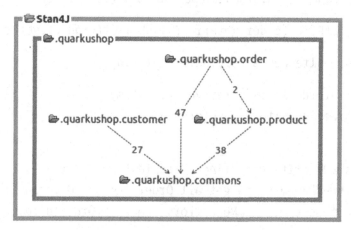

> ❶   You didn't totally break the link between the `order` and `product` packages. This is because, to calculate an order total amount, you need to have the product price. You will see how to deal with this link in future steps.

Conclusion

This is good! You just finished one of the heaviest tasks in the migration process!

Next, you can start building the standalone microservices. Before that, you need to learn more about the best practices and the microservices patterns.

## CHAPTER 10

Meeting the Microservices Concerns and Patterns

When we deal with architecture and design, we immediately start thinking about recipes and patterns. These design patterns are useful for building reliable, scalable, secure applications in the cloud.

A *pattern* is a reusable solution to a problem that occurs in a particular context. It's an idea, which has its origins in real-world architecture, that has proven to be useful in software architecture and design.

Actually, the Microservices Architecture is one of the most powerful architectural patterns. We discussed this pattern in detail in Chapter 8.

When presenting a pattern, we start by defining the context and the problem and then provide the solution given by the pattern.

Cloud Patterns

This chapter deals with these patterns:

- Externalized configuration

- Service discovery and registration

- Circuit breaker

- Database per service

- API gateway

- CQRS

- Event sourcing

277

© Nebrass Lamouchi 2021
N. Lamouchi, *Pro Java Microservices with Quarkus and Kubernetes*,
https://doi.org/10.1007/978-1-4842-7170-4_10

- Log aggregation

- Distributed tracing

- Audit logging

- Application metrics

- Health check API

Service Discovery and Registration

Context and Problem

In the microservices world, service registry and discovery plays an important role because you'll most likely run multiple instances of services and need a mechanism to call other services without hardcoding their hostnames or port numbers. In addition to that, in cloud environments, service instances may go up and down anytime. So you need an automatic service registration and discovery mechanism.

In a monolithic application, calls between components are made through language-level calls. But, in a Microservices Architecture, services typically need to call each another using REST (or other) calls. In order to make a request, a service needs to know the network location (IP address and port) of a given service instance. As mentioned in previous chapters, microservices have dynamically assigned network locations. This is due to many factors such as different deployment frequencies, for example. Moreover, a service can have more than one instance that can keep change dynamically because of autoscaling, failures, etc.

So, you must implement a mechanism that enables the clients of a given service to make requests to a dynamically changing set of service instances.

How does the client of a service discover the location of a service instance? How does the client of a service know about the available instances of a service?

Solution

You can create a service registry, which is a database of available service instances. It works like this:

- The network location of the microservice instance is registered with the service registry when the instance starts up.

- The network location of the microservice instance is removed from the service registry when the instance terminates.

- The microservice instance's availability is typically refreshed periodically using a heartbeat mechanism.

There are two varieties of this pattern:

- **Client-Side Discovery Pattern**: The requesting service (client) is responsible for seeking the network locations of the available service instances. The client queries a service registry and then selects, using some load-balancing algorithms, one of the available service instances and makes a request. This mechanism follows the client-side discovery pattern.

- **Server-Side Discovery Pattern**: The server-side discovery pattern advises that the client make a request to a service via a load balancer. It's the responsibility of the load balancer to query the service registry and to forward each request to an available service instance. So, if you want to follow this pattern, you need to have (or implement) a load balancer.

Externalized Configuration

Context and Problem

An application typically uses one or more infrastructures (a message broker and a database server, etc.) and third-party services (a payment gateway, email and messaging, etc.). These services need configuration information (credentials, for example). This configuration information is stored in files that are deployed with the application.

In some cases, it's possible to edit these files to change the application behavior after it's been deployed. However, changes to the configuration require the application to be redeployed, often resulting in unacceptable downtime and other administrative overhead.

Local configuration files also limit the configuration to a single application, and sometimes it would be useful to share configuration settings across multiple applications. Examples include database connection strings and the URLs of queues and storage used by a related set of applications.

Our monolith is split into many microservices. All these microservices need the configuration information that was provided to the monolith. Imagine that we need to update the database's URL. This task needs to be done for all the microservices. If we forget to update the data somewhere, it can result in instances using different configuration settings while the update is being deployed.

Solution

Externalize all application configurations, including the database credentials and the network location. You can, for example, store the configuration information externally and provide an interface that can be used to quickly and efficiently read and update the configuration settings. You can call this configuration store a *configuration server.*

When a microservice starts up, it reads the configuration from the given configuration server.

Circuit Breaker

Context and Problem

Microservices communicate mainly using HTTP REST requests. When a microservice is synchronized with another one, there is always the risk that the other service will be unavailable or unreachable due to high latency, which means it is essentially unusable. These unsuccessful calls might lead to resource exhaustion, which would make the calling service unable to handle other requests. The failure of one service can potentially cascade to other services throughout the application.

Solution

A requesting microservice should invoke a remote service via a proxy that works in a similar mechanism to an electrical circuit breaker. When the number of consecutive failures crosses a threshold, the circuit breaker trips, and for the duration of a timeout period, all attempts to invoke the remote service will fail immediately. After the timeout expires, the circuit breaker allows a limited number of test requests to pass through. If those requests succeed, the circuit breaker resumes normal operation. If there is a failure, the timeout period will begin again.

The Circuit Breaker pattern, popularized by Michael Nygard in his book *Release It!*, can prevent an application from repeatedly trying to execute an operation that's likely to fail. This allows the application to continue without waiting for the fault to be fixed or wasting CPU cycles while it determines that the fault is long lasting. The Circuit Breaker pattern also enables an application to detect whether the fault has been resolved. If the problem appears to have been fixed, the application can try to invoke the operation.

Database Per Service

Context and Problem

In the Microservices Architecture world, services must be loosely coupled so that they can be developed, deployed, and scaled independently.

Most services need to persist data in some kind of database. In our application, `Order Service` stores information about orders and `Customer Service` stores information about customers.

What's the database architecture in a microservices application?

Solution

Keep each microservice's persistent data private to that service and accessible only via its API.

The service's database is effectively part of the implementation of that service. It cannot be accessed directly by other services.

There are a few different ways to keep a service's persistent data private. You do not need to provision a database server for each service. For example, if you are using a relational database, the options are as follows:

- `Private-tables-per-service`: Each service owns a set of tables that can only be accessed by that service.

- `Schema-per-service`: Each service has a database schema that's private to that service.

- `Database-server-per-service`: Each service has its own database server.

`Private-tables-per-service` and `schema-per-service` have the lowest overhead. Using a schema per service is appealing since it makes ownership clearer. Some high-throughput services might need their own database server.

It is a good idea to create barriers that enforce this modularity. You could, for example, assign a different database user ID to each service and use a database access control mechanism such as grants. Without some kind of barrier to enforce encapsulation, developers will always be tempted to bypass a service's API and access its data directly.

API Gateway

Context and Problem

For the QuarkuShop boutique, imagine that you are implementing the product details page. Let's imagine that you need to develop multiple versions of the product details user interface:

- **HTML5/JavaScript-based UI for desktop and mobile browsers**: HTML is generated by a server-side web application.

- **Native Android and iPhone clients**: These clients interact with the server via REST APIs.

In addition, QuarkuShop must expose product details via a REST API for use by third-party applications.

A product details UI can display a lot of information about a product. For example:

- Basic information about the product, such as name, description, price, etc.

- Your purchase history for the product.

- Availability.

- Buying options.

- Other items that are frequently bought with this product.

- Other items bought by customers who bought this product.

- Customer reviews.

Since QuarkuShop follows the Microservices Architecture pattern, the product details data is spread out over multiple services:

- **Product Service**: Basic information about the product such as name, description, price, customer reviews, and product availability.

- **Order Service**: Purchase history for a product.

- **QuarkuShop:** Customers, carts, etc.

Consequently, the code that displays the product details needs to fetch information from all of these services.

How do the clients of a microservices-based application access the individual services?

Solution

Implement an API gateway that is the single entry point for all clients. The API gateway handles requests in one of two ways. Some requests are simply proxied/routed to the appropriate service. It handles other requests by fanning out to multiple services.

Rather than provide a one-size-fits-all style API, the API gateway can expose a different API for each client. The API gateway might also implement security, e.g. verify that the client is authorized to perform the request.

CQRS

Context and Problem

In traditional data management systems, both commands (updates to the data) and queries (requests for data) are executed against the same set of entities in a single data repository. These entities can be a subset of the rows in one or more tables in a relational database such as SQL Server.

Typically in these systems, all create, read, update, and delete (CRUD) operations are applied to the same representation of the entity. For example, a data transfer object (DTO) representing a customer is retrieved from the data store by the data access layer (DAL) and displayed on the screen. A user updates some fields of the DTO (perhaps through data binding) and the DTO is then saved back in the data store by the DAL. The same DTO is used for both the read and write operations.

Traditional CRUD designs work well when only limited business logic is applied to the data operations. Scaffold mechanisms provided by development tools can create data access code very quickly, which can then be customized as required.

However, the traditional CRUD approach has some disadvantages:

- It often means that there's a mismatch between the read and write representations of the data, such as additional columns or properties that must be updated correctly even though they aren't required as part of an operation.

- It risks data contention when records are locked in the data store in a collaborative domain, where multiple actors operate in parallel on the same set of data. Update conflicts caused by concurrent updates when optimistic locking is used are also an issue. These risks increase as the complexity and throughput of the system grows. In addition, the traditional approach can have a negative effect on performance due to load on the data store and data access layer, and the complexity of queries required to retrieve information.

- It can make managing security and permissions more complex because each entity is subject to both read and write operations, which might expose data in the wrong context.

Solution

Command and Query Responsibility Segregation (CQRS) is a pattern that segregates the operations that read data (queries) from the operations that update data (commands) by using separate interfaces. This means that the data models used for querying and updates are different. The models can then be isolated.

Compared to the single data model used in CRUD-based systems, using separate query and update models for the data in CQRS-based systems simplifies design and implementation. However, one disadvantage is that, unlike CRUD designs, CQRS code can't automatically be generated using scaffold mechanisms.

The query model for reading data and the update model for writing data can access the same physical store, perhaps by using SQL views or by generating projections on the fly.

The read store can be a read-only replica of the write store, or the read and write stores can have a different structure altogether. Using multiple read-only replicas of the read store can greatly increase query performance and application UI responsiveness, especially in distributed scenarios where read-only replicas are located close to the application instances.

Event Sourcing

Context and Problem

Most applications work with data, and the typical approach is for the application to maintain the current state of the data by updating it as users work with it. For example, in the traditional create, read, update, and delete (CRUD) model, a typical data process is to read data from the store, make some modifications to it, and update the current state of the data with the new values—often by using transactions that lock the data.

The CRUD approach has some limitations:

- CRUD systems perform update operations directly against a data store, which can slow down performance and responsiveness, and limit scalability, due to the processing overhead it requires.

- In a collaborative domain with many concurrent users, data update conflicts are more likely because the update operations take place on a single item of data.

- Unless there's an additional auditing mechanism that records the details of each operation in a separate log, history is lost.

Solution

The Event Sourcing pattern defines an approach to handling operations on data that's driven by a sequence of events, each of which is recorded in an append-only store. Application code sends a series of events that imperatively describe each action that has occurred on the data to the event store, where they're persisted. Each event represents a set of changes to the data (such as AddedItemToOrder).

The events are persisted in an event store that acts as the system of record (the authoritative data source) about the current state of the data. The event store typically publishes these events so that consumers can be notified and can handle them if needed. Consumers could, for example, initiate tasks that apply the operations in the events to other systems, or perform any other associated action that's required to complete the operation. Notice that the application code that generates the events is decoupled from the systems that subscribe to the events.

Typical uses of the events published by the event store are to maintain materialized views of entities as actions in the application change them, and for integration with external systems. For example, a system can maintain a materialized view of all customer orders that's used to populate parts of the UI. As the application adds new orders, adds or removes items on the order, and adds shipping information, the events that describe these changes can be handled and used to update the materialized view.

In addition, at any point it's possible for applications to read the history of events and use it to materialize the current state of an entity by playing back and consuming all the events related to that entity. This can occur on demand to materialize a domain object when handling a request, or through a scheduled task so that the state of the entity can be stored as a materialized view to support the presentation layer.

Log Aggregation

Context and Problem

In the Microservices Architecture, our application consists of multiple services and service instances that are running on different servers and locations. Requests often cross multiple service instances.

When we had the monolith, the application was generating one log stream, which was generally stored in one log file/directory. Now, each service instance generates its own log file.

How do you identify the behavior of an application and troubleshoot problems when the log is split this way?

Solution

Use a centralized logging service that aggregates logs from each service instance. When the log is aggregated, the users can search and analyze the logs. They can configure alerts that are triggered when certain messages appear in the logs.

Distributed Tracing

Context and Problem

In the Microservices Architecture, requests often span multiple services. Each service handles a request by performing one or more operations, e.g. database queries, message publishing, etc.

When a request fails, how do you identify the behavior and troubleshoot the problems?

Solution

Instrument services with code that:

- Assigns each external request a unique external Request ID

- Passes the external Request ID to all services that are involved in handling the request

- Includes the external Request ID in all log messages

- Records information (e.g., start time and end time) about the requests and operations performed when handling an external request in a centralized service

Audit Logging

Context and Problem

In a Microservices Architecture, we need more visibility about our services to monitor how things are going, in addition to the logging system.

How do you monitor the behavior of users and the application and troubleshoot any problems?

Solution

You can record user activity in a database or in some special dedicated logging system.

Application Metrics

Context and Problem

In a Microservices Architecture, we need more visibility about the services to see what's going on, in addition to the indicators that we already have.

How do you identify and articulate an application's behavior?

Solution

The recommended solution is to have a centralized metrics service that gathers and stocks the decision-enabling statistics of each service operation. Microservices can push their metrics information to the metrics service. On the other side, the metrics service can pull metrics from the microservices.

Health Check API

Context and Problem

It's a good practice, and often a business requirement, to monitor web applications and backend services, in order to ensure they're available and performing correctly. However, it's more difficult to monitor services running in the cloud than it is to monitor on-premises services. There are many factors that affect applications, such as network latency, the performance and availability of the underlying compute and storage systems, and the network bandwidth. A service can fail entirely or partially due to any of these factors. Therefore, you must verify at regular intervals that the service is performing correctly to ensure the required level of availability.

Solution

Implement health monitoring by sending requests to an endpoint on the application. The application should perform the necessary checks and return an indication of its status.

A health monitoring check typically combines two factors:

- The checks (if any) performed by the application or service in response to the request to the health verification endpoint.

- Analysis of the results by a tool or framework that performs the health verification check.

The response code indicates the status of the application and, optionally, any components or services it uses. The latency or response time check is performed by the monitoring tool or framework.

Security Between Services: Access Token

Context and Problem

In a Microservices Architecture and with the use of the API gateway pattern, the application is composed of numerous services. The API gateway is the single entry point for client requests. It authenticates requests and forwards them to other services, which might in turn invoke other services.

How do you communicate the requestor's identity to the services that handle the request?

Solution

The API gateway authenticates the request and passes an access token (e.g., a JSON web token) that securely identifies the requestor in each request to the services. A service can include the access token in requests it makes to other services.

Conclusion

Now that you have split the QuarkuShop monolith and learned about some useful patterns, you can start building the standalone microservices.

CHAPTER 11

Getting Started with Kubernetes

Introduction

To deploy our (so huge, so big) application, 😊 we will be using 🐳 Docker. We will deploy our code in a container, so we can enjoy the great features provided by 🐳 Docker.

🐳 Docker has become the standard used to develop and run containerized applications.

Using 🐳 Docker is quietly simple, especially during the development stages. Deploying containers in the same server (`docker-machine`) is simple, but when you need to deploy many containers to many servers, things become complicated (managing the servers, managing the container state, etc.).

This is when the orchestration system comes into play, and it provides many great features:

- Orchestrating resources between running tasks

- Scheduling and matching containers to machines based on many factors like resources needs, affinity requirements, etc.

- Handling replications

- Handling failures

For this tutorial, we use 🌐 Kubernetes, the star of container orchestration.

© Nebrass Lamouchi 2021
N. Lamouchi, *Pro Java Microservices with Quarkus and Kubernetes*,
https://doi.org/10.1007/978-1-4842-7170-4_11

What Is Kubernetes?

✹ Kubernetes (aka K8s) is a project that spun out of **G** Google as a open-source next-gen container scheduler. It's designed using the lessons learned from developing and managing Borg and Omega.

Kubernetes is designed to have loosely coupled components centered on deploying, maintaining, and scaling applications. K8s abstracts the underlying infrastructure of the nodes and provides a uniform layer for the deployed applications.

The Kubernetes Architecture

A Kubernetes cluster is composed of two items:

- **Master node**: The main control plane for Kubernetes. It contains an API server, a scheduler, a controller manager (K8s cluster manager), and a datastore to save the cluster state called `Etcd`.

- **Worker node**: A single host, physical or virtual machine, that runs a *pod*. It's managed by the master node.

Let's look inside the master node:

- **Kube API-Server**: Allows communication, through REST APIs, between the master node and its clients, such as the worker nodes, `kube-cli`, etc.

- **Kube Scheduler**: The scheduler is like a restaurant waiter who assigns you the "first available" table based on a specific logic (aka, a policy). The Kube Scheduler assigns newcomers to the most suitable node based on a specific policy.

- **Kube Controller Manager**: A permanent running process that is responsible for ensuring that the Kubernetes cluster state is the same as requested by the administrator. If the admin made some configuration commands, the Kube Controller Manager is responsible for verifying that these commands are applied all over the cluster.

- Etcd: A key-value database used by Kubernetes to save the cluster configuration.

Let's look inside the worker node:

- **Kubelet**: An agent that is running on each node in the cluster. It ensures that the node is correctly registered in the master node, along with verifying that the POD is running without problems.

- **Kube-Proxy**: An agent that is running on each node in the cluster. It ensures that the networking rules are correctly applied in the node.

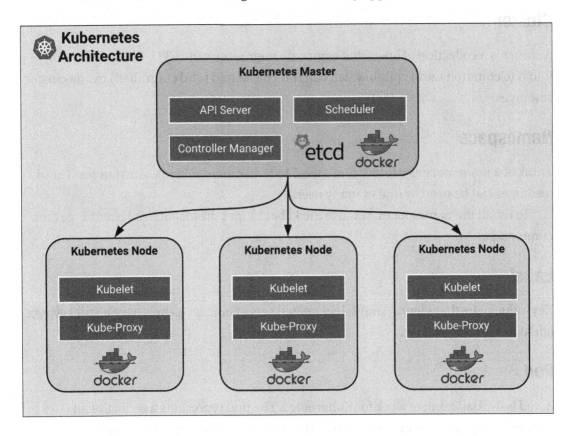

> 💡 The container runtime that we use is Docker. Kubernetes is compatible with many others, such as `cri-o`, `rkt`, etc.

Kubernetes Core Concepts

The K8s ecosystem covers many concepts and components. The next sections briefly discuss them.

Kubectl

The `kubectl` is a CLI for executing commands on configured Kubernetes clusters.

Cluster

A *cluster* is a collection of hosts that aggregate their resources (CPU, RAM, disks, etc.) into one common usable pool, which can then be shared (and controlled) by the cluster resources.

Namespace

Think of a *namespace* as a folder that's used to hold different kinds of resources. These resources can be used by one or many users.

To list all the namespaces, you use the `kubectl get namespace` or `kubectl get ns` commands.

Label

Key-value pairs that identify and select related sets of objects. Labels have a strict syntax and defined character set.

Pod

A *pod* is the basic unit of work for Kubernetes. The pod represents a collection of containers that share resources, such as IP addresses and storage. See Listing 11-1.

Listing 11-1. Pod Example

```
apiVersion: v1
kind: Pod
metadata:
  name: example-pod
  labels:
    app: example
spec:
  containers:
  - name: example-container
    image: busybox
    command: ['sh', '-c', 'echo Hello World :) !']
```

To list all the pods, run the kubectl get pod or kubectl get po command.

ReplicaSet

This component is responsible for running a desired number of replica pods at any given time. See Listing 11-2.

Listing 11-2. ReplicaSet Example

```
apiVersion: apps/v1
kind: ReplicaSet
metadata:
  name: mongodb
  labels:
    app: mongodb
spec:
  replicas: 2
  selector:
    matchLabels:
      app: mongodb
  template:
    metadata:
      labels:
```

```
      app: mongodb
   spec:
     containers:
     - name: mongodb
       image: mongo:4.4
       imagePullPolicy: Always
```

To list all ReplicaSets, run the kubectl get replicaset or kubectl get rs commands.

Deployment

This includes a pod template and a replicas field. Kubernetes will make sure the actual state (the amount of replicas and the pod template) always matches the desired state. When you update a deployment, it will perform a "rolling update." See Listing 11-3.

Listing 11-3. Deployment Example

```
apiVersion: apps/v1
kind: Deployment
metadata:
  name: nginx-deployment
  labels:
    app: nginx
spec:
  replicas: 3
  selector:
    matchLabels:
      app: nginx
  template:
    metadata:
      labels:
        app: nginx
    spec:
      containers:
```

```
  - name: nginx
    image: nginx:1.9.1
    ports:
    - containerPort: 80
```

To list all the deployments, use the `kubectl get deployment` command.

StatefulSet

This component is responsible for managing pods that must persist or maintain state. The pod identity, including hostname, network, and storage, will be persisted. See Listing 11-4.

Listing 11-4. StatefulSet Example

```
apiVersion: apps/v1
kind: StatefulSet
metadata:
  name: web
spec:
  selector:
    matchLabels:
      app: nginx
  serviceName: "nginx"
  replicas: 3
  template:
    metadata:
      labels:
        app: nginx
    spec:
      terminationGracePeriodSeconds: 10
      containers:
      - name: nginx
        image: k8s.gcr.io/nginx-slim:0.8
        ports:
        - containerPort: 80
          name: web
```

```
        volumeMounts:
        - name: www
          mountPath: /usr/share/nginx/html
  volumeClaimTemplates:
  - metadata:
      name: www
    spec:
      accessModes: [ "ReadWriteOnce" ]
      storageClassName: "my-storage-class"
      resources:
        requests:
          storage: 1Gi
```

To list all StatefulSets, run the kubectl get statefulset command.

DaemonSet

This component creates an instance of each pod on all (or some by choice) nodes in the cluster. See Listing 11-5.

Listing 11-5. DaemonSet Example

```
apiVersion: apps/v1
kind: DaemonSet
metadata:
  name: fluentd-elasticsearch
  namespace: kube-system
  labels:
    k8s-app: fluentd-logging
spec:
  selector:
    matchLabels:
      name: fluentd-elasticsearch
  template:
    metadata:
      labels:
        name: fluentd-elasticsearch
```

```
spec:
  tolerations:
    - key: node-role.kubernetes.io/master
      effect: NoSchedule
  containers:
    - name: fluentd-elasticsearch
      image: gcr.io/google-containers/fluentd-elasticsearch:1.20
  terminationGracePeriodSeconds: 30
```

To list all DaemonSets, run the kubectl get daemonset or kubectl get ds commands.

Service

This defines a single IP/port combination that provides access to a group of pods. It uses label selectors to map groups of pods and ports to a cluster-unique virtual IP. See Listing 11-6.

Listing 11-6. Service Example

```
apiVersion: v1
kind: Service
metadata:
  name: my-nginx
  labels:
    run: my-nginx
spec:
  ports:
    - port: 80
      protocol: TCP
  selector:
    run: my-nginx
```

To list all services, run the kubectl get service or kubectl get svc command.

Ingress

An ingress controller is the primary method for exposing a cluster service (usually http) to the outside world. These are load balancers or routers that usually offer SSL termination, name-based virtual hosting, etc. See Listing 11-7.

Listing 11-7. Ingress Example

```
apiVersion: networking.k8s.io/v1
kind: Ingress
metadata:
  name: test-ingress
  annotations:
    nginx.ingress.kubernetes.io/rewrite-target: /
spec:
  rules:
    - http:
        paths:
          - path: /testpath
            backend:
              service:
                name: test
                port:
                  number: 80
```

To list all ingresses, use kubectl get ingress.

Volume

This represents storage that is tied to the pod lifecycle and is consumable by one or more containers within the pod.

PersistentVolume

A PersistentVolume (PV) represents a storage resource. PVs are commonly linked to a backing storage resource, NFS, GCEPersistentDisk, RBD, etc., and are provisioned ahead of time. Their lifecycle is handled independently from a pod.

To list all PersistentVolumes, run the `kubectl get persistentvolume` or `kubectl get pv` command.

PersistentVolumeClaim

A PersistentVolumeClaim (PVC) is a request for storage that satisfies a set of requirements. It's commonly used with dynamically provisioned storage.

To list all PersistentVolumeClaims, use the `kubectl get persistentvolumeclaim` or `kubectl get pvc` command.

StorageClass

Storage classes are an abstraction on top of an external storage resource. They include a provisioner, the provisioner configuration parameters, and a PV `reclaimPolicy`.

To list all StorageClasses, run `kubectl get storageclass` or `kubectl get sc`.

Job

The job controller ensures that one or more pods are executed and successfully terminate. It will do this until it satisfies the completion and/or parallelism condition.

To list all jobs, run `kubectl get job`.

CronJob

An extension of the job controller, the CronJob provides a method of executing jobs on a cron-like schedule.

To list all CronJobs, run `kubectl get cronjob`.

ConfigMap

A ConfigMap is externalized data stored in Kubernetes that can be referenced as a command-line argument or environment variable, or injected as a file into a volume mount. They are ideal for implementing the External Configuration Store pattern.

To list all ConfigMaps, run `kubectl get configmap` or `kubectl get cm`.

Secret

Functionally identical to ConfigMaps, but stored encoded as base64 and encrypted at rest (if configured).

To list all secrets, run `kubectl get secret`.

Run Kubernetes Locally

For this tutorial, we will not build a real Kubernetes cluster. We use Minikube.

Minikube is used to run a single-node Kubernetes cluster locally with no pain. This tool is very useful, especially for development.

For Minikube installation, visit `https://github.com/kubernetes/minikube`.

After the installation, run this command to start Minikube:

```
minikube start
```

When running Minikube, a new Kubernetes context is created and is available. The `minikube start` command creates a `kubectl context` called `minikube`.

ℹ️   A Kubernetes context contains the configuration needed to communicate with a Kubernetes cluster.

To access the Kubernetes Dashboard, run:

```
minikube dashboard
```

The Dashboard will be opened in your default browser, as shown here:

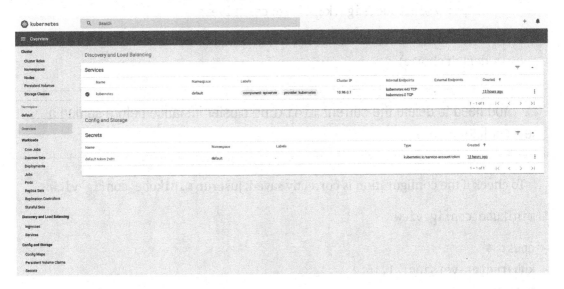

These `minikube` commands are particularly useful:

- `minikube stop`: Stops the K8s cluster and shuts down the Minikube VM without losing the cluster content.

- `minikube delete`: Deletes the K8s cluster and the Minikube VM.

You can allocate resources for `minikube` using these commands:

```
minikube config set memory 8192                    ①
minikube config set cpus 4                         ②
minikube config set kubernetes-version 1.16.2      ③
minikube config set vm-driver kvm2                 ④
minikube config set container-runtime crio         ⑤
```

Each line defines:

   ① The allocated memory to 8192MB (8GB)

   ② The allocated CPUs to 4

   ③ Kubernetes version to 1.16.2

④ The VM driver to kvm2. To learn more about drivers, visit https://minikube.sigs.k8s.io/docs/drivers/

⑤ The container runtime to use crio instead of Docker (the default choice)

⚠ **You need to delete the current minikube cluster instance before setting a new configuration.**

To check if the configuration is correctly saved, just run minikube config view:

```
$ minikube config view

- cpus: 4
- kubernetes-version: 1.16.2
- memory: 8192
- vm-driver: kvm2
- container-runtime: crio
```

Practical Summary and Conclusion

Kubernetes is the most widely used container orchestrator available in the market. ☺ Many solutions are now based on it like, the OpenShift Container Platform and the Rancher Kubernetes Engine. Kubernetes became the standard for the cloud-native architecture and infrastructure. Almost all the cloud providers have managed Kubernetes hosting the following:

- Azure Kubernetes Service

- Amazon Elastic Kubernetes Service

- Google Kubernetes Engine

- IBM Cloud Kubernetes Service

- Oracle Container Engine for Kubernetes

- Alibaba Container Service for Kubernetes

Even OVH and DigitalOcean have joined the race to provide managed Kubernetes hosting solutions. 😬

As listed in the first part of this chapter, there are many Kubernetes objects. Each can be used to satisfy a specific need. In this next section, we look at how these objects can fit our needs.

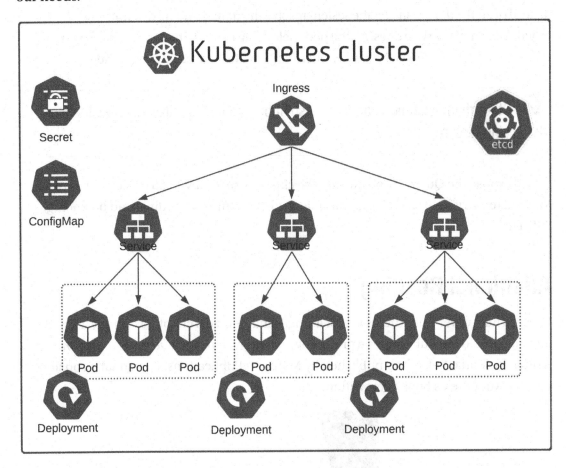

QuarkuShop is packaged as a Docker container. In Kubernetes, our application will be running inside a pod object, which is the most elementary Kubernetes object! We will maybe want to have more than one pod for a given microservice. To avoid managing them manually, you use the Deployment object, which will handle each pod set. It will also make sure that there is the desired number of instances, in case you want to have many instances of a specific pod.

To store these properties, you can use the ConfigMap. To store the credentials, you can use the SECRET object. To access them, you communicate with the Kubernetes API Server to get/read the desired data.

When we split the monolithic application into microservices, we said that the communication between them was based on the HTTP protocol (directly or indirectly). Each microservice is running inside a pod, which will have a dedicated, dynamic IP address. So if the Order microservice communicates with the Product microservice, for example, it cannot guess the IP address of its target. We need to use a DNS-like solution, to use a domain name instead of an IP address and let the system resolve the domain name dynamically. This is exactly what a K8s service does. All the pods belonging to the same service share their IP addresses under the same DNS name, where you can do load-balancing on them.

💡 Other than dynamic IP address resolution, the service also includes the load balancing feature.

To expose the QuarkuShop outside the cluster, use the INGRESS object. It exposes a Kubernetes service externally and has many great features, including load balancing, SSL, etc.

Additional Reading

I cannot fully cover Kubernetes in just a single chapter. This chapter is simply a small introduction to the Kubernetes world. I suggest that you read *Kubernetes in Action*, written by Marko Luksa and published by Manning Publications. I personally consider it the best Kubernetes book ever written.

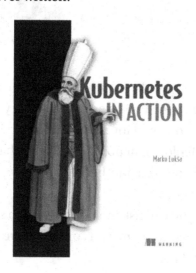

If you are more comfortable with videos, I suggest this great Kubernetes learning YouTube playlist, made by my friend Houssem Dellai, a cloud engineer at Microsoft.

CHAPTER 12

Implementing the Cloud Patterns

Introduction

You already know that you will use Kubernetes as the cloud platform in this book. In the previous chapter, you learned about the Kubernetes objects that you will use with QuarkuShop. In this chapter, you will start implementing some cloud patterns and bring the monolithic universe (the monolithic application, PostgreSQL, and Keycloak) to Kubernetes.

Bringing the Monolithic Universe to Kubernetes

Before starting to work on the application code, you need to bring the ▇ PostgreSQL database and Keycloak to the Kubernetes cluster.

Deploying PostgreSQL to Kubernetes

To deploy a ▇ PostgreSQL database instance to Kubernetes, you will use:

- A `ConfigMap` that stores the PostgreSQL username and database name
- A `Secret` that stores the PostgreSQL password
- A `PersistentVolumeClaim` that requests a storage space for the PostgreSQL pods

© Nebrass Lamouchi 2021
N. Lamouchi, *Pro Java Microservices with Quarkus and Kubernetes*,
https://doi.org/10.1007/978-1-4842-7170-4_12

- A Deployment that provides the description of the wanted the PostgreSQL pods

- A Service that is used as a DNS name pointing to the PostgreSQL pods

The ConfigMap for PostgreSQL is shown in Listing 12-1.

Listing 12-1. postgres-cm.yaml

```
apiVersion: v1
kind: ConfigMap
metadata:
  name: postgres-config
  labels:
    app: postgres
data:
  POSTGRES_DB: demo
  POSTGRES_USER: developer
```

The PostgreSQL password is stored in a Secret. The value needs to be encoded as Base64. You can encode the p4SSW0rd string using the openssl library locally:

```
echo -n 'p4SSW0rd' | openssl base64
```

The result is cDRTU1cwcmQ=. You use it inside the Secret object, as shown in Listing 12-2.

Listing 12-2. postgres-secret.yaml

```
apiVersion: v1
kind: Secret
metadata:
  name: postgres-secret
  labels:
    app: postgres
type: Opaque
data:
  POSTGRES_PASSWORD: cDRTU1cwcmQ=
```

Listing 12-3 shows the `PersistentVolumeClaim` that is used to request storage access for PostgreSQL.

Listing 12-3. postgres-pvc.yaml

```
apiVersion: v1
kind: PersistentVolumeClaim
metadata:
  name: postgres-pvc          ①
  labels:
    app: postgres
spec:
  accessModes:
    - ReadWriteMany            ②
  resources:
    requests:
      storage: 2Gi            ③
```

      ① The PVC name.

      ② Type of access. Many pods can read and write simultaneously in this PVC.

      ③ Required PVC storage.

Listing 12-4 shows the PostgreSQL `Deployment` file.

Listing 12-4. postgres-deployment.yaml

```
apiVersion: apps/v1
kind: Deployment
metadata:
  name: postgres
spec:
  replicas: 1                        ①
  selector:
    matchLabels:
      app: postgres                  ②
  template:
```

```
  metadata:
    labels:
      app: postgres
  spec:
    volumes:                        ③
      - name: data                  ③
        persistentVolumeClaim:      ③
          claimName: postgres-pvc   ③
    containers:
      - name: postgres
        image: postgres:12.3
        envFrom:
          - configMapRef:           ④
              name: postgres-config ④
          - secretRef:              ④
              name: postgres-secret ④
        ports:
          - containerPort: 5432
        volumeMounts:               ③
          - name: data              ③
            mountPath: /var/lib/postgresql/data
            subPath: postgres
        resources:
          requests:
            memory: '512Mi'         ⑤
            cpu: '500m'             ⑤
          limits:
            memory: '1Gi'           ⑥
            cpu: '1'                ⑥
```

This deployment resource will deploy PostgreSQL with the following:

　　① One pod instance.

　　② Targets the pods that have an app=postgres label.

　　③ Defines postgres-pvc as a persistence volume.

④ Loads the environment variable from `postgres-config` and `postgres-secret`.

⑤ The minimal needed resources for each pod is 512MB and 0.5 CPU unit.

⑥ The maximum allowed resources for each pod is 1GB and 1 CPU unit.

The PostgreSQL Service file is shown in Listing 12-5.

Listing 12-5. postgres-svc.yaml

```
apiVersion: v1
kind: Service
metadata:
  name: postgres
  labels:
    app: postgres
spec:
  selector:
    app: postgres
  ports:
   - port: 5432
  type: LoadBalancer
```

ℹ️ We are creating a `Service` with type `LoadBalancer`. On cloud providers that support load balancers, an external IP address would be provisioned to access the `Service`. As we are on `minikube`, the `LoadBalancer` type makes the `Service` accessible through the `minikube service` command:

```
minikube service SERVICE_NAME
```

Next, we test the deployed PostgreSQL instance using the IntelliJ Database Explorer.

Start by getting the PostgreSQL Kubernetes Service URL. You use this command to get the Kubernetes Service URL from the Minikube cluster:

```
$ minikube service postgres --url
```

```
http://192.168.39.79:31450
```

ⓘ   The command will return the Kubernetes URL for a service in the Minikube cluster. If there are many URLs, they will be printed one at a time.

We will use the following:

- `192.168.39.79:31450` as the database URL

- `developer` as the user

- `p4SSWOrd` as the password

- `demo` as the database name

Just click Test Connection to verify that everything is okay. If it's okay, you will get a ✔ that confirms that the connection was successful.

Deploying Keycloak to Kubernetes

To deploy Keycloak to the Kubernetes cluster, we will use Helm.

WHAT IS KUBERNETES HELM?

Helm is a package manager for Kubernetes that allows developers and operators to more easily package, configure, and deploy applications and services onto Kubernetes clusters.

Helm is now an official Kubernetes project and is part of the Cloud Native Computing Foundation, a non-profit that supports open-source projects in and around the Kubernetes ecosystem.

Helm can:

- Install software.

- Automatically install software dependencies.

- Upgrade software.

- Configure software deployments.

- Fetch software packages from repositories.

Helm provides this functionality through the following components:

- A command-line tool, called `helm`, which provides the user interface to all Helm functionality.

- A companion server component, called `tiller`, that runs on your Kubernetes cluster, listens for commands from `helm`, and handles the configuration and deployment of software releases on the cluster.

- The Helm packaging format, called *charts*.

WHAT IS A HELM CHART ?

Helm packages are called *charts*, and they consist of a few YAML configuration files and some templates that are rendered into Kubernetes manifest files.

The `helm` command can install a chart from a local directory, or from a `.tar.gz` packaged version of this directory structure. These packaged charts can also be automatically downloaded and installed from chart repositories or repos.

To install the Helm CLI, just go to this guide: `helm.sh/docs/intro/install`

After installing the Helm CLI, you can install the Keycloak Helm chart into your Kubernetes cluster.

The Keycloak helm chart that you need to install is available in the `codecentric` repository, so you need to add it to the Helm repositories:

```
helm repo add codecentric https://codecentric.github.io/helm-charts
```

Next, create a Kubernetes namespace to install Keycloak:

```
$ kubectl create namespace keycloak

namespace/keycloak created
```

Next, install Keycloak using this Helm command:

```
helm install keycloak --namespace keycloak codecentric/keycloak
```

To list the created objects in the keycloak namespace, use the kubectl get all -n keycloak command:

```
NAME                        READY    STATUS    RESTARTS
pod/keycloak-0              1/1      Running   0
pod/keycloak-postgresql-0   1/1      Running   0

NAME                                      TYPE         CLUSTER-IP      PORT(S)
service/keycloak-headless                 ClusterIP    None            80/TCP
service/keycloak-http                     ClusterIP    10.96.104.85    80/TCP
8443/TCP 9990/TCP
service/keycloak-postgresql               ClusterIP    10.107.175.90   5432/TCP
service/keycloak-postgresql-headless      ClusterIP    None            5432/TCP

NAME                                      READY
statefulset.apps/keycloak                 1/1
statefulset.apps/keycloak-postgresql      1/1
```

Note that we have two pods:

- keycloak-0: Contains the Keycloak application

- keycloak-postgresql-0: Contains a dedicated PostgreSQL database instance for the Keycloak application

Now you need to configure the Keycloak instance as you did in Chapter 5. To access the Keycloak pod, use *port-forwarding* from the pod to the localhost:

```
kubectl -n keycloak port-forward service/keycloak-http 8080:80
```

Now, access the Keycloak Console on `localhost:8080/auth`:

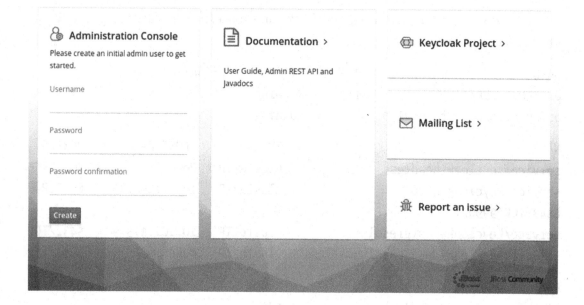

From this screen, you can create the Administrator user:

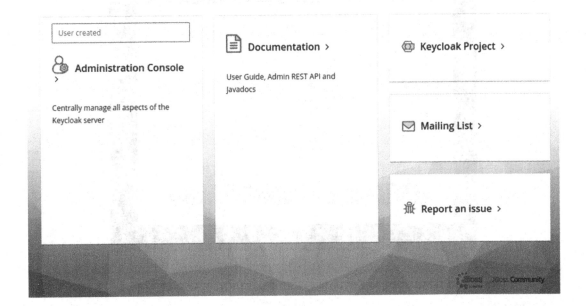

Next, click Administration Console to access the login screen:

After login, you'll land at the Keycloak Administration console:

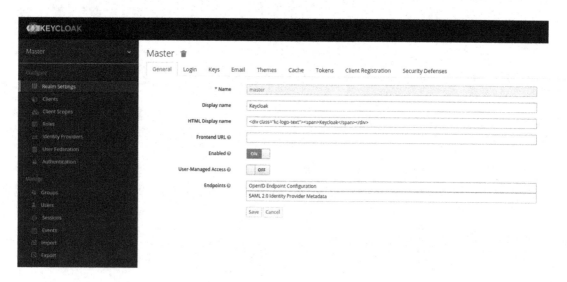

You can now use the same steps as in Chapter 5 to create the Keycloak realm.

Deploying the Monolithic QuarkuShop to Kubernetes

After bringing the 🗄 PostgreSQL database and Keycloak to Kubernetes, you can proceed to deploying the monolithic QuarkuShop application to Kubernetes. This exercise is very useful to learn how to deploy only one application to Kubernetes.

We start by adding two dependencies to the QuarkuShop pom.xml, as follows:

```
<dependency>
  <groupId>io.quarkus</groupId>
  <artifactId>quarkus-kubernetes</artifactId>
</dependency>
<dependency>
  <groupId>io.quarkus</groupId>
  <artifactId>quarkus-container-image-jib</artifactId>
</dependency>
```

When building the project using Maven, these two libraries will:

- Create the Docker image for the application

- Generate the Kubernetes objects descriptors required to deploy the application

To verify that I'm telling the truth, 😊 let's build the application and check it:

```
$ mvn clean install -Dquarkus.container-image.build=true
```

In the target directory, there are two new folders—jib and kubernetes. To check their content, run the following:

```
$ ls -l target/jib target/kubernetes

target/jib:          ①
total 32
-rw-rw-r-- 1 nebrass nebrass 1160 sept.  8 21:01 application.properties
-rw-rw-r-- 1 nebrass nebrass  427 sept.  8 21:01 banner.txt
drwxrwxr-x 3 nebrass nebrass 4096 sept.  8 21:01 com
drwxrwxr-x 3 nebrass nebrass 4096 sept.  8 21:01 db
drwxrwxr-x 7 nebrass nebrass 4096 sept.  8 21:01 io
```

```
drwxrwxr-x 7 nebrass nebrass 4096 sept.  8 21:01 javax
drwxrwxr-x 7 nebrass nebrass 4096 sept.  8 21:01 META-INF
drwxrwxr-x 4 nebrass nebrass 4096 sept.  8 21:01 org

target/kubernetes:  ②
total 12
-rw-rw-r-- 1 nebrass nebrass 5113 sept.  8 21:01 kubernetes.json
-rw-rw-r-- 1 nebrass nebrass 3478 sept.  8 21:01 kubernetes.yml
```

① The directory used by JIB while generating the Docker image.

② The directory used to store the generated Kubernetes descriptors. The same content is generated in two formats: YAML and JSON.

If you want to build the Docker image based on the native binary, run the following:

```
mvn clean install -Pnative -Dquarkus.native.container-build=true -Dquarkus.
container-image.build=true
```

You can also verify whether there is a newly created Docker image locally:

```
$ docker images
```

REPOSITORY	TAG	IMAGE ID	CREATED	SIZE
nebrass/quarkushop	1.0.0-SNAPSHOT	eb2c67d7fa27	21 minutes ago	244MB

Next, push this image to the Docker Hub:

```
$ docker push nebrass/quarkushop:1.0.0-SNAPSHOT
```

Before importing the Kubernetes descriptor, you need to make one small modification. The application is currently pointing to local PostgreSQL and Keycloak instances. You have two options:

- Change the hardcoded properties.

- Override the properties using the environment variables. This is the best solution, as it doesn't require a new build or release.

To override the properties, we will use environment variables. For example, to override the value of the `quarkus.http.port` property to 9999, you can create an environment variable called `QUARKUS_HTTP_PORT=9999`. As you can notice, it's the same capitalized string with an underscore instead of the separating dot. In this case, we want to override these properties:

- `quarkus.datasource.jdbc.url`: Pointing to the PostgreSQL URL. Its corresponding environment variable will be `QUARKUS_DATASOURCE_JDBC_URL`

- `mp.jwt.verify.publickey.location`: Pointing to the Keycloak URL. Its corresponding environment variable will be `MP_JWT_VERIFY_PUBLICKEY_LOCATION`

- `mp.jwt.verify.issuer`: Pointing to the Keycloak URL. Its corresponding environment variable will be `MP_JWT_VERIFY_ISSUER`

These three properties are pointing to `localhost` as the host for the PostgreSQL and Keycloak instances. We want them now to point to the PostgreSQL and Keycloak respective pods.

As mentioned in the previous chapter, the K8s service objects can be used as DNS names for each set of pods.

Let's list the available `Service` objects that we have in our cluster:

```
$ kubectl get svc --all-namespaces
```

NAMESPACE	NAME	PORT(S)	
default	kubernetes	443/TCP	
default	postgres	5432:31450/TCP	①
keycloak	keycloak-headless	80/TCP	②
keycloak	keycloak-http	80/TCP,8443/TCP,9990/TCP	②
keycloak	keycloak-postgresql	5432/TCP	②
keycloak	keycloak-postgresql-headless	5432/TCP	②
kube-system	kube-dns	53/UDP,53/TCP,9153/TCP	
kubernetes-dashboard	dashboard-metrics-scraper	8000/TCP	
kubernetes-dashboard	kubernetes-dashboard	80/TCP	

① The PostgreSQL `Service` is available in the `default` namespace.

② We have several Keycloak `Service` objects in the `keycloak` namespace:

- `keycloak-headless`: A headless Kubernetes service pointing to Keycloak pods. A headless service is used to enable direct communication with the matching pods without an intermediate layer. There is no proxy or routing layer involved in the communication. A headless service lists all the selected backing pods, while the other service types forward the calls to a randomly selected pod.

- `keycloak-http`: Kubernetes service that offers a load-balancing router to Keycloak pods.

- `keycloak-postgresql`: Kubernetes service that offers a load-balancing router to PostgreSQL pods.

- `keycloak-postgresql-headless`: Headless Kubernetes service pointing to PostgreSQL pods.

In this case, we will not be using the headless service, as we want to have requests load-balancing and we don't have any need to communicate directly with the pods.

The `quarkus.datasource.jdbc.url` property contains `jdbc:postgresql://localhost:5432/demo`. We will use `postgres` service with port 5432 from the `default` namespace, instead of `localhost`. So the new property definition will be:

`quarkus.datasource.jdbc.url=jdbc:postgresql://postgres:5432/demo`

The environment variable will be:

`QUARKUS_DATASOURCE_JDBC_URL=jdbc:postgresql://postgres:5432/demo`

Good! We will apply the same logic to the `mp.jwt.verify.publickey.location` and `mp.jwt.verify.issuer` properties.

```
1 mp.jwt.verify.publickey.location=http://localhost:9080/auth/realms/
quarkushop-realm/protocol/openid-connect/certs
2 mp.jwt.verify.issuer=http://localhost:9080/auth/realms/quarkushop-realm
```

Instead of the `localhost` we will use `keycloak-http` with port 80 from the `keycloak` namespace. The new `properties` values will be:

```
1 mp.jwt.verify.publickey.location=http://keycloak-http.keycloak/auth/
  realms/quarkushop-realm/protocol/openid-connect/certs
2 mp.jwt.verify.issuer=http://keycloak-http.keycloak/auth/realms/
  quarkushop-realm
```

> ℹ **Note** that for visibility, we appended the `namespace` name after the `service` name for the Keycloak services, yet we didn't do that for the PostgreSQL service. This is due to the presence of the PostgreSQL service inside the `default` namespace, where we deploy our application. The Keycloak services are available inside the `keycloak` namespace.

The `MP JWT` environment variables will be:

```
1 MP_JWT_VERIFY_PUBLICKEY_LOCATION=http://keycloak-http.keycloak/auth/
  realms/quarkushop-realm/protocol/openid-connect/certs
2 MP_JWT_VERIFY_ISSUER=http://keycloak-http.keycloak/auth/realms/
  quarkushop-realm
```

Now we need to add these new environment variables to the Kubernetes descriptor that was generated by the Quarkus Kubernetes Extension inside the `target/kubernetes/` directory.

In the Kubernetes world, if we want to pass environment variables to a pod, we pass them using the Kubernetes Deployment Object, in the `spec.template.spec.containers.env` section.

The updated `Deployment` object in the `Kubernetes.json` descriptor file is shown in Listing 12-6.

Listing 12-6. target/kubernetes/kubernetes.json

```json
{
  "apiVersion": "apps/v1",
  "kind": "Deployment",
  "metadata": { ...,
```

```
      "name": "quarkushop"
    },
    "spec": {
      "replicas": 1,
      "selector": ...,
      "template": {
        "metadata": {
          "annotations": ...,
          "labels": {
            "app.kubernetes.io/name": "quarkushop",
            "app.kubernetes.io/version": "1.0.0-SNAPSHOT"
          }
        },
        "spec": {
          "containers": [
            {
              "env": [
                { "name": "KUBERNETES_NAMESPACE",
                  "valueFrom": {
                    "fieldRef": { "fieldPath": "metadata.namespace" }
                  }
                },
                { "name": "QUARKUS_DATASOURCE_JDBC_URL",
                  "value": "jdbc:postgresql://postgres:5432/demo"
                },
                { "name": "MP_JWT_VERIFY_PUBLICKEY_LOCATION",
                  "value": "http://keycloak-http.keycloak/auth/realms/
                  quarkushop-realm/protocol/openid-connect/certs"
                },
                { "name": "MP_JWT_VERIFY_ISSUER",
                  "value": "http://keycloak-http.keycloak/auth/realms/
                  quarkushop-realm"
                }
              ],
```

```
    "image": "nebrass/quarkushop:1.0.0-SNAPSHOT",
    "imagePullPolicy": "IfNotPresent",
  ...
}
```

It's annoying to have to add these values each time, especially when the target folder is deleted each time you build the code. This is why the Quarkus team added a new mechanism of environment variables definition for Kubernetes descriptors. You can learn more about it at https://quarkus.io/guides/deploying-to-kubernetes#env-vars.

You can add the same environment variables using the application.properties file with the prefix quarkus.kubernetes.env.vars. for each environment variable:

1 quarkus.kubernetes.env.vars.quarkus-datasource-jdbc-
  url=jdbc:postgresql://postgres:5432/demo
2 quarkus.kubernetes.env.vars.mp-jwt-verify-publickey-location=http://
  keycloak-http.keycloak/auth/realms/quarkushop-realm/protocol/openid-
  connect/certs
3 quarkus.kubernetes.env.vars.mp-jwt-verify-issuer=http://keycloak-http.
  keycloak/auth/realms/quarkushop-realm

To import the generated Kubernetes descriptor, use:

```
$ kubectl apply -f target/kubernetes/kubernetes.json
```

```
serviceaccount/quarkushop created
service/quarkushop created
deployment.apps/quarkushop created
```

To verify that QuarkuShop is correctly deployed to Kubernetes, just list all the objects in the current (default) namespace, as follows:

```
$ kubectl get all
```

NAME		READY	STATUS	RESTARTS
pod/postgres-69c47c748-pnbbf		1/1	Running	3
pod/quarkushop-78c67844ff-7fzbv		1/1	Running	0

NAME	TYPE	CLUSTER-IP	PORT(S)
service/kubernetes	ClusterIP	10.96.0.1	443/TCP
service/postgres	LoadBalancer	10.106.7.15	5432:31450/TCP
service/quarkushop	ClusterIP	10.97.230.13	8080/TCP

NAME	READY	UP-TO-DATE	AVAILABLE
deployment.apps/postgres	1/1	1	1
deployment.apps/quarkushop	1/1	1	1

NAME	DESIRED	CURRENT	READY
replicaset.apps/postgres-69c47c748	1	1	1
replicaset.apps/quarkushop-78c67844ff	1	1	1

In the resource list, there is a pod called quarkushop-78c67844ff-7fzbv. To check that everything is okay, you need to access the application packaged inside it. To do that, you do a port-forward from the port 8080 of the quarkushop-78c67844ff-7fzbv pod to port 8080 of the localhost.

```
$ kubectl port-forward quarkushop-78c67844ff-7fzbv 8080:8080

Forwarding from 127.0.0.1:8080 -> 8080
Forwarding from [::1]:8080 -> 8080
```

Now open http://localhost:8080/api/health-ui, as shown on the screenshot:

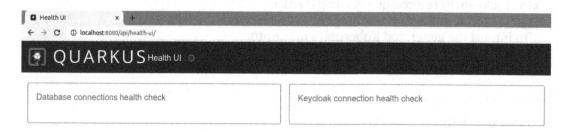

You can see that the health checks verified that the PostgreSQL database and Keycloak are reachable.

Defining environment variables using application.properties is not always a good idea. For example, if you want to change/add a property, you'll need to build and redeploy the application. There is an alternative that doesn't require all this effort to provide additional properties to the application using the ConfigMaps. The application parses the ConfigMap content as environment variables, which is an excellent way to pass properties to the application.

To do this, you need another Maven dependency:

```
<dependency>
    <groupId>io.quarkus</groupId>
    <artifactId>quarkus-kubernetes-config</artifactId>
</dependency>
```

You need to remove the ENV VARs properties that you added before:

```
quarkus.kubernetes.env.vars.quarkus-datasource-jdbc-url=jdbc:postgresql://
postgres: ...
quarkus.kubernetes.env.vars.mp-jwt-verify-publickey-location=http://
keycloak-http.k...
quarkus.kubernetes.env.vars.mp-jwt-verify-issuer=http://keycloak-http.
keycloak/a...
```

Next, you enable the Kubernetes ConfigMap access and tell the application which ConfigMap has the properties you need:

```
quarkus.kubernetes-config.enabled=true
quarkus.kubernetes-config.config-maps=quarkushop-monolith-config
```

Listing 12-7 shows how you define the new ConfigMap called quarkushop-monolith-config.

Listing 12-7. quarkushop-monolith-config.yml

```
1 apiVersion: v1
2 kind: ConfigMap
3 metadata:
4   name: quarkushop-monolith-config
5 data:
6   application.properties: |-
7     quarkus.datasource.jdbc.url=jdbc:postgresql://postgres:5432/demo
8     mp.jwt.verify.publickey.location=http://keycloak-http.keycloak/auth/
      realms/quarkushop-realm/protocol/openid-connect/certs
9     mp.jwt.verify.issuer=http://keycloak-http.keycloak/auth/realms/
      quarkushop-realm
```

You simply import quarkushop-monolith-config.yml to the Kubernetes cluster:

```
kubectl apply -f quarkushop-monolith-config.yml
```

Now, if you build the QuarkuShop application again, you will notice that in the generated Kubernetes descriptors, there is a new RoleBinding object. This object is generated by the quarkus-kubernetes-config Quarkus extension.

```
{
  "apiVersion" : "rbac.authorization.k8s.io/v1",
  "kind" : "RoleBinding",                                    ①
  "metadata" : {
    "annotations" : {
      "prometheus.io/path" : "/metrics",
      "prometheus.io/port" : "8080",
      "prometheus.io/scrape" : "true"
    },
    "labels" : {
      "app.kubernetes.io/name" : "quarkushop",
      "app.kubernetes.io/version" : "1.0.0-SNAPSHOT"
    },
    "name" : "quarkushop:view"                               ②
  },
  "roleRef" : {
    "kind" : "ClusterRole",                                  ③
    "apiGroup" : "rbac.authorization.k8s.io",
    "name" : "view"                                          ③
  },
  "subjects" : [ {
    "kind" : "ServiceAccount",                               ④
    "name" : "quarkushop"                                    ④
  } ]
}
```

① The current object is RoleBinding.

② The RoleBinding object name is quarkushop:view.

③ This will bind the ClusterRole with the view role to read ConfigMaps and Secrets.

④ This RoleBinding is applied to the ServiceAccount called quarkushop, which is generated by the quarkus-kubernetes extension.

Let's build and package the application image and deploy it again to the K8s cluster:

```
mvn clean install -DskipTests -DskipITs -Pnative \
    -Dquarkus.native.container-build=true \
    -Dquarkus.container-image.build=true
```

Next, push the image:

```
docker push nebrass/quarkushop:1.0.0-SNAPSHOT
```

Next, deploy the application again to Kubernetes:

```
kubectl apply -f target/kubernetes/kubernetes.json
```

To test the application now, just do a port-forward on the QuarkuShop pod:

```
$ kubectl get pods

NAME                         READY   STATUS    RESTARTS   AGE
postgres-69c47c748-pnbbf     1/1     Running   5          19d
quarkushop-77dcfc7c45-tzmbs  1/1     Running   0          73m

$ kubectl port-forward quarkushop-77dcfc7c45-tzmbs 8080:8080
Forwarding from 127.0.0.1:8080 -> 8080
Forwarding from [::1]:8080 -> 8080
```

Then open `http://localhost:8080/api/health-ui/`, as shown in the screenshot:

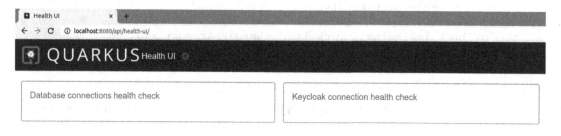

Excellent! You learned how to bring the monolithic application into Kubernetes. 😄 In the next chapter, you will use these same steps to create and bring microservices into the Kubernetes cluster.

Conclusion

This chapter tried to introduce some cloud patterns based on the Kubernetes ecosystem. The exercise of bringing the monolithic application and its dependencies into Kubernetes is the first step to creating and deploying your microservices.

## CHAPTER 13

Building the Kubernetized Microservices

Introduction

Chapter 8 discussed how to apply a data-driven design (DDD) to the monolithic application. We broke the relationships between the boundary contexts that were revealed while analyzing the project. In Stan4J, the final code structure looks like this:

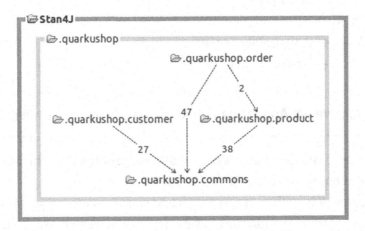

In this chapter, you will implement the three microservices—Product, Order, and Customer. These packages depend on the commons package, so, you'll need to implement it before implementing the three microservices.

© Nebrass Lamouchi 2021
N. Lamouchi, *Pro Java Microservices with Quarkus and Kubernetes*,
https://doi.org/10.1007/978-1-4842-7170-4_13

Creating the Commons Library

The commons JAR library will wrap the contents of the commons package.

We will generate a simple Maven project, where we will copy the contents of the commons package.

```
mvn archetype:generate -DgroupId=com.targa.labs.commons
-DartifactId=quarkushop-commons \
    -DarchetypeArtifactId=maven-archetype-quickstart \
    -DarchetypeVersion=1.4 -DinteractiveMode=false
```

This command generates a simple project with this contents:

```
project
|-- pom.xml
`-- src
    |-- main/java
    |        `-- com.targa.labs.commons
    |                `-- App.java
    `-- test/java
             `-- com.targa.labs.commons
                    `-- AppTest.java
```

ℹ️   We will remove the App.java and AppTest.java as we will not need them.

Then, we copy/paste the contents of the commons package from the monolithic application to our quarkushop-commons project.

Don't be scared! You will see many errors and warnings when you paste the copied classes, but the next step is to add the missing dependencies to make the IDE happy. 😄

Let's open the pom.xml file and start making the changes:

1. Start by changing maven.compiler.source and maven.compiler. target from 1.7 to 11.

2. Define the dependencies as follows:

```
<dependencies>
    <dependency>
        <groupId>org.slf4j</groupId>
```

```xml
        <artifactId>slf4j-api</artifactId>
        <version>1.7.30</version>
    </dependency>
    <dependency>
        <groupId>javax.validation</groupId>
        <artifactId>validation-api</artifactId>
        <version>2.0.1.Final</version>
    </dependency>
    <dependency>
        <groupId>org.eclipse.microprofile.openapi</groupId>
        <artifactId>microprofile-openapi-api</artifactId>
        <version>1.1.2</version>
    </dependency>
    <dependency>
        <groupId>org.jboss.spec.javax.ws.rs</groupId>
        <artifactId>jboss-jaxrs-api_2.1_spec</artifactId>
        <version>2.0.1.Final</version>
    </dependency>
    <dependency>
        <groupId>jakarta.persistence</groupId>
        <artifactId>jakarta.persistence-api</artifactId>
        <version>2.2.3</version>
    </dependency>
    <dependency>
        <groupId>jakarta.enterprise</groupId>
        <artifactId>jakarta.enterprise.cdi-api</artifactId>
        <version>2.0.2</version>
    </dependency>
    <dependency>
        <groupId>org.eclipse.microprofile.health</groupId>
        <artifactId>microprofile-health-api</artifactId>
        <version>2.2</version>
    </dependency>
```

```
<dependency>
    <groupId>org.eclipse.microprofile.config</groupId>
    <artifactId>microprofile-config-api</artifactId>
    <version>1.4</version>
</dependency>
<dependency>
    <groupId>org.eclipse.microprofile.metrics</groupId>
    <artifactId>microprofile-metrics-api</artifactId>
    <version>2.3</version>
</dependency>
<dependency>
    <groupId>com.fasterxml.jackson.core</groupId>
    <artifactId>jackson-databind</artifactId>
    <version>2.11.2</version>
</dependency>
<dependency>
    <groupId>io.quarkus.security</groupId>
    <artifactId>quarkus-security</artifactId>
    <version>1.1.2.Final</version>
</dependency>
<dependency>
    <groupId>org.projectlombok</groupId>
    <artifactId>lombok</artifactId>
    <version>1.18.16</version>
</dependency>
<dependency>
    <groupId>org.testcontainers</groupId>
    <artifactId>postgresql</artifactId>
    <version>1.15.3</version>
</dependency>
<dependency>
    <groupId>io.quarkus</groupId>
    <artifactId>quarkus-test-common</artifactId>
    <version>1.13.3.Final</version>
</dependency>
</dependencies>
```

Wow! ☺ Where did these dependencies come from? I'm sure that you are like me, and don't like writing things that you don't understand. 😊 But don't worry, these dependencies are from the Quarkus Framework. I used the IDE to add the missing dependency:

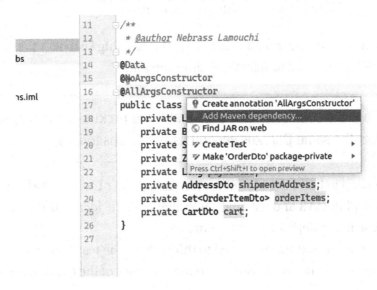

The Maven Artifact Search window will appear, as follows:

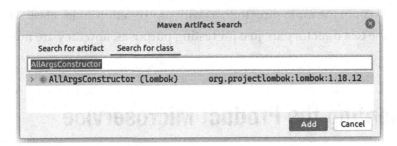

So, which version of a given dependency should you choose? You can use IntelliJ to determine which external libraries are used in the monolithic application:

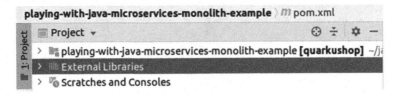

Expand the section and scroll to find the desired library. The version will be shown after the `groupId` and the `artifactId`, as follows:

Here, you can see that the monolithic application is using Lombok `v1.18.12`, so in the `Commons` project, you need to select the same version.

⚠ In order to avoid conflicts, make sure that the `quarkus-test-common` dependency has the same Quarkus version as the microservices. ☺

Finally, you need to build the Maven project using `mvn clean install`. This command will build the JAR and will make it available in the local `.m2` directory. This enables you to use it as a dependency in future steps.

Wait! You aren't finished yet! You need to think about the tests! You need to copy the `utils` package from the test classes to the main classes of the `quarkushop-commons` project.

To be able to reuse these classes outside the `quarkushop-commons` library, you need to have them in the main directory, as with any other ordinary class. The classes belonging to the test directory are just for testing purposes, and they are not intended to be reused.

Implementing the Product Microservice

In this section, you start to do the serious job: create the `Product` microservice. Let's generate a new Quarkus application called `quarkushop-product` from the code.quarkus.io:

Here are the selected extensions:

- RESTEasy JAX-RS

- RESTEasy JSON-B

- SmallRye OpenAPI

- Hibernate ORM

- Hibernate Validator

- JDBC Driver - PostgreSQL

- Flyway

- Quarkus Extension for Spring Data JPA API

- SmallRye JWT

- SmallRye Health

- Kubernetes

- Kubernetes Config

- Container Image Jib

Download the generated application skull by clicking Generate Your Application.

Then import the code to your IDE. Open the pom.xml file and add the Lombok and TestContainers dependencies to it:

```
<dependencies>
    <dependency>
        <groupId>org.projectlombok</groupId>
        <artifactId>lombok</artifactId>
        <version>1.18.16</version>
    </dependency>

    <dependency>
        <groupId>org.testcontainers</groupId>
        <artifactId>junit-jupiter</artifactId>
        <version>1.15.3</version>
        <scope>test</scope>
    </dependency>
    <dependency>
        <groupId>org.testcontainers</groupId>
        <artifactId>postgresql</artifactId>
        <version>1.15.3</version>
        <scope>test</scope>
    </dependency>

    <dependency>
        <groupId>org.assertj</groupId>
        <artifactId>assertj-core</artifactId>
        <scope>test</scope>
    </dependency>
</dependencies>
```

Next, add the most important dependency—the `quarkushop-commons`:

```xml
<dependency>
    <groupId>com.targa.labs</groupId>
    <artifactId>quarkushop-commons</artifactId>
    <version>1.0-SNAPSHOT</version>
</dependency>
```

Copy the code from the `product` package to the `quarkushop-product` microservice.

ⓘ   Don't forget to copy the banner.txt file from the monolithic application to the `src/main/resources` directory of the Product microservice.

The next step is to populate the `application.properties`:

```
1 # Datasource config properties
2 quarkus.datasource.db-kind=postgresql
3 quarkus.datasource.username=developer
4 quarkus.datasource.password=p4SSWOrd
5 quarkus.datasource.jdbc.url=jdbc:postgresql://localhost:5432/product
6 # Flyway minimal config properties
7 quarkus.flyway.migrate-at-start=true
8 # HTTP config properties
9 quarkus.http.root-path=/api
10 quarkus.http.access-log.enabled=true
11 %prod.quarkus.http.access-log.enabled=false
12 # Swagger UI
13 quarkus.swagger-ui.always-include=true
14 # Datasource config properties
15 %test.quarkus.datasource.db-kind=postgresql
16 # Flyway minimal config properties
17 %test.quarkus.flyway.migrate-at-start=true
18 # Define the custom banner
19 quarkus.banner.path=banner.txt
20 ### Security
21 quarkus.http.cors=true
```

```
22 quarkus.smallrye-jwt.enabled=true
23 # Keycloak Configuration
24 keycloak.credentials.client-id=quarkushop
25 # MP-JWT Config
26 mp.jwt.verify.publickey.location=http://localhost:9080/auth/realms/
   quarkushop-realm/protocol/openid-connect/certs
27 mp.jwt.verify.issuer=http://localhost:9080/auth/realms/quarkushop-realm
28 ### Health Check
29 quarkus.smallrye-health.ui.always-include=true
30 # Kubernetes ConfigMaps
31 quarkus.kubernetes-config.enabled=true
32 quarkus.kubernetes-config.config-maps=quarkushop-product-config
```

The properties are almost the same as the monolithic application, which is logical, as the microservice is a slice cut from the monolithic application.

❗ I changed the names of the database (line 5) and the ConfigMap (line 34). ⚠

Recall that we changed the ConfigMap, so now we need to create it. See Listing 13-1.

Listing 13-1. quarkushop-product-config.yml

```
1 apiVersion: v1
2 kind: ConfigMap
3 metadata:
4   name: quarkushop-product-config
5 data:
6   application.properties: |-
7     quarkus.datasource.jdbc.url=jdbc:postgresql://postgres:5432/product
8     mp.jwt.verify.publickey.location=http://keycloak-http.keycloak/auth/
      realms/quarkushop-realm/protocol/openid-connect/certs
9     mp.jwt.verify.issuer=http://keycloak-http.keycloak/auth/realms/
      quarkushop-realm
```

❗ I also changed the name of the database (line 7) in this ConfigMap.

I changed the database name because, as you learned in Chapter 9, it's wise to have one database per microservice.☺ This is why I created a dedicated schema for each microservice:

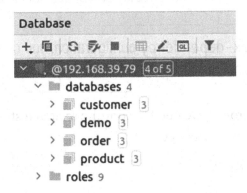

Because we are in the database context, we need to copy the Flyway scripts V1.0__Init_app.sql and V1.1__Insert_samples.sql from the monolithic application to the src/main/resources/db/migration directory of the Product microservice. We also need to clean up the SQL scripts to keep only the product bounded context-related objects and sample data.

⚠ Be sure that you clean up the scripts correctly, or the deployment will fail during the application boot process.

Next, there is a very important task to do: identify the quarkushop-commons project to the Quarkus index of the quarkushop-product.

WHAT IS THE QUARKUS INDEX?

Quarkus automatically indexes the current module. However, when you have external modules containing CDI beans, entities, and objects serialized as JSON, you need to explicitly index them.

Indexing can be done in many ways:

- Using the Jandex Maven plugin

- Adding an empty META-INF/beans.xml file

- Using Quarkus Index Dependency properties, which is my favorite choice

---

This indexing can be done using `application.properties` values:

```
quarkus.index-dependency.commons.group-id=com.targa.labs
quarkus.index-dependency.commons.artifact-id=quarkushop-commons
```

❗   Without this `index-dependency` configuration, you cannot build the native binary of the application.

Before building the project, we need to copy the related tests from the monolith to the quarkushop-product microservice:

- `CategoryResourceIT`

- `CategoryResourceTest`

- `ProductResourceIT`

- `ProductResourceTest`

- `ReviewResourceIT`

- `ReviewResourceTest`

We also need to copy the Keycloak Docker files from `src/main/docker` to the quarkushop-product microservice:

- The `keycloak-test.yml` file

- The `realms` directory

In order to be able to execute tests, we need to disable the Kubernetes support in the test environment/profile:

```
%test.quarkus.kubernetes-config.enabled=false
quarkus.test.native-image-profile=test
```

ℹ   We are defining the Native Image Test Profile as `test` in order to disable the Kubernetes support for native image tests.

Next, we need to execute the tests and build and push the quarkushop-product image:

```
mvn clean install -Pnative \
    -Dquarkus.native.container-build=true \
    -Dquarkus.container-image.build=true
```

Then we push the quarkushop-product image to the container registry, as follows:

```
docker push nebrass/quarkushop-product:1.0.0-SNAPSHOT
```

We now create the quarkushop-product-config ConfigMap:

```
kubectl apply -f quarkushop-product/quarkushop-product-config.yml
```

And deploy the Product microservice to the Kubernetes cluster:

```
kubectl apply -f quarkushop-product/target/kubernetes/kubernetes.json
```

Excellent! Now we can list the pods:

```
$ kubectl get pods
```

```
NAME                                    READY   STATUS
postgres-69c47c748-pnbbf                1/1     Running
quarkushop-product-7748f9f74c-dqnqk     1/1     Running
```

We can test the application using a port-forward on the quarkushop-product:

```
$ kubectl port-forward quarkushop-product-7748f9f74c-dqnqk 8080:8080

Forwarding from 127.0.0.1:8080 -> 8080
Forwarding from [::1]:8080 -> 8080
Handling connection for 8080
Handling connection for 8080
```

Then a curl command can count the products stored on the database:

```
$ curl -X GET "http://localhost:8080/api/products/count"
```

4

Good! Access to the database is working correctly. 😄 We can also run a health check to be sure that the Keycloak is correctly reached, by using the `curl -X GET "http://localhost:8080/api/health"` command:

```
{
    "status": "UP",
    "checks": [
        {
            "name": "Keycloak connection health check",
            "status": "UP"
        },
        {
            "name": "Database connections health check",
            "status": "UP"
        }
    ]
}
```

Excellent! Everything is working as expected! 😊😊 We can move now to the `Order` microservice.

Implementing the Order Microservice

In this section, we will generate the `Order` microservice with the same extensions as the `Product` microservice and include an extra one: the REST client extension.

We know that the `Order` microservice has a communication dependency on the `Product` microservice. This communication can be implemented as REST API calls from the `Order` microservice to the `Product` microservice. This is why we included the REST client extension in the selected dependencies.

After generating the project, we will run the same tasks as we did with the `Product` microservice:

- Copy the code from the `order` package in the monolithic application to the new `Order` microservice

- Add the Lombok, AssertJ, and TestContainers dependencies

- Add the `quarkushop-commons` dependency

- Copy the `banner.txt` file from the monolith

- Add the `application.properties` and change the database and `ConfigMap` names

- Create the `quarkushop-product-config` `ConfigMap` file

- Copy the Flyway scripts and clean up the unrelated objects and data

- Add the Quarkus Index Dependency for `quarkushop-commons` in the `application.properties`

At this point, we need to fix the code, as we still have a `ProductRepository` reference inside the `OrderItemService` class.

`OrderItemService` uses `ProductRepository` to find a product using a given ID. This programmatic call will be replaced by a REST API call to the `Product` microservice. For this, we need to create a `ProductRestClient` class that will fetch the Product data using a given ID:

```
@Path("/products")                              ①
@RegisterRestClient                             ②
public interface ProductRestClient {

    @GET
    @Path("/{id}")
    ProductDto findById(@PathParam Long id);    ③
}
```

① The `ProductRestClient` will point to the `/products` URI.

② The `@RegisterRestClient` allows Quarkus to know that this interface is meant to be available for CDI injection as a REST client.

③ The `findById()` method will do an HTTP GET on the `/products` URI.

But what's the base URL of the `Product` microservice API? The `ProductRestClient` needs to be configured in order to work correctly. The configuration can be done using these properties:

```
1 product-service.url=http://quarkushop-product:8080/api
2 com.targa.labs.quarkushop.order.client.ProductRestClient/mp-rest/
url=${product-service.url}      ①
3 com.targa.labs.quarkushop.order.client.ProductRestClient/mp-rest/
scope=javax.inject.Singleton    ②
```

① The base URL configuration of the ProductRestClient.

② Defines the scope of the ProductRestClient bean as Singleton.

We will refactor the OrderItemService class to change:

```
@Inject
ProductRepository productRepository;
```

To the new:

```
@RestClient
ProductRestClient productRestClient;
```

ℹ️   @RestClient is used to inject a REST client.

Then, we change the productRepository.getOne() call to productRestClient. findById(). 😊 The JPA Repository fetches have been replaced by a REST API call.

Because we have an external dependency to the Product microservice, we need to create a health check that will verify that the Product microservice is reachable, the same way we did with PostgreSQL and Keycloak. The ProductServiceHealthCheck looks like this:

```
@Slf4j
@Liveness
@ApplicationScoped
public class ProductServiceHealthCheck implements HealthCheck {

    @ConfigProperty(name = "product-service.url", defaultValue = "false")
    Provider<String> productServiceUrl;
```

```java
@Override
public HealthCheckResponse call() {

    HealthCheckResponseBuilder responseBuilder =
            HealthCheckResponse.named("Product Service connection
            health check");

    try {

        productServiceConnectionVerification();
        responseBuilder.up();

    } catch (IllegalStateException e) {
        responseBuilder.down().withData("error", e.getMessage());
    }

    return responseBuilder.build();
}

private void productServiceConnectionVerification() {
    HttpClient httpClient = HttpClient.newBuilder()
            .connectTimeout(Duration.ofMillis(3000))
            .build();

    HttpRequest request = HttpRequest.newBuilder()
            .GET()
            .uri(URI.create(productServiceUrl.get() + "/health"))
            .build();

    HttpResponse<String> response = null;

    try {
        response = httpClient.send(request, HttpResponse.BodyHandlers.
        ofString());
    } catch (IOException e) {
        log.error("IOException", e);
    } catch (InterruptedException e) {
        log.error("InterruptedException", e);
        Thread.currentThread().interrupt();
    }
```

```
    if (response == null || response.statusCode() != 200) {
        throw new IllegalStateException("Cannot contact Product Service");
    }
  }
}
```

We need to copy these related tests from the monolith to the quarkushop-order microservice:

- AddressServiceUnitTest

- CartResourceIT

- CartResourceTest

- OrderItemResourceIT

- OrderItemResourceTest

- OrderResourceIT

- OrderResourceTest

We also need to copy the Keycloak Docker files from src/main/docker to the quarkushop-order microservice:

- The keycloak-test.yml file

- The realms directory

Then we add the properties needed to execute the tests:

```
%test.quarkus.kubernetes-config.enabled=false
quarkus.test.native-image-profile=test
```

The quarkushop-product doesn't rely on any other microservice, so the modifications that we made for the quarkushop-order were enough for quarkushop-product. However, the quarkushop-order reply on the quarkushop-product microservice means that the tests also rely on the quarkushop-product microservice.

We have many solutions here—here are my two choices:

- Mock the RestClient

- Add a testing instance of quarkushop-product

I will use the second choice for quarkushop-order and will mock the RestClient for quarkushop-customer, as it replies on another microservice.

Recall that we used the TestContainers Framework to provision a Keycloak instance for the integration tests. The provision was made using a docker-compose file, where a keycloak service was created. We can use this same method to provision a quarkushop-product instance, using the same docker-compose file. But we must first create a new QuarkusTestResourceLifecycleManager class instead of using KeycloakRealmResource, as it's made to provision Keycloak only.

Let's rename the src/main/docker/keycloak-test.yml file to src/main/docker/context-test.yml. Then we can add two services: quarkushop-product and postgresql-db.

ℹ   Why do we add the postgresql-db service? The answer is simple; ☺ it's needed by the quarkushop-product (our microservices need database storage and a Keycloak tenant to work). ☺

The contents of src/main/docker/context-test.yml will be as follows:

```
version: '3'
services:
  keycloak:
    image: jboss/keycloak:latest
    command:
      [
        '-b','0.0.0.0',
        '-Dkeycloak.migration.action=import',
        '-Dkeycloak.migration.provider=dir',
        '-Dkeycloak.migration.dir=/opt/jboss/keycloak/realms',
        '-Dkeycloak.migration.strategy=OVERWRITE_EXISTING',
        '-Djboss.socket.binding.port-offset=1000',
        '-Dkeycloak.profile.feature.upload_scripts=enabled',
      ]
    volumes:
      - ./realms-test:/opt/jboss/keycloak/realms
```

```
    environment:
      - KEYCLOAK_USER=admin
      - KEYCLOAK_PASSWORD=admin
      - DB_VENDOR=h2
    ports:
      - 9080:9080
      - 9443:9443
      - 10990:10990
  quarkushop-product:
    image: nebrass/quarkushop-product:1.0.0-SNAPSHOT
    environment:
      - QUARKUS_PROFILE=test
      - QUARKUS_DATASOURCE_JDBC_URL=jdbc:postgresql://postgresql-db:5432/
        product
      - MP_JWT_VERIFY_PUBLICKEY_LOCATION=http://keycloak:9080/auth/realms/
        quarkushop-realm/protocol/openid-connect/certs
      - MP_JWT_VERIFY_ISSUER=http://keycloak:9080/auth/realms/quarkushop-
        realm
    depends_on:
      - postgresql-db
      - keycloak
    ports:
      - 8080:8080
  postgresql-db:
    image: postgres:13
    volumes:
      - /opt/postgres-volume:/var/lib/postgresql/data
    environment:
      - POSTGRES_USER=developer
      - POSTGRES_PASSWORD=p4SSWord
      - POSTGRES_DB=product
      - POSTGRES_HOST_AUTH_METHOD=trust
    ports:
      - 5432:5432
```

> **ⓘ**   Note that used the available Keycloak instance via the environment variables
> for quarkushop-product. 😬

Excellent! Now, TestContainers will provision Keycloak/PostgreSQL/quarkushop-product instances, which is what the quarkushop-order needs for these integration tests. 😊😊

Next, we need to create a new QuarkusTestResourceLifecycleManager class, called ContextTestResource. This class will provision Keycloak and quarkushop-product and pass their properties to the application. See Listing 13-2.

Listing 13-2. src/test/java/com/targa/labs/quarkushop/order/util/ContextTestResource.java

```java
public class ContextTestResource implements
QuarkusTestResourceLifecycleManager {

    @ClassRule
    public static DockerComposeContainer ECOSYSTEM = new
    DockerComposeContainer(
            new File("src/main/docker/context-test.yml"))
            .withExposedService("quarkushop-product_1", 8080,    ①
                    Wait.forListeningPort().withStartupTimeout(
                    Duration.ofSeconds(30)))
            .withExposedService("keycloak_1", 9080,               ①
                    Wait.forListeningPort().withStartupTimeout(
                    Duration.ofSeconds(30)));

    @Override
    public Map<String, String> start() {
        ECOSYSTEM.start();

        String jwtIssuerUrl = String.format("http://%s:%s/auth/realms/
        quarkus-realm",
                ECOSYSTEM.getServiceHost("keycloak_1", 9080),
                ECOSYSTEM.getServicePort("keycloak_1", 9080)
        );
```

```
        TokenService tokenService = new TokenService();
        Map<String, String> config = new HashMap<>();

        try {

            String adminAccessToken = tokenService.
            getAccessToken(jwtIssuerUrl,
                    "admin", "test", "quarkus-client", "mysecret");
            String testAccessToken = tokenService.getAccessToken(
            jwtIssuerUrl, "test", "test", "quarkus-client", "mysecret");

            config.put("quarkus-admin-access-token", adminAccessToken);
            config.put("quarkus-test-access-token", testAccessToken);

        } catch (IOException | InterruptedException e) {
            e.printStackTrace();
        }

        config.put("mp.jwt.verify.publickey.location", jwtIssuerUrl
                                + "/protocol/openid-connect/certs");   ②
        config.put("mp.jwt.verify.issuer", jwtIssuerUrl);              ②

        String productServiceUrl = String.format("http://%s:%s/api",
                ECOSYSTEM.getServiceHost("quarkushop-product_1", 8080),
                ECOSYSTEM.getServicePort("quarkushop-product_1", 8080)
        );
        config.put("product-service.url", productServiceUrl);         ②

        return config;
    }

    @Override
    public void stop() {
        ECOSYSTEM.stop();
    }
}
```

① Defines the provisioned services.

② Defines the properties needed by Keycloak and quarkushop-product.

Then we refactor the tests to include the ContextTestResource:

```
@DisabledOnNativeImage
@QuarkusTest
@QuarkusTestResource(TestContainerResource.class)
@QuarkusTestResource(ContextTestResource.class)
class CartResourceTest {
...
}
```

ℹ️   When running the refactoring steps, I removed the customer creation. I'm using a randomly generated customer ID.

Let's take a closer look at the microservice creation process: 😄

- Build the quarkushop-order image and push it to the container registry:

```
$ mvn clean install -Pnative \
    -Dquarkus.native.container-build=true \
    -Dquarkus.container-image.build=true

$ docker push nebrass/quarkushop-order:1.0.0-SNAPSHOT
```

- Create the quarkushop-order-config ConfigMap file:

```
1 apiVersion: v1
2 kind: ConfigMap
3 metadata:
4   name: quarkushop-order-config
5 data:
6   application.properties: |-
7     quarkus.datasource.jdbc.url=jdbc:postgresql://postgres:5432/
     order
8     mp.jwt.verify.publickey.location=http://keycloak-http.
     keycloak/auth/realms/quarkushop-realm/protocol/openid-
     connect/certs
9     mp.jwt.verify.issuer=http://keycloak-http.keycloak/auth/
     realms/quarkushop-realm
```

355

- Create the `quarkushop-order-config` `ConfigMap` in Kubernetes:

  `kubectl apply -f quarkushop-order/quarkushop-order-config.yml`

- Deploy the `quarkushop-order` application to Kubernetes:

  `kubectl apply -f quarkushop-order/target/kubernetes/kubernetes.json`

- Check the `quarkushop-order` pod using the health checks, a `port-forward`, and a simple `curl` GET command to the `/health` API:

```
{
    "status": "UP",
    "checks": [
        {
            "name": "Keycloak connection health check",
            "status": "UP"
        },
        {
            "name": "Product Service connection health check",
            "status": "UP"
        },
        {
            "name": "Database connections health check",
            "status": "UP"
        }
    ]
}
```

Good! The `Order` microservice is working as expected. Next, let's do the same thing to the `Customer` microservice. 😋

Implementing the Customer Microservice

To implement the `Customer` microservice we will apply the same steps as we did for the `Order` microservice. Again, we will:

- Copy the code from the `customer` package in the monolithic application to the new `Customer` microservice

- Add the Lombok, AssertJ, and TestContainers dependencies

- Add the `quarkushop-commons` dependency

- Copy the `banner.txt` file from the monolith

- Add the `application.properties` and change the database and `ConfigMap` names

- Copy the Flyway scripts and clean up the unrelated objects and data

- Add the Quarkus Index Dependency for `quarkushop-commons` in the `application.properties`

Then, we need to copy these related tests from the monolith to the `quarkushop-customer` microservice:

- `CustomerResourceIT`

- `CustomerResourceTest`

- `PaymentResourceIT`

- `PaymentResourceTest`

We also need to copy the Keycloak Docker files from `src/main/docker` to the `quarkushop-order` microservice:

- The `keycloak-test.yml` file

- The `realms` directory

Then we add the properties needed to execute the tests:

```
%test.quarkus.kubernetes-config.enabled=false
quarkus.test.native-image-profile=test
```

Next, we mock the `OrderRestClient`. We create a new class called `MockOrderRestClient`, as shown in Listing 13-3.

Listing 13-3. src/test/java/com/targa/labs/quarkushop/customer/utils/
MockOrderRestClient.java

```java
@Mock                                                              ①
@ApplicationScoped
@RestClient
public class MockOrderRestClient implements OrderRestClient {     ②

    @Override
    public Optional<OrderDto> findById(Long id) {                 ③
        OrderDto order = new OrderDto();
        order.setId(id);
        order.setTotalPrice(BigDecimal.valueOf(1000));
        return Optional.of(order);
    }

    @Override
    public Optional<OrderDto> findByPaymentId(Long id) {
        OrderDto order = new OrderDto();
        order.setId(5L);
        return Optional.of(order);
    }

    @Override
    public OrderDto save(OrderDto order) {
        return order;
    }
}
```

① Annotation used to mock beans injected in tests.

② The Mock class implements the RestClient interface.

③ The Mock methods were implemented to return results suitable
for tests.

That's all! Mocking is very easy and the mocked components will automatically be injected into the tests. 😄 The microservice creation process is as follows:

- Build the `quarkushop-customer` image and push it to the container registry

- Create the `quarkushop-customer-config` `ConfigMap` file

- Create the `quarkushop-customer-config` `ConfigMap` in Kubernetes

- Check the `quarkushop-customer` pod using the health checks, a `port-forward`, and a simple `curl` GET command to the `/health` API

ℹ   You will find all the code and resources in the book's ○ GitHub repositories.

Implementing the User Microservice

What, an extra microservice? I know I did not mention this one at the start of the chapter. 😲

Don't worry, this is not a huge microservice. It's used for authentication and will hold the user section REST APIs listed in the Quarkushop Swagger UI monolith:

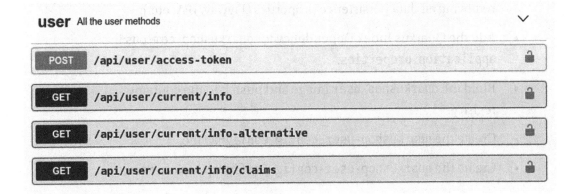

Let's generate a new Quarkus application with these extensions:

- RESTEasy JAX-RS

- RESTEasy JSON-B

- SmallRye OpenAPI

- SmallRye JWT

- SmallRye Health

- Kubernetes

- Kubernetes Config

- Container Image Jib

ℹ There are no persistence-related extensions, as you won't interact with the database in this microservice.

The steps to implement the User microservice are as follows:

- Copy the user-related content. This microservice is very minimal, so it will only hold the UserResource class.

- Add the Lombok dependency.

- Add the quarkushop-commons dependency.

- Copy the banner.txt file from the monolith.

- Add application.properties, changing the ConfigMap name and removing all data persistence properties (Flyway, JPA, etc.).

- Add the Quarkus Index Dependency for quarkushop-commons in application.properties.

- Build the quarkushop-user image and push it to the container registry.

- Create the quarkushop-user-config ConfigMap file.

- Create the quarkushop-user-config ConfigMap in Kubernetes.

- Check the quarkushop-user pod using the health checks, a port-forward, and a simple curl GET command to the /health API.

ℹ You will find all the code and resources in the book's ○ GitHub repositories.

After deploying the `quarkushop-user` microservice, you can use it to get an `access_token` and communicate with the secured APIs of the other three microservices:

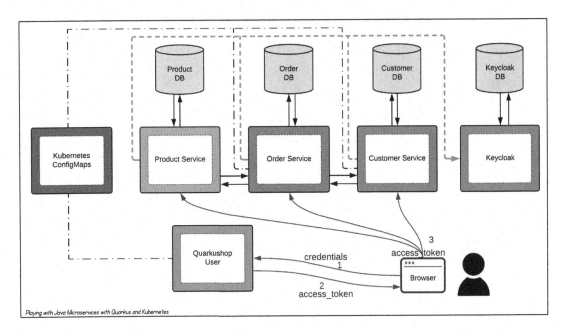

Playing with Java Microservices with Quarkus and Kubernetes

Good! The microservices are correctly deployed and working! 😄

Conclusion

In this chapter, you learned how to create the microservices and deploy them to Kubernetes. During this heavy task, you implemented patterns introduced in Chapter 9. But you did not implement the most wanted patterns. This is what you will do in the next chapter.😄

CHAPTER 14

Flying All Over the Sky with Quarkus and Kubernetes

Introduction

Starting in Chapter 9, you learned about cloud-native patterns and even implemented some of them:

- **Service discovery and registration**: Made using the Kubernetes `Deployment` and `Service` objects

- **Externalized configuration**: Made using the Kubernetes `ConfigMap` and `Secret` objects

- **Database per service**: Made while splitting the monolith codebase using DDD concepts

- **Application metrics**: Implemented using the SmallRye Metrics Quarkus extension

- **Health Check API**: Implemented using the SmallRye Health Quarkus extension

- **Security Between Services**: Implemented using the SmallRye JWT Quarkus extension and Keycloak

© Nebrass Lamouchi 2021
N. Lamouchi, *Pro Java Microservices with Quarkus and Kubernetes*,
https://doi.org/10.1007/978-1-4842-7170-4_14

In this chapter, you learn how to implement more popular patterns:

- Circuit Breaker

- Log Aggregation

- Distributed Tracing

- API Gateway

Implementing the Circuit Breaker Pattern

The Circuit Breaker pattern is useful for making resilient microservices that use faulty communication protocols (like HTTP). The idea of the pattern is to handle any communication problems between microservices.

This implementation of the Circuit Breaker pattern will only impact the `Order` and `Customer` microservices, where we used the REST client to make external calls.

Implementing this pattern in a Quarkus-based application is very easy. The first step is to add this dependency to the `pom.xml` file:

```
<dependency>
    <groupId>io.quarkus</groupId>
    <artifactId>quarkus-smallrye-fault-tolerance</artifactId>
</dependency>
```

Now we enable the Circuit Breaker feature on the REST client components. Let's say that we want our REST clients to stop making API calls for 15 seconds if we have a 50% failing request from the last 10 requests. This can be done using this line of code:

```
@CircuitBreaker(requestVolumeThreshold = 10, failureRatio = 0.5, delay = 15000)
```

In the `Order` microservice:

```
@Path("/products")
@RegisterRestClient
public interface ProductRestClient {
```

```
@GET
@Path("/{id}")
@CircuitBreaker(requestVolumeThreshold = 10, failureRatio = 0.5,
delay = 15000)
ProductDto findById(@PathParam Long id);
}
```

@CircuitBreaker has many attributes:

- failOn: The list of exception types that should be considered failures; the default value is {Throwable.class}. All exceptions inheriting from Throwable, thrown by the annotated method, are considered failures.

- skipOn: The list of exception types that should not be considered failures; the default value is {}.

- delay: The delay after which an open circuit will transition to a half-open state; the default value is 5000.

- delayUnit: The unit of the delay. The default value is ChronoUnit.MILLIS.

- requestVolumeThreshold: The number of consecutive requests in a rolling window. The default value is 20.

- failureRatio: The ratio of failures within the rolling window that will trip the circuit to open. The default value is 0.50.

- successThreshold: The number of successful executions before a half-open circuit is closed again. The default value is 1.

ℹ️ The Circuit Breaker pattern has three states:

- Closed: All requests are made normally

- Half-open: Transition state where verifications are made to check if the problem is still occurring

- Open: All requests are disabled until the delay is due

In the `Customer` microservice:

```
@Path("/orders")
@RegisterRestClient
public interface OrderRestClient {

    @GET
    @Path("/{id}")
    @CircuitBreaker(requestVolumeThreshold = 10, delay = 15000)
    Optional<OrderDto> findById(@PathParam Long id);

    @GET
    @Path("/payment/{id}")
    @CircuitBreaker(requestVolumeThreshold = 10, delay = 15000)
    Optional<OrderDto> findByPaymentId(Long id);

    @POST
    @CircuitBreaker(requestVolumeThreshold = 10, delay = 15000)
    OrderDto save(OrderDto order);
}
```

The SmallRye Fault Tolerance extension offers many other useful options to deal with faults, in order to be strong resilient microservices. We have for example these mechanisms:

- **Retry mechanism**: Used to make a number of retries if an invocation fails:

  ```
  @Path("/products")
  @RegisterRestClient
  public interface ProductRestClient {

      @GET
      @Path("/{id}")
      @CircuitBreaker(requestVolumeThreshold = 10, delay = 15000)
      @Retry(maxRetries = 4)
      ProductDto findById(@PathParam Long id);
  }
  ```

ⓘ @Retry(maxRetries = 4) will run up to four retries if the invocation fails.

- **Timeout mechanism**: Used to define a method execution timeout. It can be easily implemented:

```
@Path("/products")
@RegisterRestClient
public interface ProductRestClient {

    @GET
    @Path("/{id}")
    @CircuitBreaker(requestVolumeThreshold = 10, delay = 15000)
    @Retry(maxRetries = 4)
    @Timeout(500)
    ProductDto findById(@PathParam Long id);
}
```

ⓘ @Timeout(500) will make the application throw a TimeoutException if the findById() invocation takes more than 500 milliseconds.

- **Fallback mechanism**: Used to invoke a fallback (or backup) method if the main method fails. An annotation is here to do the job:

```
public class SomeClass {

    @Inject
    @RestClient
    ProductRestClient productRestClient;

    @Fallback(fallbackMethod = "fallbackFetchProduct")
    List<ProductDto> findProductsByCategory(String category){
        return productRestClient.findProductsByCategory(category);
    }
```

```
        public List<ProductDto> fallbackFetchProduct(String category) {
            return Collections.emptyList();
        }
    }
```

ⓘ   If `productRestClient.findProductsByCategory()` fails, you get the response from the `fallbackFetchProduct()` method instead of `findProductsByCategory()`. You can tune this powerful mechanism even more. You can, for example, configure it to switch to the fallback method after defined exceptions or after a certain timeout.

Note that the Circuit Breaker pattern and the Fault Tolerance patterns are perfectly implemented in the Quarkus Framework.

Implementing the Log Aggregation Pattern

For the Log Aggregation pattern, we use the famous ELK (Elasticsearch, Logstash, and Kibana) stack. These are three open-source projects:

- Elasticsearch is a search and analytics engine.

- Logstash is a server-side data processing pipeline that ingests data from multiple sources simultaneously, transforms it, and then sends it to a "stash" like Elasticsearch.

- Kibana lets users visualize data with charts and graphs in Elasticsearch.

Together, these tools are most commonly used to centralize and analyze logs in distributed systems. The ELK stack is popular because it fulfills a need in the log analytics space.

The use case of the ELK stack in this chapter is as follows:

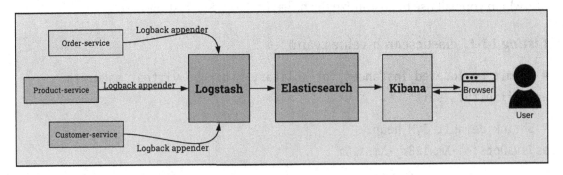

All the microservices will push their respective logs to Logstash, which will use Elasticsearch to index them. The indexed logs can be consumed later by Kibana.

Quarkus has a great extension called `quarkus-logging-gelf`, which is described as a "log using the Graylog Extended Log Format and centralizing your logs in ELK or EFK." 😊

WHAT IS THE GRAYLOG EXTENDED LOG FORMAT?

Based on the `Graylog.org` website: "The Graylog Extended Log Format (GELF) is a uniquely convenient log format created to deal with all the shortcomings of classic plain Syslog. This enterprise feature allows you to collect structured events from anywhere, and then compress and chunk them in the blink of an eye."

Good! Logstash natively supports the Graylog Extended Log Format. You need just to activate it during the configuration process.

Step 1: Deploying the ELK Stack to Kubernetes

How do you install the ELK stack in your Kubernetes cluster? 😕 That's a big question!

It's an extremely easy task: as we did with Keycloak, we will use Helm to install the ELK stack. 😊

Start by adding the official ELK Helm Charts Repository to our Helm client:

```
helm repo add elastic https://helm.elastic.co
```

Next, we need to update the references:

```
helm repo update
```

If you are on Minikube like me, you need to create an `elasticsearch-values.yaml` file, which you will use to customize the `helm install`. See Listing 14-1.

Listing 14-1. elasticsearch-values.yaml

```
# Permit co-located instances for solitary minikube virtual machines.
antiAffinity: "soft"

# Shrink default JVM heap.
esJavaOpts: "-Xmx128m -Xms128m"

# Allocate smaller chunks of memory per pod.
resources:
  requests:
    cpu: "100m"
    memory: "512M"
  limits:
    cpu: "1000m"
    memory: "512M"

# Request smaller persistent volumes.
volumeClaimTemplate:
  accessModes: [ "ReadWriteOnce" ]
  storageClassName: "standard"
  resources:
    requests:
      storage: 100M
```

♀ This configuration file is the recommended configuration to use while installing Elasticsearch on Minikube: `https://github.com/elastic/helm-charts/blob/master/elasticsearch/examples/minikube/values.yaml`

Now we install Elasticsearch:

```
helm install elasticsearch elastic/elasticsearch -f
./elasticsearch-values.yaml
```

We can see what was created using this command:

```
$ kubectl get all -l release=elasticsearch
```

NAME	READY	STATUS	RESTARTS
pod/elasticsearch-master-0	1/1	Running	0
pod/elasticsearch-master-1	1/1	Running	0
pod/elasticsearch-master-2	1/1	Running	0

NAME	TYPE	CLUSTER-IP	PORT(S)
service/elasticsearch-master 9300/TCP	ClusterIP	10.103.91.46	9200/TCP,
service/elasticsearch-master-headless 9300/TCP	ClusterIP	None	9200/TCP,

NAME	READY
statefulset.apps/elasticsearch-master	3/3

ⓘ   The three masters are here for high-availability purposes. I know that we don't have a problem now, but think about Black Friday! ☺

The pods are in running status, so we can test the Elasticsearch 9200 port. We can do a port-forward and a curl:

```
$ kubectl port-forward service/elasticsearch-master 9200
Forwarding from 127.0.0.1:9200 -> 9200
Forwarding from [::1]:9200 -> 9200

$ curl localhost:9200
{
  "name" : "elasticsearch-master-1",
  "cluster_name" : "elasticsearch",
  "cluster_uuid" : "UkYbL4KsSeK4boVr4rOe2w",
  "version" : {
    "number" : "7.9.2",

    ...
```

```
    "lucene_version" : "8.6.2",
    "minimum_wire_compatibility_version" : "6.8.0",
    "minimum_index_compatibility_version" : "6.0.0-beta1"
  },
  "tagline" : "You Know, for Search"
}
```

Excellent! We can deploy Kibana:

```
helm install kibana elastic/kibana --set fullnameOverride=quarkushop-kibana
```

We can see what was created using this command:

```
$ kubectl get all -l release=kibana
```

NAME		READY	STATUS		
pod/quarkushop-kibana-696f869668-5tcvz		1/1	Running		

NAME	TYPE	CLUSTER-IP	EXTERNAL-IP	PORT(S)
service/quarkushop-kibana	ClusterIP	10.107.223.6	<none>	5601/TCP

NAME	READY	UP-TO-DATE	AVAILABLE
deployment.apps/quarkushop-kibana	1/1	1	1

NAME	DESIRED	CURRENT	READY
replicaset.apps/quarkushop-kibana-696f869668	1	1	1

We will do a port-forward on the Kibana service:

```
kubectl port-forward service/quarkushop-kibana 5601
```

Then open the Kibana UI to check that everything is working correctly:

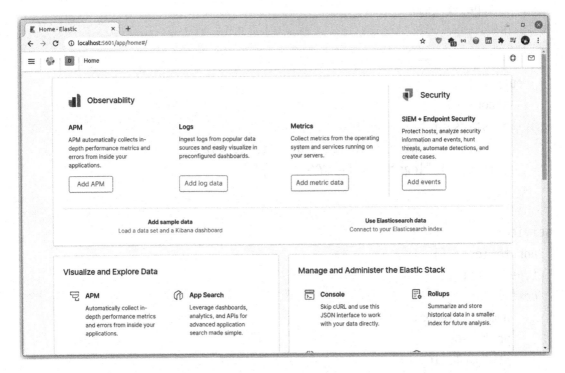

Good! We need to install Logstash, but we will need to customize the installation using a Helm `logstash-values.yaml` file; see Listing 14-2.

Listing 14-2. logstash-values.yaml

```
logstashConfig:
  logstash.yml: |
    http.host: "0.0.0.0"
    xpack.monitoring.elasticsearch.hosts: [ "http://elasticsearch-master:9200" ]
    xpack.monitoring.enabled: true
  pipelines.yml: |
    - pipeline.id: custom
      path.config: "/usr/share/logstash/pipeline/logstash.conf"
logstashPipeline:
  logstash.conf: |
    input {
      gelf {
```

```
      port => 12201
      type => gelf
    }
  }

  output {
    stdout {}
    elasticsearch {
      hosts => ["http://elasticsearch-master:9200"]
      index => "logstash-%{+YYYY-MM-dd}"
    }
  }
service:
  annotations: {}
  type: ClusterIP
  ports:
    - name: filebeat
      port: 5000
      protocol: TCP
      targetPort: 5000
    - name: api
      port: 9600
      protocol: TCP
      targetPort: 9600
    - name: gelf
      port: 12201
      protocol: UDP
      targetPort: 12201
```

This `values.yaml` file is used to configure:

- The Logstash pipeline. Enabling the `gelf` plugin, exposing the default
  12201 port, and defining the Logstash output pattern and flow to the
  Elasticsearch instance

- The Logstash service definition and exposed ports

Now, let's install the Logstash:

```
helm install -f ./logstash-values.yaml logstash elastic/logstash \
    --set fullnameOverride=quarkushop-logstash
```

To list the created objects, run the following:

```
$ k get all -l chart=logstash
```

NAME	READY	STATUS	RESTARTS
pod/quarkushop-logstash-0	1/1	Running	0

NAME	TYPE	CLUSTER-IP	PORT(S)
service/quarkushop-logstash	ClusterIP	10.107.204.49	5000/TCP,
9600/TCP,12201/UDP			
service/quarkushop-logstash-headless	ClusterIP	None	5000/TCP,
9600/TCP,12201/UDP			

NAME	READY
statefulset.apps/quarkushop-logstash	1/1

Excellent! Now the ELK stack is correctly deployed. The next step is to configure the microservices to log into the ELK stack.

Step 2: Configuring the Microservices to Log Into the ELK Stack

The modifications that we will do in this step are applicable to:

- quarkushop-product

- quarkushop-order

- quarkushop-customer

- quarkushop-user

Let's add the extension to the pom.xml file:

```
<dependency>
    <groupId>io.quarkus</groupId>
    <artifactId>quarkus-logging-gelf</artifactId>
</dependency>
```

We need to define the Logstash server properties to each microservice `ConfigMap` file, as shown in Listing 14-3.

Listing 14-3. quarkushop-order-config.yml

```
apiVersion: v1
kind: ConfigMap
metadata:
  name: quarkushop-order-config
data:
  application.properties: |-
    quarkus.datasource.jdbc.url=jdbc:postgresql://postgres:5432/order
    mp.jwt.verify.publickey.location=http://keycloak-http.keycloak/auth/
    realms/quarkushop-realm/protocol/openid-connect/certs
    mp.jwt.verify.issuer=http://keycloak-http.keycloak/auth/realms/
    quarkushop-realm
    quarkus.log.handler.gelf.enabled=true
    quarkus.log.handler.gelf.host=quarkushop-logstash        ①
    quarkus.log.handler.gelf.port=12201                      ②
```

    ① The Logstash host is the Kubernetes service that's exposing Logstash.

    ② The Logstash Port is defined in the Logstash Kubernetes service.

Let's build, push the containers, and deploy again to our Kubernetes cluster. We need to import the `ConfigMaps` again in order to update them.

Step 3: Collecting Logs

Once everything is deployed and configured, we need to access the Kibana UI to parse the collected logs:

```
kubectl port-forward service/quarkushop-kibana 5601
```

Go to Management ➤ Stack Management ➤ Index Management ➤ Kibana ➤ Index Patterns:

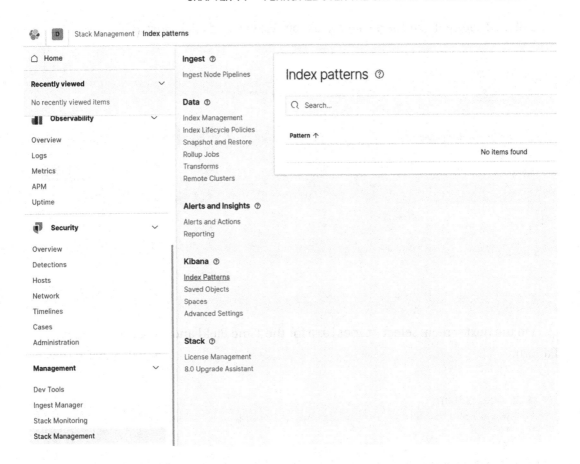

From here, click Create Index Pattern to create a new index pattern. A new screen will appear:

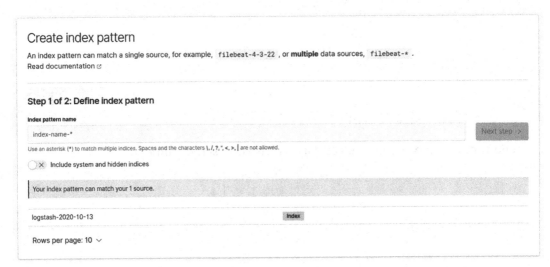

Fill the Index Pattern Name field with `logstash-*` and click Next Step:

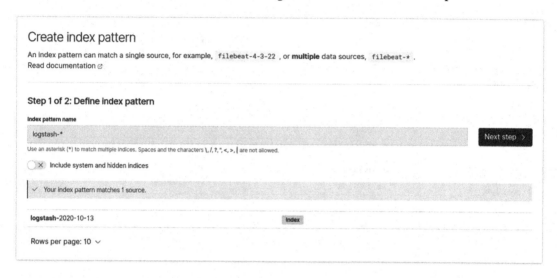

On the next screen, select `@timestamp` for the Time Field and click Create Index Pattern:

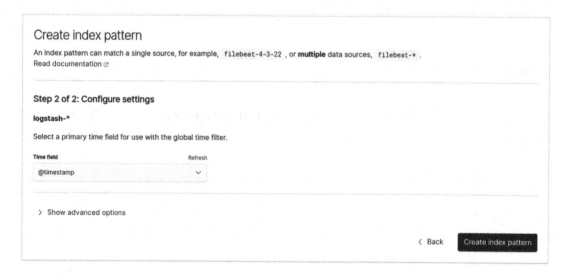

A new index pattern is created and a confirmation screen appears:

★ logstash-*

Time Filter field name: '@timestamp'   Default

This page lists every field in the **logstash-*** index and the field's associated core type as recorded by Elasticsearch. To change a field type, use the Elasticsearch Mapping API⌀

Fields (35)   Scripted fields (0)   Source filters (0)

🔍 Search   All field types ⌄

Name	Type	Format	Searchable	Aggregatable	Excluded	
@timestamp ⊙	date		●	●		✎
@version	string		●	●		✎
LoggerName	string		●			✎
LoggerName.keyword	string		●	●		✎
Severity	string		●			✎
Severity.keyword	string		●	●		✎
SourceClassName	string		●			✎
SourceClassName.keyword	string		●	●		✎
SourceMethodName	string		●			✎
SourceMethodName.keyword	string		●	●		✎

Rows per page: 10 ⌄   ‹ **1** 2 3 4 ›

Now, if you click the Discover menu in the Kibana section, you will see a list of the logs: 😁

Excellent! 😁 Now we can keep an eye on all the logs produced in all our microservices. We can enjoy the powerful features of the ELK stack. For example, we can create a custom query to monitor specific kinds of errors in the log streams.

Implementing the Distributed Tracing Pattern

The Distributed Tracing pattern has a dedicated extension in Quarkus called quarkus-smallrye-opentracing. ☺ Just like with the Log Aggregation pattern, we will need a distributed tracing system for the Distributed Tracing pattern.

A *distributed tracing system* is used to collect and store the timing data needed to monitor communication requests in a microservices architecture, in order to detect latency problems. There are many distributed tracing systems available on the market, such as Zipkin and Jaeger. In this book, we will use Jaeger, because it's the default tracer supported by the quarkus-smallrye-opentracing extension.

We need to install Jaeger and configure the microservices to support it in order to collect request traces.

Before starting the installation, here are the components of the Jaeger ecosystem:

- **Jaeger Client**: Includes language-specific implementations of the OpenTracing API for distributed tracing.

- **Jaeger Agent**: A network daemon that listens for SPANS sent over UDP.

- **Jaeger Collector**: Receives SPANS and places them in a queue for processing. This allows the collector to immediately return to the client/agent instead of waiting for the SPAN to make its way to storage.

- **Query**: A service that retrieves traces from storage.

- **Jaeger Console**: A user interface that lets you visualize your distributed tracing data.

The Jaeger components architecture looks as follows:

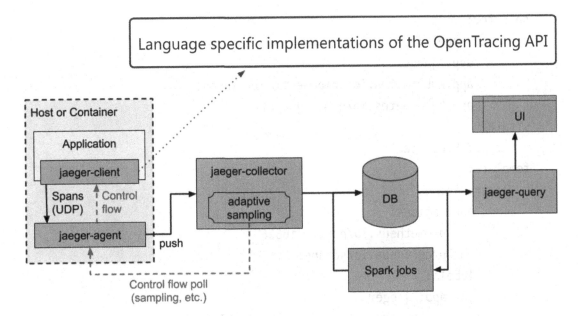

Step 1: Deploying the Jaeger All-in-One to Kubernetes

We start by creating the jaeger-deployment.yml file with the content shown in Listing 14-4.

Listing 14-4. jaeger/jaeger-deployment.yml

```
apiVersion: apps/v1
kind: Deployment
metadata:
    labels:
        app: jaeger
        app.kubernetes.io/component: all-in-one
        app.kubernetes.io/name: jaeger
    name: jaeger
spec:
    progressDeadlineSeconds: 2147483647
    replicas: 1
    revisionHistoryLimit: 2147483647
```

```
selector:
    matchLabels:
        app: jaeger
        app.kubernetes.io/component: all-in-one
        app.kubernetes.io/name: jaeger
strategy:
    type: Recreate
template:
    metadata:
        annotations:
            prometheus.io/port: "16686"
            prometheus.io/scrape: "true"
        labels:
            app: jaeger
            app.kubernetes.io/component: all-in-one
            app.kubernetes.io/name: jaeger
    spec:
        containers:
            - env:
                - name: COLLECTOR_ZIPKIN_HTTP_PORT
                  value: "9411"
              image: jaegertracing/all-in-one
              imagePullPolicy: Always
              name: jaeger
              ports:
                - containerPort: 5775
                  protocol: UDP
                - containerPort: 6831
                  protocol: UDP
                - containerPort: 6832
                  protocol: UDP
                - containerPort: 5778
                  protocol: TCP
                - containerPort: 16686
                  protocol: TCP
```

```
            - containerPort: 9411
              protocol: TCP
          readinessProbe:
            failureThreshold: 3
            httpGet:
                path: /
                port: 14269
                scheme: HTTP
            initialDelaySeconds: 5
            periodSeconds: 10
            successThreshold: 1
            timeoutSeconds: 1
          resources: {}
          terminationMessagePath: /dev/termination-log
          terminationMessagePolicy: File
      dnsPolicy: ClusterFirst
      restartPolicy: Always
      schedulerName: default-scheduler
      securityContext: {}
      terminationGracePeriodSeconds: 30
```

Next, import this file into the Kubernetes cluster:

```
kubectl apply -f jaeger/jaeger-deployment.yml
```

This Deployment resource will deploy all of Jaeger backend components and UI in one container.

We now need to create a load-balanced Kubernetes service object called jaeger-query, as shown in Listing 14-5.

Listing 14-5. jaeger/jaeger-query-service.yml

```
apiVersion: v1
kind: Service
metadata:
    name: jaeger-query
```

```
    labels:
        app: jaeger
        app.kubernetes.io/name: jaeger
        app.kubernetes.io/component: query
spec:
    ports:
        - name: query-http
          port: 80
          protocol: TCP
          targetPort: 16686
    selector:
        app.kubernetes.io/name: jaeger
        app.kubernetes.io/component: all-in-one
    type: LoadBalancer
```

We also need to create another service called `jaeger-collector`, as shown in Listing 14-6.

Listing 14-6. jaeger/jaeger-collector-service.yml

```
apiVersion: v1
kind: Service
metadata:
    name: jaeger-collector
    labels:
        app: jaeger
        app.kubernetes.io/name: jaeger
        app.kubernetes.io/component: collector
spec:
    ports:
        - name: jaeger-collector-tchannel
          port: 14267
          protocol: TCP
          targetPort: 14267
```

```
      - name: jaeger-collector-http
        port: 14268
        protocol: TCP
        targetPort: 14268
      - name: jaeger-collector-zipkin
        port: 9411
        protocol: TCP
        targetPort: 9411
  selector:
      app.kubernetes.io/name: jaeger
      app.kubernetes.io/component: all-in-one
  type: ClusterIP
```

Listing 14-7 shows the last one we need to create, called `jaeger-agent`.

Listing 14-7. jaeger/jaeger-agent-service.yml

```
apiVersion: v1
kind: Service
metadata:
    name: jaeger-agent
    labels:
        app: jaeger
        app.kubernetes.io/name: jaeger
        app.kubernetes.io/component: agent
spec:
    ports:
        - name: agent-zipkin-thrift
          port: 5775
          protocol: UDP
          targetPort: 5775
        - name: agent-compact
          port: 6831
          protocol: UDP
          targetPort: 6831
```

```
      - name: agent-binary
        port: 6832
        protocol: UDP
        targetPort: 6832
      - name: agent-configs
        port: 5778
        protocol: TCP
        targetPort: 5778
  clusterIP: None
  selector:
      app.kubernetes.io/name: jaeger
      app.kubernetes.io/component: all-in-one
```

We are exposing many ports via TCP and UDP protocols for the Jaeger agent. The 6831 on UDP consumes the SPANS. This is the one that we will be using to communicate with the Jaeger agent.

Next, let's create the Kubernetes objects:

```
kubectl apply -f jaeger/jaeger-query-service.yml
kubectl apply -f jaeger/jaeger-collector-service.yml
kubectl apply -f jaeger/jaeger-agent-service.yml
```

Excellent now, let's check if Jaeger is correctly installed. We need to do a port-forward on the jaeger-query service:

```
kubectl port-forward service/jaeger-query 8888:80
```

Then open the localhost:8888, as shown in the screenshot:

Excellent! We can move to the microservices configuration now. 😊

Step 2: Enabling Jaeger Support in Our Microservices

The first step is to add the quarkus-smallrye-opentracing dependency to our microservices:

```
<dependency>
    <groupId>io.quarkus</groupId>
    <artifactId>quarkus-smallrye-opentracing</artifactId>
</dependency>
```

Then, we need to define the Jaeger configuration in every microservice's ConfigMap:

```
1 apiVersion: v1
2 kind: ConfigMap
3 metadata:
```

```
4    name: quarkushop-user-config
5 data:
6    application.properties: |-
7      mp.jwt.verify.publickey.location=http://keycloak-http.keycloak/auth/
       realms/quarkushop-realm/protocol/openid-connect/certs
8      mp.jwt.verify.issuer=http://keycloak-http.keycloak/auth/realms/
       quarkushop-realm
9      quarkus.log.handler.gelf.enabled=true
10     quarkus.log.handler.gelf.host=quarkushop-logstash
11     quarkus.log.handler.gelf.port=12201
12     quarkus.jaeger.service-name=quarkushop-user
13     quarkus.jaeger.sampler-type=const
14     quarkus.jaeger.sampler-param=1
15     quarkus.log.console.format=%d{HH:mm:ss} %-5p traceId=%X{traceId},
       spanId=%X{spanId}, sampled=%X{sampled} [%c{2.}] (%t) %s%e%n
16     quarkus.jaeger.agent-host-port=jaeger-agent:6831
```

The new Jaeger properties are as follows:

- `quarkus.jaeger.service-name`: The service name, which is the name used by the microservice to present itself to the Jaeger server.

- `quarkus.jaeger.sampler-type`: The sampler type in the example is const. We will constantly send the quota defined in `quarkus.jaeger.sampler-param`.

- `quarkus.jaeger.sampler-param`: Sample quota defined between 0 and 1, where 1 is 100% of the requests.

- `quarkus.log.console.format`: Add trace IDs to the log message.

- `quarkus.jaeger.agent-host-port`: The hostname and port for communicating with the Jaeger agent via UDP. We make it point on the `jaeger-agent` as the host and 6831 as the port.

Good. Let's build, push the containers, and deploy them all again to our Kubernetes cluster. We also need to import the `ConfigMaps` again in order to update them.

Step 3: Collecting Traces

After deploying the Jaeger server and updating the microservices, we need to make some requests to generate traces. Then we can see what Jaeger is catching.

For example, we can use `quarkushop-user` to request an `access_token` from Keycloak:

```
kubectl port-forward service/quarkushop-user 8080
```

Then run a `curl` to request the `access_token` from the `quarkushop-user` microservice:

```
curl -X POST "http://localhost:8080/api/user/access-token?password=password&username=nebrass"
```

Good! Let's do a `port-forward` and access Jaeger to see what's going on there:

```
kubectl port-forward service/jaeger-query 8888:80
```

Then open the `localhost:8888`, as shown in the screenshot:

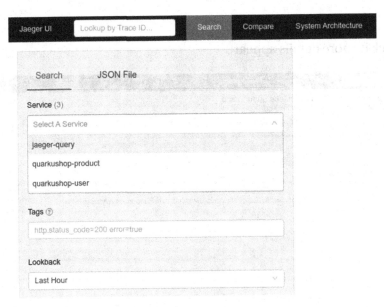

As you can see in the Service section, there are three elements. Just select `quarkushop-user` and click Find Traces:

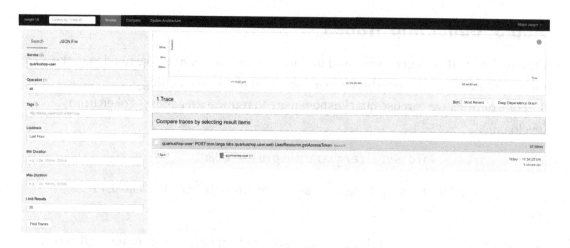

One SPAN is shown:

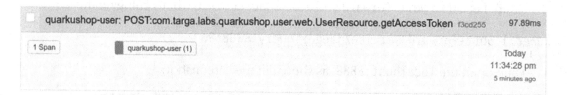

If you click it, more details appear:

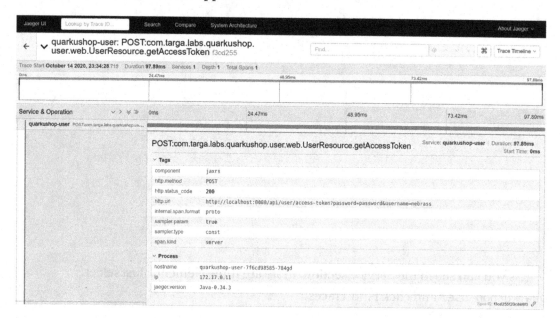

You can see that all the details of the request are shown here:

- The URL

- The HTTP verb

- The duration

- And so on; everything is here 😄

Done! We finished implementing the Distributed Tracing pattern in Quarkus in a very efficient and easy way! I'm really happy! 😄

Implementing the API Gateway Pattern

An *API Gateway* is a programming facade that sits in front of APIs and acts as a single point of entry for a defined group of microservices.

To implement Kubernetes, an *Ingress* manages external access to the services in a cluster, typically `facadeHTTP`. Ingress can provide load balancing, SSL termination, and name-based virtual hosting.

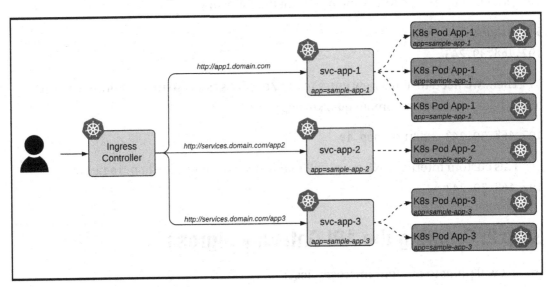

An *Ingress* is a collection of rules that allow inbound connections to reach the cluster services. It can be configured to give services externally-reachable URLs, load-balanced traffic, terminate SSL, name-based virtual hosting, and more.

An *Ingress Controller* is responsible for fulfilling the ingress, usually with a load-balancer, although it may also configure your edge router or additional frontends to help handle the traffic in a high-availability manner.

Let's bring the API Gateway pattern to Kubernetes. 😁

Step 1: Enabling Ingress Support in Minikube

The first step is to enable Ingress support in Minikube. This step is not required for those (lucky people) using real Kubernetes clusters. 😁

To enable Ingress support in Minikube, just start your minikube instance and then run this command:

```
minikube addons enable ingress
```

 Ingress is available as an add-on to Minikube. ☺

We need a domain name for Ingress; let's use the quarkushop.io domain name. We get the IP address of Minikube by typing the following:

```
$ minikube ip
192.168.39.243
```

Then, we need to add a new entry to the /etc/hosts file to this IP address, in order to use it for our custom domain quarkushop.io:

```
192.168.39.243   quarkushop.io
```

This custom internal DNS entry will make any call to quarkushop.io target 192.168.39.243. 😁

Step 2: Creating the API Gateway Ingress

Ingress will point to our four microservices:

- quarkushop-product
- quarkushop-order
- quarkushop-customer
- quarkushop-user

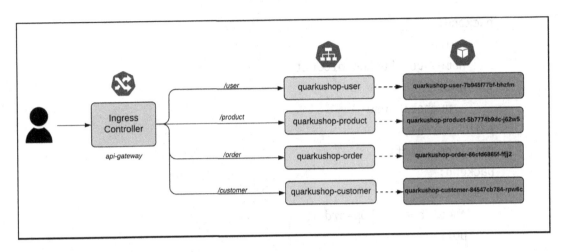

The Ingress descriptor is shown in Listing 14-8.

Listing 14-8. api-gateway-ingress.yml

```
apiVersion: networking.k8s.io/v1
kind: Ingress
metadata:
  name: api-gateway
  annotations:
    nginx.ingress.kubernetes.io/rewrite-target: /$1
spec:
  rules:
  - http:
      paths:
      - path: /user
        pathType: Prefix
        backend:
          service:
            name: quarkushop-user
            port:
              number: 8080
      - path: /product
        pathType: Prefix
```

```
      backend:
        service:
          name: quarkushop-product
          port:
            number: 8080
    - path: /order
      pathType: Prefix
      backend:
        service:
          name: quarkushop-order
          port:
            number: 8080
    - path: /customer
      pathType: Prefix
      backend:
        service:
          name: quarkushop-customer
          port:
            number: 8080
```

Just save this content to api-gateway-ingress.yml and create the resource with this command:

```
kubectl create -f api-gateway-ingress.yml
```

Ingress has been created successfully! Let's check on it:

```
$ kubectl get ingress

NAME           CLASS     HOSTS           ADDRESS          PORTS    AGE
api-gateway    <none>    quarkushop.io   192.168.39.243   80       7m46s
```

Excellent! As you can see, the ADDRESS is the same as the Minikube IP. ☺

Step 3: Testing Ingress

Now we can enjoy our Ingress. We can use it to request an `access_token` from the quarkushop-user microservice:

```
$ curl -X POST "http://quarkushop.io/user/api/user/access-token?password=pa
ssword&username=nebrass"

eyJhbGciOiJSUzI1NiIsIn...
```

Hurrah! We got the `access_token` request! 😀 Ingress is working like a charm! 😎

Conclusion

In this chapter, we implemented many patterns using different Quarkus extensions coupled with Kubernetes objects. This task was quite easy, especially because we delegated many tasks to Kubernetes.

Hakuna matata! 😀 We successfully implemented our cloud-native microservices. I'm so happy about the extensions available and the great documentation offered.

AFTERWORD

Final Words and Thoughts

I hope that you enjoyed reading this book. I tried to share my personal experience with the Quarkus Framework.

When I started writing this book, I just wanted to dig more into this new framework. I never imagined that Quarkus would be so excellent! I really appreciated the wide range of available libraries implementing many patterns.

The GraalVM support in Quarkus is just incredible as well! I'm really excited by the performance and by the implementation abstraction of the native image.

© Nebrass Lamouchi 2021
N. Lamouchi, *Pro Java Microservices with Quarkus and Kubernetes*,
https://doi.org/10.1007/978-1-4842-7170-4

Index

© Nebrass Lamouchi 2021
N. Lamouchi, *Pro Java Microservices with Quarkus and Kubernetes*,
https://doi.org/10.1007/978-1-4842-7170-4

E, F

G, H

Printed in the United States
by Baker & Taylor Publisher Services